Insular Destinies

In this collection, an eminent authority on the history of political thought and on the intellectual history of modern Hellenism employs his twin academic specializations in political science and in intellectual history to understand the intricacies of the historical experience of his native island. Writing in a perspective inspired by the work of Fernand Braudel, he attempts in a series of studies in cultural and social history to recover lost and overlooked aspects of the collective destinies of Cyprus and the Cypriot diaspora in the centuries of Ottoman rule, a period of critical significance for the survival of the people of the island. He then turns to a penetrating analysis of the politics of the Cyprus Question. The pertinent studies collected in this volume bear the imprint of the deep soul-searching by the younger generation of Cypriot scholars at the time of the tragedy of 1974 over what went so wrong that their country was exposed to foreign invasion, occupation and division. The hints at answers to these questions offered by the author's interdisciplinary and critical treatment of the subject make this work an indispensable aid to anyone wishing to grasp the deeper antinomies and dilemmas immanent in the Cyprus Question.

Paschalis M. Kitromilides, PhD Harvard University, is Professor Emeritus of Political Science at the University of Athens and Director of the Centre for Asia Minor Studies. From 2000 to 2011 he was Director of the Institute of Neohellenic Research at the National Hellenic Research Foundation. His recent books in English include: *Adamantios Korais and the European Enlightenment* (2010); *Enlightenment and Revolution: The Making of Modern Greece* (2013); *Enlightenment and Religion in the Orthodox World* (2016).

British School at Athens – Modern Greek and Byzantine Studies
Volume number 8
Series editor: Professor John Bennet
Director, British School at Athens, Greece

The study of modern Greek and Byzantine history, language and culture has formed an integral part of the work of the British School at Athens since its foundation. This series continues that pioneering tradition. It aims to explore a wide range of topics within a rich field of enquiry which continues to attract readers, writers, and researchers, whether their interest is primarily in contemporary Europe or in one of the many dimensions of the long Greek post-classical past.

Allegory of the Island of Cyprus, evoking her aspiration to recover her lost sovereignty. Engraving from Kyprianos, *Chronological History of the Island of Cyprus*, Venice 1788.

Insular Destinies

Perspectives on the history and politics of modern Cyprus

Paschalis M. Kitromilides

 Routledge
Taylor & Francis Group

LONDON AND NEW YORK

First published 2020
by Routledge
2 Park Square, Milton Park, Abingdon, Oxon OX14 4RN

and by Routledge
52 Vanderbilt Avenue, New York, NY 10017

Routledge is an imprint of the Taylor & Francis Group, an informa business

British Library Cataloguing-in-Publication Data
A catalogue record for this book is available from the British Library

Library of Congress Cataloging-in-Publication Data
A catalog record has been requested for this book

ISBN: 978-0-8153-5660-8 (hbk)
ISBN: 978-1-351-12782-0 (ebk)

Typeset in Times New Roman
by Integra Software Services Pvt. Ltd.

Contents

Illustrations

Foreword

For the student of the history of Cyprus, the essays collected together in this book are of especial interest. They are so in their own right, which is to say as self-standing analyses of the various topics with which they are concerned, extending from the sixteenth century through to our own times. This is hardly surprising. Paschalis Kitromilides is one of the leading historians of the intellectual and social trajectory of modern Greek culture.

More especially, however, their fascination derives from the fact that they trace a personal odyssey of engagement with modern Cypriot evolution against the backdrop of the contemporary travails of the island, above all defined by the tragedy of 1974. It is the inherent interplay between the past and present, the then and now, which gives them in retrospect real importance as a sort of document of the shifting contexts in which they emerged.

That document is of a particular kind. Kitromilides's own background, not least educational, defines him as the product of a liberal, cosmopolitan, self-consciously modern and European strand running through Cypriot society during the decades following the Second World War. Religious attachment to Orthodoxy — so central to Kitromilides's personal scholarship — has been perfectly compatible with secular values, just as deeply rooted Greek identity can run alongside an essentially diverse and open concept of the natural character of life within the island itself.

Yet there have been other powerful elements at work in (and on) late colonial and postcolonial Cyprus jarring with such a worldview and which drove a future at an awkward tangent to it. Kitromilides's call at various junctures in these essays for a self-critical understanding of how Cyprus has found itself painfully wounded by internal division, and exposed to the manipulation of hostile or wholly self-interested outsiders, may be seen as a lament for roads not taken, those "alternative possibilities" identified at one point (p. 106), and characterized by tolerance, flexibility and experimentalism too often spurned for something narrower, harsher and ultimately self-defeating. The author shows himself keenly aware, however, that such a "self-awareness" can come more easily to a long-time Cypriot expatriate — even one in Athens — than to those caught up in the immediate struggles within the island.

One of the striking aspects of this collection is the remarkable consistency of the critique, and the vision of Cyprus itself that emerges from it. I shall just underline a few dimensions. Key, as a preliminary to everything else, is the cultural exceptionalism of the island in its relationship to the hugely varied pattern of societies and political structures in the Aegean and eastern Mediterranean worlds. The island was always pushed and pulled in multiple directions. In Kitromilides's understanding, any mono-vision of Cypriot identity and destiny shows scant understanding of the deep historical currents involved.

What follows is an emphasis on what the author terms on several occasions the "creative osmosis" inherent in Cypriot affairs over centuries, a process rooted in the internal dialogue amongst Cypriots themselves. This is something that has gone on, almost without interruption, despite those forms of external conquest and domination to which Cyprus has recurrently been subject. Not even the era of Ottoman rule after 1571 froze it completely, though it slowed down the pace at which it proceeded; the rigidity and limitations of the post-1960 constitution, paradoxically, had a similar effect. The tragedy of 1974, apart from the purely physical and scarring realities of invasion and partition, lies in the way in which a natural dialogue amongst the diversity of Cypriots has been frozen in aspic.

In terms of ethnicity, Kitromilides's interpretation of Cypriot reality stresses throughout the persisting dynamic of coexistence between the main communities. This arose from the material necessities of a peasant world; but it was also bound up with the social customs and impulses natural to ordinary Cypriots. When this dynamic foundered, it was invariably due to pressures "from above", not below, and to the bewilderment arising from sudden changes of regime and social order in which fear and anxiety are liable to invert normal criteria.

In these essays monolithic nationalisms — and the ethnic and cultural loyalties attached to them — emerge as the great temptation, but also the great destroyer. Their opportunity comes with the bewilderment of change, and the manipulation of it by others. Again paradoxically, despite the many subjections and distortions of Ottoman overlordship, this was a danger that the nature of the millet system kept at bay. The real challenge came with that reconnection with the full blast — or something like the full blast — of modernity through the accident of British control after 1878.

The coming of modernity to Cyprus progressively uprooted the old peasant world in which coexistence was the natural default mechanism. It produced a new social order, but one still very fragile, and where some cadres and individual actors were liable to pull any lever that served their ends. Kitromilides can hardly here tell this story in any detail, but his various treatments of this theme — one essay cowritten with the distinguished political scientist Theodore A. Couloumbis — come back, either implicitly or explicitly, to what one may term a bastardized form of modernity as a looming danger over the island.

This is why, it seems to me, that the theme of leadership haunts these essays. The nature and quality of a leading cadre was critical to steering Cypriot communities away from the cliff edges of transition in post-Ottoman, and finally postcolonial, circumstances. "The problem of ethnic conflict, becomes, therefore", Kitromilides states (pp. 123–124) "one of direction ... [requiring] courage, imagination, and generosity to accomplish, especially on the part of the stronger, majority community". Self-criticism within the latter was vital to achieving a binational secular society which, for all its messy aspects and cultural compromises, was better than any likely alternative.

Again, as these essays exemplify, it is in underlining more contemporary challenges by harking back to critical historical episodes that Kitromilides's own form of critical method is best illustrated. His portrayal of Archbishop Kyprianos confronted by the perils of his own day sum this up most meaningfully. In the two pastoral letters issued prior to his brutal execution by the Ottoman authorities in 1821, and aware of how high the stakes were, the Archbishop called for submission and prudence on the part of his flock, a call defined by that sense of responsibility which is, the author argues, the mark of true leadership. Kyprianos did not save himself, but he did perhaps cushion the Greek of Cyprus from the full force of what might otherwise have happened — a Chios or Psara.

The circumstances of 1821 were not those of 1950–1951 or 1973–1974. But the parallels can implicitly be made. For submission and prudence in relation to the Ottomans might be substituted a keenly judged caution in relation to the rather different challenges of a later day, where fundamental risks still confronted Cypriots. It was a matter of constraining options, and discriminating between those likely to mutilate the very fabric of the island, and those which kept alive as much as possible of the essential traditions of the insular society.

In formulating such a critique of the insular destinies of Cyprus — the title is key — Kitromilides does not in any way push to the margins the role played by exogenous factors, or the externality of the island's fate at any given time. But what he does do is to focus on the critical interplay between the inside and the outside. He is in no doubt, for example, with regard to the unfolding events from the late 1950s onwards of a malign Turkish hostility to a plural, exceptionalist Cyprus, or of the sheer indifference of other involved Powers. But it was precisely because of these threats that it was so essential to pin the future to the success of intercommunal dialogue. The necessarily unresolved question in this analysis is whether Greek-Cypriots in particular — as the stronger community — were prepared to pay the price for ensuring this was achieved before the looming "accident" of events made it too late.

It would be wrong, however, to say that Kitromilides's version of Cypriot history embodied in these essays is a story of failure. Indeed, it is the very opposite, whereby the inherently resilient character of a small, diverse, culturally enriched mix of religions and ethnicities in the end has invariably charted a viable path through the complexity of the eastern Mediterranean region. Sometimes, this means going forwards directly; sometimes it has meant having to double back to pick up at some earlier point a missed turning or an alternative future. What Kitromilides regards as the fundamental success of the Republic of Cyprus (p. 126), that is, the survival of the island itself in its basic make-up and predisposition, regardless of others, means that this still remains the case today.

Not everybody by any means will agree with the thrust of the arguments and vision in this book. At times it is at odds with dominant approaches amongst the Greeks of Cyprus, or at least segments of that community. But as a persuasive account of a liberal, secular, modern Cypriot mind — written with honesty and forthrightness from a position of a certain detachment from the pitilessness that struggles of any kind always induce — it is an important collection that merits profound reflection from a moral just as much as a historical point of view.

Robert Holland
Centre for Hellenic Studies
King's College London

Acknowledgements

In compiling this collection I incurred many debts and I am very happy indeed to acknowledge them in this note. My greatest debt is to my friend Robert Holland, the leading authority on modern Cyprus in the United Kingdom, for his generosity in providing a Foreword to this book. I feel truly honoured by his presence in these pages. Many friends and colleagues responded to my requests and questions very promptly and graciously and it is a great pleasure to record my gratitude to Daniele Conversi, Amaury Faivre d'Arcier, Vassilis Gounaris, Maria Hadjipavlou, Alexis Heraclides, Robert Holland, Eleni Kanthou, Nota Kourou, Petros Papapolyviou, Andrei Pippidi, Alexis Rappas, Ioannis Stefanidis, Anastasia Yiangou. Some of them may not even remember that they helped me with my research on the history of Cyprus but my gratitude to them for various kindnesses over the years has remained with me as one of the most precious rewards of our profession.

I am very grateful to my respected friend Professor Theodore Coulombis for his generous agreement to include our coauthored article as chapter 10 in this collection.

I am deeply grateful to the British School at Athens, its Publications Committee and the Director, Professor John Bennet, for agreeing to include this work in BSA's *Modern Greek and Byzantine Studies.*

Grateful acknowledgement is also made to the editors and publishers of the collective volumes and professional journals in which the writings that compose this collection originally appeared, for hosting my work and for their permission to reprint. The sources of original publication are recorded in detail in the Bibliographical and Critical Notes in Part III of this book.

The A. G. Leventis Foundation has extended its support for this project with its usual generosity. My work on the project has been supported very effectively by my collaborators at the Centre for Asia Minor Studies in Athens. The Hellenic Observatory at The London School of Economics and Political Science has included me among its Research Associates since 2017 and this association gave me access to the resources of the British Library of Political and Economic Science, which has greatly facilitated my work on the present collection.

It is a great pleasure to acknowledge the generosity of the Sylvia Ioannou Foundation for supplying a digital copy of Lusignan's 1575 map of Cyprus; to the Abbot Bishop of Ledra Epiphanios and the brotherhood of the Holy Monastery of Macheras for permission to use the portrait of Archbishop Kyprianos from the monastery museum; the Telemachos Kanthos Foundation for digital copies and permission to use the two woodcuts from their collections.

A more enduring debt that goes back more deeply in time is owed to my mentor at Wesleyan University, Fred I. Greenstein, who supervised my earliest major research project on Cyprus, my B.A. Honours thesis on the first multiparty election in the Republic of Cyprus in 1970. From Fred I learnt the principles of professionalism and critical thinking in political science that have stayed with me. His passing away in December 2018, while this book was in the making, reminded me of this enduring debt.

PMK
February 2019

Abbreviations

Introduction

The present collection brings together fourteen studies in the history of modern Cyprus and the Cyprus Question. It is divided into three parts. Part I includes eight studies in rough chronological order, of which the first is an essay of historical reflection surveying the history of Cyprus from pre-history to independence in the mid-twentieth century. The remaining seven chapters in Part I are studies in the intellectual and social history of early modern Cyprus. Chapters 2 and 3 are directly related to the major research project I was able to devote to the history of Cyprus in my research career, the project that produced the work *Κυπριακή λογιοσύνη 1571–1878*, which was published as Vol. XLIII in the collection *Texts and Studies of History of Cyprus* of the Cyprus Research Centre in 2002. This was a study of Cypriot intellectual life during the centuries of Ottoman rule over the island. My motivation in undertaking the project was to include Cyprus in my work on the intellectual history of post-Byzantine and modern Hellenism, which was the main object of my research and writing about in the broad area of the history of ideas and had produced a number of books and articles primarily dealing with the various aspects and expressions of the Enlightenment in the Greek cultural tradition. As a Cypriot I wished to delve in depth in the study of pertinent phenomena in the history of Cyprus during the early modern period, thus extending the purview of my research to the Eastern-most cultural frontier of the Greek-speaking Orthodox world. Up until the 1990s, when I undertook this research project, my writings on Cyprus had been mostly motivated by the politics of the Cyprus Question. A selection of these early studies make up Part II of this collection and I will refer to them in due course below.

The undertaking of the study of Cypriot learning was due to the initiative of Dr. George S. Georghallides, director of the Cyprus Research Centre at the time, who encouraged me to devote part of my research efforts to the study of Cyprus. This led to a formal research programme under the aegis of the Cyprus Research Centre, which eventually produced the book *Κυπριακή λογιοσύνη* referred to above. The research effort that went into this project lasted much longer than originally planned, due to the complexity of the subject and the diversity and dispersal of the primary source material all over Europe. As a byproduct of the programme a collection of primary sources of Cypriot learning and history was initiated at the National Hellenic Research Foundation in 2008. The collection has produced five books to date which make available hitherto unpublished or rare and inaccessible material in modern critical editions.

To give the reader of the present collection an idea of the work connected with the project on Cypriot learning, an extensively revised and updated section of the introduction to that work is included in the present collection as Chapter 2. Chapter 3 provides a reading of the works of the three most important authors treated in the project from the perspective of the experience and culture of exile and its impact on social thought.

Chapters 4 and 5 represent attempts to look in a different light at neglected aspects of the social history of Cyprus in the long centuries of Ottoman rule. The revolt ignited in October 1764 by the maltreatment of the bishops of the Church of Cyprus by governor Chil Osman has always intrigued me as an instance of a premodern, prenational rebellion in which both religious communities on the island joined against the rapacity of the governor. The discovery and publication of the Venetian Consul's report further motivated my interest to look for additional evidence on the events and over the years visits to the Archives Nationales in Paris and to the National Archives at Kew Gardens in England produced additional material. The report of the French Consul Benoît Astier is published as an appendix to Chapter 4. The evidence collected at the British National Archives clearly suggests that the uprising kept the island in turmoil for about two years until the end of 1766. It is hoped that on the basis of this evidence the complete story of Cypriot unrest in the years 1764–1766 will be written one day pointing out the social dynamics and interreligious networks and interactions on the island.

In Chapter 5 the occasion of commenting on the visual evidence supplied by the wall painting of the family of Dragoman Christophakis at the church of Saint George of Arpera (Tersephanou, Larnaca) invites the observer of Cypriot social history to direct attention to issues of gender and to the multiple and subtly disguised forms of inequality in premodern society. To my knowledge this aspect of the social history of Cyprus has remained in obscurity and did not attract the attention of historians concerned with the history of the island before the contemporary period. In this case too it is desirable to look for evidence that might enrich our understanding of this aspect of the social structure of this insular society. By focusing on issues like the structure of gender relations and the symbolic forms of handling inequality and oppression we are led in the direction of writing a history of mentalities, even, a history of social sentiments. Many years ago in commenting on a selection of twelve documents from the correspondence of the Venetian Consulate in Larnaca during the eighteenth century, I had attempted to suggest such a history of mentalities and feelings in looking at early modern Cyprus, beyond the formalism of political history or the technocratic character of economic history, in order to recover the human content of historical experience. I believe that this remains an important desideratum in the historiography of modern Cyprus.

Chapters 6 and 7 of this collection direct attention to an emblematic presence in the history of modern Cyprus, Archbishop Kyprianos (1810–1821). On account of his martyrdom in 1821, Archbishop Kyprianos became an iconic figure in the Greek nationalist reading of the history of modern Cyprus. The studies presented in the two chapters on Kyprianos attempt to suggest that beyond a nationalist icon, which privileges his capacity as an ethnomartyr, his story can be read and narrated on many other levels of analysis as well. Such additional or alternative readings might contribute to more effectively recovering the complexity of a significant personality and his work. Chapter 6 attempts to document in some detail Kyprianos's relation to the Enlightenment, a connection that shaped his archiepiscopal strategy in the service of reform and cultural change. Kyprianos of Cyprus was one of a number of senior Orthodox prelates in the late eighteenth and early nineteenth centuries who understood their mission and their service to their Church not in terms of conservatism and resistance to change but as an obligation to bring Orthodox society and the flock that was entrusted to their pastoral care, into the age of Lights and reason. This task, they believed, could be transacted primarily through educational reform, without compromising the essentials of the faith. They thus formed an Orthodox "ecclesiastical Enlightenment", which should be recognized as an important component of the cultural and intellectual history of the Orthodox East, beyond earlier bipolar and Manichean readings of the historical record.

Chapter 7 brings to light the report written by the Counsul of the Levant Company in Cyprus on 31 December of the fateful year 1821. It refers to Kyprianos's martyrdom and it can be seen as one of the many testimonies that set in motion the elaboration of historical memory that produced the iconic image with which Kyprianos has been identified in Cypriot collective conscience. It was this iconic image that was canonized by Cyprus's national poet, Vassilis Michaelides in his great epic in Cypriot Greek, "The ninth of July in Nicosia Cyprus", written late in the nineteenth century.

This work, a truly great achievement of narrative poetry in modern Greek literature as a whole, forms the point of departure of the short study presented in Chapter 8 on the politics that went into the construction of the poetic tradition of modern Cyprus. A great deal more could and has been written on this important subject but the present study was one of the earliest attempts to conceptualize the interplay of poetry and politics in the context of Cypriot literature. Its claim for inclusion in this collection is based primarily on its precocious appearance that adds a certain historiographical interest to it.

Part II of the collection focuses on the politics of the Cyprus Question. Most of the studies in this Part were published earlier than the studies that appear in Part I, but to be consistent with the chronological principle adopted in the organization of the collection they had to follow the mostly historical first part since they refer primarily to contemporary politics. Studies IX and X are my earliest writings on the Cyprus Question. They represent the strivings of a young political scientist to come to terms with and understand the reasons for the tragedy that befell his native island in 1974.

Study IX discusses the internal dynamics of the ethnic conflict that arose as a consequence of the growth of two nationalist movements on the island in the period of British rule. The logic of the approach adopted was to direct attention to the internal factors of the problem in an effort to enhance understanding through a serious conversation with the social and cultural history of the island.

This motivation was also dictated by the wish, amidst the feelings of distress and loss caused by the disaster of 1974, to develop a critical perspective that might invite reconsideration of many of the ideological stereotypes and one-sided truths that prevailed in the political discourse whipped up in the bosom of both communities of the island. The deeper motivating question was whether it might be possible to see and appraise things differently in the hope that an attempt at self-criticism might lead to more responsible political attitudes and thus make possible some form of transcendence of the conflict, its sources and consequences.

As is made clear in Chapter 10, the original motivation and groping for a different understanding did not exclude or underplay the weight of external factors, beyond the Cypriots' own control, but still the self-critical understanding of the politics of the Cyprus Question remained a constant in my subsequent writing, as suggested by Chapters 12 and 13. The critical and revisionist approach has not been unrelated to an understanding of what the mission of a self-respecting social science and particularly of a serious and self-aware "science" of politics should be, if it wishes to retain its integrity and remain true to the long tradition of political reflection that goes back to Thucydides and Plato.

The studies in the collection were written over an extensive period of time, from the late 1970s to the second decade of the twenty-first century. Writing on Cyprus, especially on the Cyprus Question and on the endless series of abortive attempts to produce a solution, has grown exponentially in this period. This scholarly output comprises some works of high quality, including writings of first-rate scholarship, but also a considerable amount of writing of indifferent quality, very often motivated not by independent academic concern but by political and other partisan considerations and intentions. In putting together this collection, therefore, and primarily out of respect for the historicity of scholarship, I decided to reproduce the studies in their original form as they first appeared in print. Looking at things from the distance of almost half a century, I believe that many of the studies, especially those in Part II, present a certain historiographical interest as testimonies of the early historiography of the Cyprus Question and as attempts to introduce the analytical perspectives of the social sciences into the writing of the history of modern Cyprus. Accordingly the fourteen studies in the collection were left intact. In Part III, nevertheless, which is composed of a bibliographical comment on each of the studies in the collection, an effort has been made to converse with the scholarship that has been produced on the respective subject since the original publication and to bring to the reader's attention writings that in my judgment advance and carry forward our knowledge of the particular subject. It is to be hoped that in its small way this collection will contribute to the recognition of some neglected aspects of the history of modern Cyprus and to a clearer sense of the destiny of an island that remains a challenge to historical understanding.

* * *

Rereading and pondering the essays that make up this collection, my own retrospective feeling, as the author, is that they are best understood and interpreted in an intellectual history perspective. But intellect, emotion and personal experience can never be clearly demarcated, and it is therefore perhaps appropriate to say something briefly about my own background and professional development in relation to the themes of this book. I was born on an island that had remained for millennia on the southeastern periphery—mentally as much as physically—of the continent of Europe. Although the island is on the threshold of Asia and shares many of the physical features of the neighbouring Near-Eastern landmass, it has always considered and understood itself as a European outpost, speaking as it does the oldest European language. The sense of the European heritage of his island has been a weighty determinant of the present author's outlook and academic interests. He grew up in an intensely intellectual environment dominated by the classics and by the national aspirations connected with an ongoing liberation struggle from colonialism. His earliest political memories are associated with the strong emotions, hopes and fears connected with that struggle and have always remained with him as a substratum of his later effort to understand the historical experience of his island. Independence came in 1960, but it remained rather uncelebrated in the public culture of the island because it was seen as a sacrifice of the essential and authentic goal of the liberation struggle, union with the motherland in the distant West. Thus the nationalist rhetoric did not subside and continued to form the unquestioned normative framework of life, culture and thought on the island. Things were compounded by the flare-up of ethnic conflict between the two national communities inhabiting the island. Nationalism, unreflective and unthinking, stifled all dissenting voices in both communities and excluded social and political criticism as a form of public expression. This was the culture of the "dialectic of intolerance" in which I grew up.

A birthday gift of two beautiful ancient Cypriot pots by my archaeologist aunt, Angeliki Pieridou, directed my interest towards archaeology and to the ancient history of the island and this motivated me to start collecting

Cypriot pottery, at the time a quite legal pastime since these artefacts were put on the market by the Republic's Department of Antiquities from multiple copies they did not need for their collections. This interest survived throughout high school but when archaeology was raised as a prospect of higher education it was drastically discouraged by the then director of antiquities who said there were no job prospects for archaeologists in Cyprus. During my summer vacation as a boy at the age of 16, I read Aeschylus's *Prometheus Bound* in the original and I was so deeply moved by the beauty of the language and the poetry that I made up my mind to study classics and live a life in conversation with the ancients. This would have been the obvious career choice for a young person growing up in a family environment dedicated to education and dominated by the belief in the values of the classical tradition. My maternal grandfather, Paschalis Paschalides, an Asia Minor Greek, was a classicist and headmaster of the Greek Gymnasium at Paphos. Both of my parents, Mikis and Magda, were also trained in the classics at the University of Athens and served Greek education in Cyprus, at Paphos and at the Pancyprian Gymnasium, my own high school as well. I still meet people who had been their students and they are remembered by all for their dedication and lofty idealism. My mother in particular, headmistress of the Pancyprian Gymnasium for girls at Pallouriotissa, a Nicosia suburb, is remembered for her determination to reopen her school in 1975, which on account of its location on the Green Line dividing the city, had been closed and turned into a National Guard outpost following the invasion in 1974. Such was the milieu of a highly educated, liberally minded, Europe-conscious Cypriot family, which provided the early background for my initial understanding of the world.

Less than a year after that memorable summer of reading *Prometheus*, a major political development in the country which our island considered its motherland set processes in motion that led me on a radically different life trajectory. The development in question, which set a major national and countless personal crises in motion, was the coup of 21 April 1967 and the imposition of military dictatorship in Greece. On account of the dictatorship I decided to avoid Greece as a place for my university studies and applied instead to the Fulbright programme for a scholarship at an American university. This eventually brought me to the USA—something completely unplanned and uncontemplated even a few months before I found myself on a plane flying to the USA from the Eastern Mediterranean in what turned out to be the longest day of my life. In the US I did not follow my original wish to study classics or archaeology. I was sent by Fulbright to one of the very top liberal arts colleges in the country, Wesleyan University, where I majored in political science and minored in modern European history. Ever since the history of modern Europe has remained one of my foremost intellectual inspirations. Studying political science and European history beyond the Atlantic in an environment of critical thinking in the early 1970s was an eye-opener: among other things, reading international politics, theories of democratic government, theories of political change, I gradually realized that back home we had been living in a culture of half-truths as far as the island's "national problem" was concerned. The rhetorical nationalist culture I had known in the 1950s and 1960s sounded increasingly hollow especially in connection with its adamant claims that for the island's troubles and misfortunes all blame should be placed on outsiders, never on the local society itself and its internal contradictions.

That realization became dramatic indeed a few years later, specifically in 1974, when the Greek military dictatorship engaged in a completely irresponsible and reckless adventure of intervention in the island that precipitated an invasion by neighbouring Turkey, which brought one third of the island under military occupation, uprooted amidst terrible atrocities more than two hundred thousand people from their ancestral hearths and homes and caused endless suffering and humanitarian problems. The invasion and the human suffering it caused, especially the tragedy of missing and unaccounted persons, the division of Cyprus and the sense of loss this involved and also the pain over the looting and destruction of the island's splendid cultural heritage, have been another emotional burden that has remained with the author and has in many ways shaped his writing on the insular destinies that form the subject of the following studies. What was the root cause of all that but nevertheless continued to provide the normative framework for explaining it in the insular society was the inexorable and self-destructive power of nationalist ideology. Nationalism of course as an ideology and as normative discourse had been discredited by the uses to which it had been put by the Greek military dictatorship in its policies of repression and authoritarianism, but among the island's society it lingered on as an unquestioned doctrine of political morality, solidified by the injustice of foreign occupation.

That was the diagnosis of the disaster in his homeland, which the author had reached by living through and trying to understand the crisis, and which he recorded in his early writings on the Cyprus Question. By then I was a graduate student at the greatest university in America and my judgement as to what had happened to the island and in my mother country was determined by my training in a field in which I felt I had found my life's vocation—the history of political thought.

At the time, in the 1970s, the only place in America to seriously study the history of political thought was Harvard University. In the Faculty of Arts and Sciences the field had been systematically cultivated as the backbone of training in political science for generations since the earliest years of the twentieth century. A succession of great scholars, Charles McIlwain, Carl J. Friedrich, Louis Hartz had established the parameters of the field. Their successors, European-born Judith Shklar and Michael Walzer became my supervisors and shaped my thinking through their teaching and intellectual influence. To theirs other influences were added, most notably that of another European-born scholar, Stanley Hoffmann, who during his long career at Harvard, remained an authentic voice of European thought and sensibility at the university and in American academia more broadly. From Harvard I also remember Herbert Kelman, professor of social psychology, whose interest in the psychology of conflict resolution and reconciliation drew his attention to Cyprus. He developed an active interest in the psychological aspects of the Cyprus problem and organized a series of workshops, which were important experiences in self-reflection for Greek and Turkish Cypriot participants. Recalling my graduate school years I cannot avoid the strong impression that the huge intellectual span of Harvard's faculty and the influences to which I was exposed produced the bent of mind that I brought to the study of Cyprus.

In this intellectual environment, as a graduate student from the Eastern Mediterranean I developed my intellectual interests and became conscious of the significance of the Enlightenment as the central expression of European modernity and the matrix of the modern idea of liberty. Within the broader culture of the Enlightenment I turned to the significant corpus of sources expressing the ideas and values of the movement of intellectual change and criticism in the Greek language, unnoticed and ignored in international scholarship on the subject and focused on this material for my doctoral research. This became a lifelong commitment. In this research orientation, I was encouraged by another great scholar, Elie Kedourie, professor of political science at the London School of Economics. Kedourie had published a seminal book on nationalism in 1960 and had discovered the significance of the political thought of Adamantios Korais in the worldwide process of transmission of the ideas of liberal nationalism.

The deeper motivation of my own intellectual choices was not unrelated to the crises of the period 1967–1974 that had nurtured my early critical reflection on nationalism. The Enlightenment and its universalist values appeared as an alternative to the parochialism and the partialities of nationalism. In the context of the later Greek intellectual tradition the presence of the extensive source material of the eighteenth and the early nineteenth centuries that bore an Enlightenment imprint, supplied evidence of alternative possibilities and patterns of political and intellectual development, hints of what might have happened. To the destructive rhetorical intolerance of nationalism, the Enlightenment juxtaposed the model of criticism and the prospect of freedom. That is why it appeared so attractive and gripping as a research project to a young mind seeking intellectual emancipation through criticism and understanding.

Later on, gradually moving away from youth, its emotions and its enthusiasms, the author returned in 1980 from the US and became a professor not in his island but in Greece. The choice to settle in Greece rather than in Cyprus was dictated by family and professional reasons. I thus lived my entire professional life as an expatriate, a diaspora Cypriot. This helped me in many ways to understand intuitively the psychology of the diaspora scholars who have been the protagonists in my historical study of Cypriot intellectual life in the early modern period. In Greece I soon realized that in a cultural environment dominated, despite the recent antijunta struggle, by a taste for authoritarian ideologies, which besides nationalism included the authoritarian populism of an ideologically ascendant Left which despised liberal democracy and its values as "bourgeois" concoctions, teaching political theory and the history of political thought was a task that required patient but sustained work of lecturing, supervising, writing and also translation of the classics of liberal political thought in an effort to clarify and restore the credibility and significance of the value of liberty. And this, next to the criticism of nationalism and the effort to expand the canon of the Enlightenment, became a lifelong project involving hard work along a rather solidary path.

Another professional engagement of the author that has turned into a lifelong commitment has been his service at the Centre for Asia Minor Studies. This private, nonprofit institute is one of the oldest continuously functioning research establishments in Greece and it is dedicated to the study of the Greek communities in Asia Minor before 1922. Its largest research resource is an oral history archive that records in great detail the life of 1375 Greek Orthodox communities, Greek-speaking or Turkish-speaking. The evidence is eloquent in many respects and also instructive on how to approach an emotionally highly charged subject with academic responsibility and allow the source material to speak and relate the epic story of ethnological survival and revival to its tragic dénouement in 1922 and the eventual uprooting and resettlement of the Greeks of Asia Minor in Greece. My experience at the Centre for Asia Minor Studies taught me that scholarship does not need and cannot proceed through either rhetoric or emotion, let alone by resorting to slogans and polemics against various forms of otherness. Scholarship can remain credible only by staying within the bounds of reason, moderation and tolerance. History, no matter how tragic the content of the evidence, should respect these principles. This is the only way to transact its job with dignity and also to narrate its story effectively. These lessons of Asia Minor research have been important, indeed salutary sources of caution, in contextualizing the history of modern Cyprus as a parallel historical trajectory.

The long connection with the Centre for Asia Minor Studies has been significant for me in another respect as well. The Centre was the child of the French Institute in Athens and of the Merlier couple, Melpo and Octave, both of whom played a leading role in Greek cultural and intellectual life in the interwar and post-World War II period. Their many-sided cultural activities and initiatives represented the extent and depth of French intellectual influence in Greece. My association with the Centre strengthened a predilection for French culture, which had its distant roots in my high school training in French in Cyprus and was strengthened in America, especially at the Centre for European Studies at Harvard. Despite my American training, at the Centre for Asia Minor Studies I maintained

French as the institute's foreign language. This was motivated both by respect for the founders and the tradition of the Centre but also as a gesture in support of cultural pluralism in the face of the levelling pressures of globalization. Beyond these formalities, however, my interest in the French intellectual tradition has been deep and genuine and since my graduate school years I had been looking at French scholarship in history and the "human sciences" as an alternative to the often unreflective positivism and behaviouralism of American social science. All this is reflected I think in some aspects of the work that is included in this volume.

So perhaps it is by now clearer how the research effort embodied in this collection was shaped by the intellectual and political experiences marking my individual life story, experiences which have determined the choice of topics and the interpretative perspective, a sense of crisis being often a distant or a deeper motivation. My account may have transmitted an impression of an arduous and rather embattled trajectory but there have been rewards and consolations as well. Rewards of the kind that Machiavelli felt in his conversations with the ancients have invariably been part of the journey. Of course, the Augustinian reminder of the workings of evil in the world has equally been ever present but next to it there has been the possibility of self-understanding through introspection and taking stock of the factors that shaped one's intellectual development, a possibility offered by reading Marcus Aurelius, Michel de Montaigne and John Stuart Mill. Such rewards and consolations, in the Boethian sense, could never be possible outside a life in the history of political thought. It has been this perspective that has informed the following studies with their limitations and shortcomings, which I cheerfully acknowledge. They illustrate the engagement of a concerned Cypriot with the dilemmas arising from the political adventures of his island and record his conviction that only the values of the Enlightenment, liberty and reason, can provide the catharsis that the island's destinies seem to have been yearning for, for so long.

Part One
Culture and society on a captive island

1   Cyprus in history

Cyprus is an important island, one of the self-contained "small continents" as Fernand Braudel describes the islands of the Mediterranean. The much acknowledged significance of the geographical factor that has placed the island on the crossroads of continents, civilizations and maritime routes, has also made it an abode of human habitation that goes back in time for about twelve millennia. The earliest traces of human habitation have in the recent past been dated to the tenth millennium before the Christian era on the evidence of finds at Akrotiri-Aetogremnos, near the site of ancient Kourion in southern Cyprus.

This pushes back by three millennia the conventional dating of Cypriot prehistory associated with the Neolithic settlement of Khirokitia with its impressive cyclical architecture and stone age art (7000 to 6000 BC). The Khirokitia culture was associated with a pattern of human settlement that was to develop into a regularity in the prehistory and ancient history of Cyprus. This was the attraction of settlers to the island from the neighbouring continents. The original settlers came to Khirokitia from the Syro-Palestinian coast in the Eastern Mediterranean.

After the decline of Khirokitia around 6000 BC, the Neolithic culture of Cyprus revived about 4000 BC at Sotira, just inland from the south coast, in the neighbourhood of the Akrotiri peninsula. The Sotira culture was marked by the earliest appearance of handmade pottery in the material culture of the island, a major step forward in the evolution of civilization. In the course of the next one and a half millennium, another major turning point was reached with the appearance of the earliest metal objects in Cyprus, attested to in the culture of Erimi, next door to Sotira. This development ushered in the Chalcolithic Age, which led on to the greatest period of prehistoric Cyprus, the Bronze Age. Meanwhile new settlers from across the sea made their appearance, this time from the north, from the southern coast of Asia Minor. Their presence is attested to in the culture of Philia in north-western Cyprus, where pottery and metalwork show strong affinities with the art of southern Asia Minor.

The Bronze Age was the great epoch of Cypriot prehistory (2500–1050 BC). The splendours of the Bronze Age are reflected in the exquisite pottery which adorns the greatest museums of the world. The discovery of copper and its economic consequences made the island a focal point of trade with Egypt, the Near East and the world of the Aegean. During this period ancient Near Eastern sources refer to the island by the name of Alasia, a toponym that can be associated with the site of Enkomi in eastern Cyprus. Toward the end of that period the major development in the historical destinies of Cyprus was set in motion: the island became a pole of attraction for immigrants from the west for the first time. From the end of the twelfth century BC onward, major waves of Greek immigration brought the Greek language and Mycenaean civilization to Cyprus. This was the background of the legends recounting the arrival of heroes of the Trojan War after the fall of Troy and the foundation of Cyprus's main cities that were to develop into the focal centres of Hellenic culture in the island: Salamis, Paphos, Lapithos, Kyrenia, Kourion. A major development connected with the settlement of the Acheans, the Mycenaean Greeks, in Cyprus was the abandonment of the Cypro-Minoan script of the late Bronze Age, in which the pre-Hellenic languages of Cyprus were written, and the adoption of the Cypro-Syllabic, in which the Greek language of the island was recorded.

After about 1050 BC and down to 750, a period described by archaeologists as Cypro-Geometric set in. Geometric pottery was produced, and the use of iron is attested to in the material culture. A major development marking this period was yet another immigration wave from the east which brought the Phoenicians to Cyprus and their settlement at the site of Kition, which became the major stronghold of this Near Eastern seafaring and trading people on the island.

In the subsequent Archaic (750–480 BC) and Classical (480–323 BC) periods the historical physiognomy of ancient Cyprus took shape with the emergence of the city-kingdoms. Their number fluctuated around ten and they were centred upon the ancient cities connected with the settlement of the Greeks and Phoenicians and the important city of Amathus, which emerged as the focus of the pre-Hellenic ethnic element in Cyprus, the so-called Eteocypriots. Besides the important coastal cities mentioned above, other city-kingdoms, like Idalion and Tamasos, emerged inland and a new Greek city, Soloi, was founded in the sixth century in honour of the great Athenian lawmaker, Solon, whose name was thus permanently commemorated in Cyprus. Despite their autonomy from each other, the kingdoms in the course of the Archaic period found themselves under a succession of foreign overlords as the empires ruling the Asian mainland extended their control over the insular territory across the sea. Assyria (709–669 BC), Egypt (570–545 BC) and Persia (545 BC onward) came to dominate Cyprus, leaving, especially the Assyrians and the Egyptians, a strong impression on ancient Cypriot art, particularly on sculpture and also important written records that inform us about the Cypriot kingdoms and their kings.

The Cypriot kingdoms, nevertheless, even under foreign overlordship, retained their individuality and grew in prosperity based on extensive commercial exchanges overseas and among themselves. Cypriot pottery and metalwork dating from this period and discovered around the Mediterranean supply ample evidence of this. Toward the end of the sixth century the kingdoms began to strike their own coinage, which has been a very important source of historical evidence, transmitting to posterity the names of their kings.

Ancient Cyprus emerged as a land of diversity punctuated by occasional conflict but also by creative osmosis, with an ever-changing identity. Ancient sources, Greek, Assyrian and Egyptian as well as the material remains of ancient Cypriot art attest to the pluralism and creative richness of the civilization of ancient Cyprus. Pluralism was inscribed within a framework defined by the dominant Hellenic element in the demographic, linguistic and cultural make-up of ancient Cyprus. The information supplied by the Greek historian Herodotus of Halicarnassus very vividly documents in characteristic detail this overall impression.

The Hellenic identity of Cyprus, which was particularly pronounced in some of the most important city-kingdoms like Salamis and Paphos, was actively expressed in the momentous decision of the Cypriots to join the Greek cities of Ionia in their revolt against Persian rule in 499/8 BC. This initiative brought to the surface deeper ethnic divisions and conflicts simmering on the island as the city kingdom of Amathus refused to join the revolt and was besieged by Onesilos, the king of Salamis, who was killed in battle. The revolt was crushed by Persia both in Ionia and in Cyprus and this became the cause of the Persian Wars fought between invading Persian forces and the mainland Greeks between 490 and 479 BC.

Cyprus remained a point of confrontation between the Greek world and Persia throughout the Classical period. Despite the Greek victory on the mainland, Persian rule returned to Cyprus and in 450/449 BC an Athenian fleet under Cimon tried to liberate the island from the Persian empire, but was resisted by the Phoenician-controlled city of Kition. Cimon died in the siege of Kition and became an emblematic figure of the Hellenic affinities of ancient Cyprus.

These affinities were reasserted by the most important of the ancient Cypriot kings, Evagoras I of Salamis (411–374 BC). His great ambition was to cement the Hellenic identity of Cypriot culture as part of affirming his own and his kingdom's independence from Persia. His son and successor Nicocles continued his policies, gaining the praise of the Athenian orator Isocrates, who also extolled Evagoras himself as one of the great leaders of the Hellenic world.

The cities of Cyprus, rallied to Alexander the Great after the Battle of Issus in 333 BC and specifically during the siege of Tyros on the opposite Phoenician coast in 332. Thus two hundred years of Persian rule and intermittent intervention in Cyprus came finally to a definite end. In the subsequent Hellenistic period (323–30 BC) Cyprus eventually became part of the kingdom of the Ptolemies (294 BC), who had inherited Egypt from Alexander's empire. The city-kingdoms came to an end and older cities were renamed with Ptolemaic names, like Marion, which became Arsinoe. Cyprus enjoyed a long period of peace and comparative prosperity and the Hellenization of the island as attested by its art was strengthened and deepened. This period witnessed the emergence of the greatest intellectual personality of Cypriot antiquity, or even perhaps of the entire history of the island, Zeno of Kition, who in 321 BC settled in Athens and taught philosophy at the Stoa Poikile, becoming the founder of Stoic philosophy, the most important current in Greek philosophy after Aristotle.

Cyprus was annexed by Rome in 58 BC and became part of the Roman province of Cilicia and Cyprus. For a brief period in 51/50 BC it was ruled by Cicero but Julius Ceasar returned the island to Cleopatra VII of Egypt. Roman rule returned permanently for a very long period in 30 BC when Anthony and Cleopatra were defeated by Octavian, the future Augustus and first Roman emperor.

Under Rome the island was ruled by a Proconsul with his seat at Paphos. The island entered a long period of peace and prosperity and Roman rule in many ways strengthened the Hellenic character of the civilization of the island. This is evident in the remains of its twelve cities in this period, which have the distinct appearance of Greek cities. The cities of Cyprus were organized into a loose cooperative system, the *Koinon Kyprion*, which struck its own coinage.

The most important development of the period of Roman rule was the introduction of the new religion of Christianity in 45 AD by the Apostle Paul, who made Cyprus the first stopover on his first evangelizing mission to the Gentiles. He was accompanied by the Cypriot Barnabas, who became the founder of the Church of Cyprus. At Paphos the two apostles converted the Proconsul Sergius Paulus to the new religion. Later on bishops of the new faith were consecrated in various cities and thus the structure of the Christian church was introduced in Cyprus. Cypriot bishops, most notably Spyridon of Tremithus, participated in the first Ecumenical Council convoked at Nicea by Emperor Constantine I in the year 325 AD

In the year 116/117 AD a major revolt of the Jewish population of Cyprus against Roman rule caused considerable bloodshed and loss of life. This upheaval led to the disappearance of the Jewish presence in the island, as a consequence of the measures of the Roman military authorities for the repression of the revolt.

On the division of the Roman Empire into east and west in 395 AD, Cyprus was included in the eastern Roman Empire and this, along with the recognition of Christianity as the Empire's official religion, opened a new era in the island's history and civilization. Cyprus was now part of the Byzantine world and Byzantine culture left its traces in art all over the island from the impressive paleo-Christian basilicas and exquisite mosaics of Late Antiquity to the painted churches of the late Byzantine period.

For the rest of the island's history the most important institution in its life became its Christian Church. The Church of Cyprus was organized in fourteen dioceses and although originally under the Patriarchate of Antioch it was granted autocephaly, that is independence, from all neighbouring ecclesiastical jurisdictions, by the Third Ecumenical Council of Ephesus in 431. Autocephaly was confirmed by the Emperor Zeno in 488. From then onward the Church of Cyprus ranked after the five original patriarchates of the unified Church of the first millennium of the Christian era (Rome, Constantinople, Alexandria, Antioch and Jerusalem) as an independent ecclesiastical entity in the communion of Christian faith.

From the year 647, and during the subsequent three centuries, Cyprus was exposed to repeated raids and invasions by the Arab followers of the new faith of Islam. The Arab raids devastated the coastal regions of the island and pushed the population to the highlands. The Arabs also extracted tribute from the Cypriots. To safeguard the islanders, Emperor Justinian II in 690/1 transferred a considerable number of Cypriots, led by their archbishop, to the city of Nova Justiniana next to Cyzicus on the Sea of Marmara. In retaliation the Arab Khalif Abd al Malik forced another population group to be transferred from Cyprus to Syria. These were the first forced mass migrations in the history of Cyprus. The forced migration did not last very long. An understanding between Byzantines and Arabs in 705 made possible the return of the Cypriots from Bithynia and Syria to their island. The forced migration left its memory in the title of the head of the Church who since then has been called the Archbishop of Nova Justiniana and all of Cyprus.

Byzantine rule returned in a stable form in Cyprus in the year 965 during the reign of Emperor Nicephoros Phocas. This ushered in a period of two and a half centuries of continuous Byzantine rule. It was a very important period for the Church with the introduction of cenobitic monasticism in the island. This was the age of the foundation of the island's most important monasteries that have survived to this date. It was also an age of flowering of religious art marked by the decoration of many churches, especially in the mountainous regions of central Cyprus, with exquisite frescos.

Byzantine rule came to an abrupt end when a new wave of invasions engulfed Cyprus at the end of the twelfth century, this time from the west. Since the late eleventh century western Christendom was engaged in military expeditions for the recovery of the Holy Sepulche and other holy sites in the land of Palestine from the Muslim Arab conquerors. The Third Crusade in 1191 snatched Cyprus away from Byzantine control and delivered it to a succession of western rulers. The island was conquered in 1191 by one of the leaders of the Third Crusade, Richard I Lionheart, king of England. This first English occupation was of very limited duration, but was marked by the marriage of the new conqueror, Richard, to Berengaria of Navarre in

Limassol, where she was also crowned Queen of England. Richard was not interested in holding on to an island so distant from his other possessions in Britain and France and the following year he sold it to the Knights Templar, whom the Arabs had expelled from Jerusalem following the second conquest of the city by Saladin. The Templars found it difficult to bring the island under control and soon resold it to the deposed king of Jerusalem, Guy de Lusignan. Their transient presence is recalled by the beautiful tower at Kolossi, west of Limassol.

The establishment of the Lusignan dynasty brought Cyprus under western rule and turned the island into an independent kingdom in the state system of Medieval Europe for three centuries (1192–1489). The Lusignans, originally a noble family from Poitou in western France, were given the crown of the Crusader kingdom of Jerusalem, their claim on which they never relinquished and continued to be crowned kings of Jerusalem in the cathedral of Famagusta. They introduced the feudal political and social organization of medieval France in Cyprus. Feudalism reduced the island's Greek Orthodox population to serfdom and subjected them to multiple forms of oppression, including the abolition of their autocephalous Orthodox Church. The *Bulla Cypria* of Pope Alexander IV in 1260 subjected the Church of Cyprus to a Latin hierarchy, reduced the number of episcopal districts of the Orthodox Church from fourteen to four and made the four Greek bishops suffragans to the Latin prelates, who ruled the island's four dioceses from the main cities (Nicosia, Famagusta, Limassol and Paphos), whereas the Greek bishops were removed to distant sees in the countryside.

One remarkable aspect of the social history of the medieval kingdom of Cyprus was the attraction it exercised on Christian groups from the Levant and from further inland in the Near East to relocate in Cyprus. Obviously Cyprus as a Christian state appeared to be a refuge of security and stability to Christian communities who wished to escape Muslim rule following the collapse of the Crusader states. Thus the city of Famagusta, as witnessed by surviving Christian monuments, grew into a multiethnic metropolis inhabited not only by Greek Orthodox and Latin Christians, but also by Nestorians, Copts, Armenians and others.

The most important wave of immigration from the Near East to Cyprus during the Lusignan period was that of the Maronites from Mount Lebanon. They settled in the cities but mainly in the countryside north-west of Nicosia in the area of Kormakitis, where their villages and monasteries, speaking an archaic form of Arabic peculiar to their community, have survived into the twenty-first century, despite the adversities of Turkish occupation since 1974.

The history of the medieval Kingdom of Cyprus was one of oppression and inequality as was the case everywhere else in medieval Europe, but it was also a period of osmosis and of cultural encounters with creative outcomes. After the confrontations and religious conflicts of the thirteenth century, which in 1231 involved the martyrdom of the thirteen monks of

Kantara monastery who resisted conversion to Roman Catholicism and sought to remain steadfast in their Orthodox faith, Cypriot society gradually proceeded to a new synthesis. This was evident in the last century of Lusignan rule. By then the royal dynasty and feudal aristocracy implanted in Cyprus had become Greek-speaking, the laws of the Kingdom of Jerusalem (*Assises*) which were used as the legal code of the Kingdom of Cyprus as well, were translated into Greek, the two Churches had found a way of accommodation with each other. This was the background of the emergence of a Cypriot version of the Renaissance that becomes perceptible both in the art and architecture of Cyprus during the fifteenth century but also in the emergence of a significant literature in Cypriot Greek.

Following the establishment of the Kingdom, the major cities of Cyprus were adorned by imposing monuments of Gothic architecture, such as the cathedrals of Saint Sophia in Nicosia and Saint Nicholas in Famagusta and the Abbey of Bellapais on the northern slopes of Pentadaktylos mountains, in the vicinity of Kyrenia. Later, influences of Renaissance styles become evident in many Cypriot monuments and western styles also influenced religious painting and the remarkable art of glazed ceramics that developed in the period of the medieval kingdom.

In literary production an important chronographical literature emerged especially in the fifteenth century, recording the self-awareness of the Cypriots concerning their identity and their sense of the past of their island and its fortunes. The two most significant representatives of this genre of vernacular prose in Cypriot Greek were Leontios Machairas and George Boustronios.

The medieval Kingdom of Cyprus had played a noticeable role in European interstate politics during the time of the later Crusades. King Louis IX of France settled in Cyprus for a period in 1248 on his way to Jerusalem at the head of the Seventh Crusade. The fame of the Kingdom was such that Thomas Aquinas dedicated his treatise *De regimine principum* to King Hugo III of Cyprus (1267–1284). Later on in the fourteenth century, King Peter I (1359–1369) by his wars and his travels in the west as far as London, made Cyprus a recognizable factor in European power politics in the Eastern Mediterranean. Following Peter's reign the kingdom entered a period of disorder that eventually led to the occupation by Genoa of the island's main port city Famagusta, which had developed into the major emporium in the Levant after the taking of Accra by the Arabs in 1291. The Genoese occupation of Famagusta lasted from 1372 to 1464 and was never recognized by the kings of Cyprus. It remained a constant source of conflict and disorder on the island and turned out to be the major cause of the decline of the medieval Kingdom.

In the course of the fifteenth century the power of the dynasty declined and the Kingdom of Cyprus came increasingly under the tutelage of the dominant power of the epoch, the Venetian Republic. In the fifteenth century, Venice was a world power comparable to what Britain was to become in the nineteenth and was in possession of an important insular empire in the Mediterranean. Cyprus inevitably attracted the interest of the Republic of Saint Mark both for geopolitical and for economic reasons. By the mid-fifteenth century the Kingdom of Cyprus was a Venetian protectorate and this status was formalized when a Venetian patrician lady, Caterina Cornaro, succeeded her husband, James II, as sovereign Queen of Cyprus. By 1489 Queen Caterina ceded the island kingdom to Venice. Thus an eighty-year period of Venetian rule was ushered in.

The Venetian period (1489–1571) was a relatively short period but it was a very important phase in the historical evolution of Cyprus. Venetian rule preserved the feudal organization of society, but economically the island moved on to a form of "colonial" economy as has been suggested by specialists in this period of its history. Thus some incipient forms of modernity began penetrating the insular society. Commercial development was accompanied by gropings toward modernity in cultural life. Extensive western influences marked a significant revival of religious painting in the sixteenth century, an exquisite lyric poetry carrying Petrarchan models into the Cypriot Greek vernacular made its appearance, in all likelihood connected with the court of Caterina Cornaro in exile, and interest in the ideas of the Protestant Reformation led Cypriots before the Venetian Inquisition. Books by Erasmus and Brucioli could be found in private libraries in Nicosia in the mid-sixteenth century, while a remarkable humanist culture can be documented on the basis of Greek manuscript witnesses from monastic libraries in the island.

Venice was primarily interested in Cyprus as a military bastion and an advanced naval outpost to shield the rest of its insular empire and the maritime routes of its commerce in the Mediterranean against the Ottoman threat. Extensive fortification works went on with the construction of new walls around the capital on the latest models of military architecture. The island's major port and naval base, Famagusta, was made impregnable by new fortifications, with the famous tower of Othello, immortalized in Shakespeare's play, as their emblem.

The Ottoman threat was not averted by the new state-of-the-art military architecture. Venice had been in decline since the early sixteenth century and could only with great exertion hold on to its insular empire in the Eastern Mediterranean. The invasion came in the summer of 1570. The Ottoman forces landed at Salines, the land around the salt lakes west of Larnaca. They proceeded almost unopposed to the capital Nicosia, which held out for about two months. On 9 September 1570 the final assault on the besieged city took place and by sunset on that day the city was taken after the entire male population, military and civilian, including the Latin and Greek clergy in the capital, fell fighting on the walls.

From Nicosia the Ottoman forces made their way east, across the Mesaoria plain, to Famagusta. They camped outside the land walls of the city and laid siege on it for almost a year. Despite repeated assaults and mining the *rivellini* of the outer walls, the city would not fall. By August 1571 a protracted naval blockage by the Ottoman fleet achieved what the land forces could not do: the city was starved and the Venetian military commander, Marcantonio Bragadino, gave himself up to the chief of the Ottoman forces, who had promised safe passage to him and his remaining troops in exchange for the surrender of the city. Promises were broken and Bragadino was subjected to atrocious tortures prior to his execution. An Augustinian monk, abbot of the monastery of St Antony in Famagusta, left an eyewitness account of Bragadino's martyrdom.

Thus western rule came to an end in Cyprus after four centuries and the island became an Ottoman province. The conquest of Cyprus and especially the news of the events of the fall of Famagusta and the martyrdom of Bragadino, propagated widely throughout Europe by a literature of pamphlets and broadsides (*avvisi*), stirred considerable concern and feelings of shock and fear. Christian Europe, at the initiative of Pope Pius V rallied its forces against the Ottoman threat and the naval forces of the three major Mediterranean powers, Spain, Venice and the Holy See, sailed to the east and fought the Ottoman navy, off the town of Lepanto, in the Corinthian Gulf on 7 October 1571. The annihilation of the Ottomans at the Battle of Lepanto, extensively commemorated in European art at the time, boosted European morale but did not change the fate of Cyprus. The island remained in Ottoman hands for the following three centuries. Venice and the Ottoman Empire eventually concluded a peace treaty in 1573.

Ottoman rule was to last in Cyprus from 1571 to 1878. The island was governed either by the admiral of the Ottoman fleet through a representative or directly by the Sublime Porte through a governor (pasha) appointed by the Ottoman Grand Vezir. In the three centuries of Ottoman rule important changes took place in the society of the island. The feudal system was abolished and the former serfs became free agricultural property holders paying the capital tax and many other levies to their new masters. A part of the conquering troops were settled and given land in the island and thus for the first time a Muslim Turkish-speaking population group emerged in the population of Cyprus. These were the ancestors of the Turkish Cypriot minority. The numbers of the minority increased over the years with periodical conversions of Christians, initially from the Latin population of Venetian Cyprus, who did so in order to keep their lands. Whole Orthodox villages also converted in order to escape the capital tax. Thus the Muslim community in Cyprus grew in numbers and overtime became for the most part Greek-speaking, especially in distant and isolated areas like Paphos in the west and the Karpass peninsula in the east.

A net beneficiary of the conquest was the Orthodox Church of Cyprus. At the conquest the Latin Church and Roman Catholic religious orders were expelled from the island. Their great cathedrals and monasteries were turned into mosques. The Orthodox Church, however, was restored and its autocephaly reaffirmed. The Patriarchate of Constantinople consecrated a new Orthodox archbishop, Timotheos and three bishops for the dioceses of Cyprus and communion of the Church of Cyprus with the rest of Orthodoxy was re-established. The Orthodox Church and its monasteries became the focal institutions around which Christian society in the island cohered during the long centuries of foreign rule. The Church cared for its flock by providing material sustenance and spiritual solace and in the later phases of the Ottoman period by leading the effort to introduce education in a mostly illiterate society. The attachment and confidence the flock felt in its Church was reflected in the widespread practice of giving over to the Church agricultural land, that might be confiscated on account of inability to pay the taxes imposed by the Ottoman authorities. This explains the massive landholdings of the Church and the monasteries in Cyprus.

The period of Ottoman rule, particularly in the eighteenth century was marked by considerable brutality and corruption, especially as a consequence of the decline of central control on the outlying provinces which encouraged the rapacity and repressiveness of local governors and officials. Cyprus repeatedly experienced such behaviour on the part of its Ottoman rulers and occasionally this motivated violent outbreaks of protest in which Christian and Muslim Cypriots joined together in order to resist oppression and rapacious taxation. One major such instance of repression and protest occurred in 1764–1765, but other occasions of common Muslim and Christian forms of resistance to authority are also recorded for the years 1665, 1680, 1712, 1783, 1804.

The year 1821 was a particularly tragic year for Cyprus. The local pasha used the pretext of the outbreak of the Greek war of Independence in order to settle his accounts with the Archbishop and to break the power of the Church. On 9 July 1821 Archbishop Kyprianos and the three other bishops were executed without any pretence of trial or other judicial procedure, followed by a hecatomb of other clerical dignitaries and lay notables. Those few who managed to escape the slaughter and take refuge abroad gathered in Rome and then proceeded to Marseille, where on 6 December 1821 they issued the first formal declaration of the wish to have Cyprus join with Greece in the struggle for its liberation from the Ottoman yoke.

The last fifty years of Ottoman rule witnessed attempts to put in place the programme of Ottoman reforms known as the Tanzimat. Some relevant measures were introduced in Cyprus and certainly a greater degree of order and security was achieved. Progress was especially made in the field of education with a sustained effort led by the Church to establish schools in the main cities of the island. The main attempts at reform were undertaken during the tenures of Archbishops Panaretos (1827–1840) and Makarios I (1855–1865) and introduced some improvements in the administration, judicial procedures and taxation of the Greek community.

Ottoman rule came to a close in 1878. A secret convention between Great Britain and the Sublime Porte signed on 4 June 1878 provided, among other things, the cession of the administration of Cyprus to Britain in exchange for military support in the event of a Russian attack on the provinces of the Ottoman empire bordering on the Caucasus. Sovereignty was retained by the Porte and Britain occupied the island as a "place of arms" in order to strengthen its strategic position in the Eastern Mediterranean. Britain had risen to an undisputed position of a major world power following the defeat of Napoleon at Waterloo in 1815. The major motivation of its strategy in the Mediterranean following the opening of the Suez Canal in 1869 had been the construction and the naval security of the road to India, the mainstay of its world empire. In the Mediterranean a maritime route was built to serve this geostrategic objective with its main naval outposts at Gibraltar, Malta, the Ionian Islands for a period (1815–1864). Cyprus was the last bastion added to this route, which continued on the southern side of Suez with the occupation of Aden, the island of Socotra and the opposite African coast that made up the British colony of Somalia. Such was the breadth and depth of the British strategic interest that remained a constant determinant of Britain's imperial policy concerning Cyprus and of its subsequent position in the politics of the Cyprus Question.

British rule abruptly exposed Cyprus to modernity. The backward and dormant province of the Ottoman Empire was suddenly endowed with a modern administration, with order and security and with a remarkable range of political freedoms, that encouraged the emergence of a free and vocal Greek press. The first Cypriot newspaper was published in Larnaca the very first year of the British occupation. In 1881 the British administration established a Legislative Council, which gave the Cypriots their first experience of representative government, despite its undemocratic and divisive structure.

Society remained extremely backward and no signs of economic development could be remarked on for most of the British period. The rural population, which formed the island's vast majority, remained exposed to poverty and multiple forms of exploitation by moneylenders.

Modernity in Cyprus was primarily expressed in the form of the emergence and rapid growth of nationalism among the Greek Cypriots, who from the very first day of the British occupation declared without equivocation their wish to see their island united with Greece on the precedent of the cession of the seven Ionian Islands by Britain to Greece in 1864. The strength of Greek feeling in favour of union with Greece was acknowledged by Winston Churchill during his visit in Cyprus in October 1907 as Undersecretary of State for the Colonies.

In 1914 upon Turkey's entry into the First World War on the side of the Central powers, Britain annexed Cyprus. The island was made a Crown colony in 1925 following the Treaty of Lausanne of July 1923, whereby Turkey renounced its rights on Cyprus (article 20).

The strength of national feeling was reinforced by widespread dissatisfaction over the payment of the Tribute, the annual sum extracted from Cypriot society in order to pay the Ottoman Empire for the cession of the island and which continued to be collected even after the island's annexation. Deep economic malaise in the island under the impact of the international financial crisis of 1929 and the continuing grievances caused by poverty in rural society, acted as motivating factors of the nationalist rising of October 1931 claiming immediate union with Greece. The rising was crushed and extensive repression followed, including the exile of the main nationalist leaders from Cyprus.

When the Second World War broke out and for a period Britain was fighting Nazi Germany alone with Greece as its only ally in the whole of Europe, British authorities in Cyprus appealed to the Cypriots to join the British armed forces and fight for "freedom and for Greece". A considerable number of Cypriot volunteers responded to the appeal and fought in the war. In the aftermath of the war, however, Britain failed to live up to its promises to grant self-determination to Cyprus and convoked a "Consultative Assembly" to discuss a project of self-government as a transitional ten-year period to self-determination. Failures in communication, a mutual hardening of positions, British obsession with strategic concerns that had lost their *raison d'être* following Indian independence and deep divisions within the Greek Cypriots set the preconditions of the decision to resort to armed revolt against British rule on 1 April 1955, demanding union with Greece.

The revolt was terminated in 1958. Despite remarkable acts of heroism and self-sacrifice by the young Cypriot fighters, union was precluded as a solution largely due to the objections of Turkey, which emerged with British encouragement as a party to the conflict. Eventually after an understanding between Greece and Turkey was reached in Zurich in February 1959, the London Agreements of the same month declared Cyprus an independent republic. In December 1959, the Archbishop of Cyprus, Makarios III, was elected the first President of the new republic. Independence was officially proclaimed on 16 August 1960. After half a millennium of foreign rule, the island rose again to sovereign statehood, vindicating a prophesy of the eighteenth-century historian, the Archimandrite Kyprianos, who commented in 1788 on the Venetian takeover of 1489 saying "who can tell whether the island in three hundred more years will not again rise to the status of an independent realm?"

2 Early modern Cypriot learning (1571–1878)

Cypriot intellectual life during the three centuries bracketed by Ottoman conquest and British occupation is comprised of a web of expressions, mainly in the diaspora. It was initially defined by a centrifugal tendency which, after the conquest, transported the intellectual residue of the remarkable civilization of the Cypriot Renaissance to the diaspora. It flourished outside Cyprus and it reproduced a succession of creative generations spanning three centuries. Eventually it manifested the first indications of centripetal tendencies from the eighteenth century onwards culminating in the restoration of the centre of gravity of intellectual creation from the diaspora to Cyprus after 1878.

These broader fluctuations in Cypriot intellectual life can be distinguished in shorter, historically articulated periods according to the following periodization scheme:

The "lost renaissance"

The splendid achievements of the Cypriot Renaissance, mainly those of the sixteenth century, provide the basis for all Cypriot intellectual life during the three centuries that followed the conquest of 1570–1571. This early period witnessed the amalgamation of trends, quests and traditions[1] expressed through creative works in the Greek language. Its most remarkable feature consisted in registering the intersection of East and West in Cypriot culture and society,[2] which thus acquired self-awareness and developed its own distinct self-definition, founded on the discovery of the island's relationship with Greek antiquity.[3] This creative osmosis of civilizations on sixteenth-century Cyprus was violently interrupted by the Ottoman conquest. As research delves deeper into the multiple expressions of Cypriot Renaissance culture and enriches our knowledge of its achievements, the destruction wrought by the conquest looms larger and harsher. Because the emergence of the Cypriot Renaissance culture was disrupted violently, abruptly and definitively, this is precisely why I believe "the lost Renaissance" is an apt description of this foundational period in Cypriot learning.

Intellectual life and diaspora

This period is represented by the transfer of Cypriot intellectual life outside Cyprus after the conquest and spans the remainder of the sixteenth
century (from 1571 onwards) and the seventeenth century. The extent of
this period justifies its division into subperiods initially defined by the
presence of the Cypriot diaspora's first great scholars — Stefano
Lusignan, Giason Denores, Enrico-Caterino Davila — in the immediate
wake of the conquest and subsequently by the presence of the successive
generations of their intellectual descendants through the end of the seventeenth century.

A notable geographic dimension of the Cypriot intellectual diaspora,
which can no longer elude the attention and comment of scholarly analysis,
consists in its articulation of effectively two diasporas, one of which
was oriented towards the West, primarily towards Italy, while the other was
oriented towards the East, primarily towards Palestine. It is worth noting
the vivid preservation of Cypriot self-awareness in the bosom of intellectual
life in the diaspora — an evocative heritage of the lost Cypriot Renaissance
which, nonetheless, did survive for generations in people's consciousness.
Characteristically, Giason Denores appends the cognomen "Cyprius" to his
name;[4] his son Pietro and grandson Giorgio remained preoccupied with the
fortunes of their island and the ambitions of the European powers in regard
to claims to the kingdom and crown of Cyprus. In Paris Davila frequented
Lusignan's social circle at the Dominican monastery of Saint Jacques.[5] The
Holy Sepulchre monks in Palestine's lavras never ceased to remind the
readers of their manuscripts that they were Cypriot, despite revealing absolutely nothing else about themselves. In the climate of calamity, finally, and
while seeking out, in the Mediterranean slave bazaars, Cypriot relatives who
had been taken captive during the conquest so he might buy them,[6] Brother
Stefano Lusignan offers a means for recovering the lost paradise, into which
Cyprus now had been transformed, looming in the Cypriot refugees' consciousness, through his *Chorograffia*.

The case of Stefano Lusignan is exceptional from every perspective. He
was not only the most prolific Cypriot writer of the sixteenth century, with
a volume of work that can only be matched by that of Giason Doneres, he
was exceptional mainly because he consciously detached Cypriot historiography from the earlier tradition of the Medieval Frankish kingdom's chronicles and instead entered into a dialogue with discourse associated with the
Greek chronographers of the fifteenth century. Indeed, he emphasized that
critics of the first edition of his *Chorograffia* had faulted him for not simply
settling for repeating the chronicles written by George Boustronios and
others up to 1490.[7] Lusignan obviously intended to incorporate the historiography of Cyprus into the Renaissance culture of the *litterae humaniores*
he had sampled upon in Cyprus before the conquest by studying the manuscripts of the Ancient Greek and Latin authors in the library of Nicosia's

Dominican monastery,[8] but especially while seeking refuge in Italy, where he encountered the humanist scholars in Rome, Bologna, Padua and Venice.

In those intellectual milieus, especially, he came into contact with Renaissance cosmography, particularly through the work of Enea Silvio Piccolomini, later Pope Pius II (1458–1564).[9] These intellectual pathways led Lusignan to the ancient geographers, Claudius Ptolemy and Strabo, from whom he borrowed the term "chorograffia"[10] to title his work. It is worth noting that this Latin cleric consciously attempted to restore the historical bonds between Cyprus and its pre-Christian past and link it to Greek antiquity by studying Plutarch[11] and subsequently through Aristotle[12] and Diogenes Laërtius,[13] when he supplemented and expanded his work for the French edition. Continuing the intellectual quests that had begun with the work of Florio Bustron, Lusignan's method of going beyond the medieval chronographic tradition highlights the Ancient Greek past of Cyprus.[14] Stefano Lusignan's historiographical approach places his work in the sphere of contemporaneous French humanist historiography and historical criticism represented by Jean Bodin and Guillaume Budé.[15]

However, the originality of Lusignan's historical text, both in its first Italian edition and its later more complete French version, stems mainly from the author's interest in the natural and social environment of his natal island, whose loss he silently experiences and relives in his pages through the dramatic descriptions of the quality of the climate, the population's beauty, the land's fertility, the abundant flora and products, the unique dietary habits and local traditions — all of which indeed create the feeling of a paradise lost. It is, I believe, this dimension of Lusignan's historical composition that casts his work as seminal to Cypriot self-awareness during the centuries of enslavement and simultaneously keeps alive interest in this work as a source of the historiography of the Mediterranean world from the author's time to the twentieth century.[16]

The epigones of the diaspora

The complete assimilation into Venetian society and the Italian-speaking world in the seventeenth century of the descendants of those Cypriot families who abandoned the island after 1571 did not in general mean the end of the Cypriot intellectual diaspora. In diaspora circles, especially in Venice,[17] there are indications, albeit sporadic and indirect, that not only did the descendants of Cypriot refugees preserve among themselves an awareness of their Cypriot heritage but also a special sensitivity for the distinctive components of their Cypriot identity as codified in the island's historical heritage. How else can one interpret, a half century after the conquest, the passion and emotion, perhaps even a faint feeling of *nostos* that permeated Savvas Kappis on 1 March 1634 when he received, in Venice, the impressive codex in which the chronicles of Leontios Machairas and George Boustronios had been copied? Perhaps Savvas Kappis had made arrangements for the famed *Chronica* to be sent to him from Cyprus so he would have a "voice of the homeland" in his foreign sojourn. The note at the end of the text[18] could, I believe, be read in this spirit.

αχλδ΄ μαρτηω –α– Ἐφέρανε τὴ
Κρώνιχαν
ἀπὸ τὴν Κύπρων ἔμενα τοῦ σαβα
Κάππη
1634 March 1
They brought the
Chronica
From Cyprus to me Savva
Kappi

This could be considered the backdrop against which the outlook of the Cypriot intellectual diaspora shaped up, at least in the West, during the centuries of the island's Ottoman occupation. It was in this emotional environment that the young Cypriots were socialized while, in Venice, they crossed the threshold into Europe and its civilization of fledging modernity.

New mobility mechanisms, new institutions, the unabated passion for education that helped the Ottoman-occupied society survive, even the political interests and indeterminate hopes directed towards the European powers in the wake of the Battle of Lepanto created a plexus of root causes that operated after the conquest and contributed to the continual replenishment of the intellectual diaspora, while the old, long tradition of Cypriot students at the University of Padua, which had decisively helped shape the spirit of the Cypriot Renaissance,[19] remained vital. In addition, the return of normalcy during the first two centuries of the Ottoman period and the emergence of new institutions reinforced, but also differentiated, the educational experience of Cypriots in Italy. As for Padua, the founding of the Cottunian College, with an endowment from Ioannis Cottunius in 1653, created an institution for welcoming Greek students that encouraged their influx to the city's university. The sons of Matthaios Kigalas, the vicar of Venice's Greek community, were among the boarding school's first students. In these new circumstances, the offspring of Ottoman-held Cyprus that had retained a bent for education continued to attend the esteemed University of Padua until the turn of the eighteenth century towards the nineteenth.[20]

From the perspective of Cypriot learning, the founding of the Cottunian College presents further interest on account of the involvement of Hilarion Kigalas in its administration from the outset. A genius, dynamic and resourceful, Hilarion Kigalas graduated from the Greek College of Saint Athanasios in Rome in 1648 and in 1657 was summoned by Ioannis Cottunius to serve as the first dean of the new college in Padua.[21] The Cypriot cleric remained at that post for three years, during which he proposed revisions to the college's rules of operation. Archival research has not yielded the text of his proposals, but it can be inferred from the surviving, albeit unpublished, responses of the Cottunian College's commissioners who effectively rejected Hilarion's recommendations.[22]

In any case, the founding in Venice itself in 1661 of the Flanginian School on an endowment by Thomas Flanginis created another mechanism for attracting Cypriots by providing priority status for students of Cypriot descent on account of the Flanginis family's Medieval Cypriot origin.[23] The Flanginian's benevolence towards Cypriots was bolstered in 1666 with the endowment of the Cypriot noble Bernardo Acris that provided two scholarships for Cypriot boarding school students.[24] The document from Acris to the University of Padua's supervisors reveals the spirit and expectations linked to the benefactor's gesture, who expresses the certainty that the "Greek nation" (*nazione greca*) which *"in questo Serenissimo Impero ha ritrovato l'aqffeto de suoi Cesari, et la Giustitia del suo Aeropago, non habbia ne anchie più da ricercare fuor di Venezia la sua Atene"*.[25]

The most important institution, however, that contributed to the reproduction of the Cypriot intellectual diaspora in Italy throughout the seventeenth century was the Pontifical Greek College of St Athanasius in Rome. A product of the Counter-Reformation, the Greek College was founded in 1576 and its first students included Cypriots who remained a fixed presence throughout the seventeenth century. It is estimated that from 1576 to 1700, a total of fifty-one Cypriots, from all-over Cyprus, attended the Greek College.[26]

From its earliest days, the college was linked to the presence in Rome of the Cypriot cleric Germanos Kouskounaris (Coscounari), bishop of Amathus and a former abbot of the Monastery of Saint John Chrysostomos at Koutsovendis. Following the fall of Famagusta, where he had participated in the defence of the city during the long Ottoman siege in 1570–1571, Germanos of Amathus sought refuge in Rome under the protection of Cardinal Giulio Santoro, whose interest in the Eastern Church was instrumental in the founding of the College.[27] His links to Santoro's milieu introduced the Cypriot bishop into the sphere of the Greek College and he became closely associated with its liturgical life during his years in Rome (1581–1600). Germanos Kouskounaris's activity at the Greek College and later among Sicily's "Greek-rite" communities, mainly Albanian-speaking, linked him to the creation of Uniate churches in whose history he occupies the position of their first recorded bishop.[28]

This is precisely why Germanos Kouskounaris's confession of faith and submission to the Church of Rome is of such historical interest. The relevant text is transmitted in a codex at the National Library of Naples.[29]

Among the numerous Cypriots who either studied or were otherwise associated with the Greek College, the most important is undoubtedly Neophytos Rodinos, who may unreservedly be described as the most significant Cypriot writer of the seventeenth century. A rather elusive figure, misunderstood and misinterpreted especially by his admirers,[30] Rodinos's voluminous unpublished work still awaits systematic study by researchers. Paraphrased religious texts steeped in the principles of the Counter-Reformation, the manuscripts of Neophytos Rodinos in the libraries of Rome are excellent monuments of vernacular Greek speech; some, such as the unpublished biography of Saint Ignatius, Patriarch of Constantinople, are outstanding feats of narrative prose.[31]

The comprehensive study of his surviving texts is the prerequisite for redeeming Neophytos Rodinos's intellectual profile not only as a representative of Cypriot learning but also as a contributor to the shaping of modern Greek prose.

Neophytos Rodinos's impressive handling of modern Greek vernacular speech and vibrant tone are not accidental, but stem from the depth of his education and the humanistic culture for which he was admired by his contemporaries, including Leo Allatius, who ranks Neophytos Rodinos among the "bees of civilisation".[32] Allatius's admiration certainly derived from his ascertainment of Rodinos's excellent command of the Greek language. Two exceptional documents, attesting to the Cypriot scholar's knowledge of Ancient Greek, survive: the epigrams he composed about the image and library of Lucas Holstensius (1659–1661), a humanist geographer and custodian of the Apostolic Library of the See of Rome.[33] The publication of these two short but remarkable texts establishes Rodinos's place in Cypriot learning not only on account of his skill in the vernacular, but in addition his command of learned Greek as a long tradition of creative expression.[34]

Neophytos Rodinos's intellectual authority among his contemporaries is reflected in the epigram written in his honour by Iosepho-Maria Suaresio as it appears in the manuscript[35] of Rodinos's *Spiritual Armour* and is reproduced in the printed version of the work.

Ἤΰτε ἐν κήπῳ ἀθροίσας ἄνθεα πολλὰ
ἁβρὸς ἀνὴρ τούτων δεσμὸν ἔτευξε καλόν,
οὕτως ἐξ ἱερῶν Παραδείσου δόγματα τευχῶν
συλλέξας Ῥοδινὸς τὴνδ' ἐπόνησε Βίβλον.
Εἰ τοίνυν ποθέεις τῶν ὀσφραίνεσθ' ἀμαράντων
πόνων, ἠνὶ ῥόδων, ἠνὶ τε πλῆθος ἴων.

As in a garden the gracious man collected many flowers and bundled them up in a bouquet likewise from the sacred rolls of Paradise Rodinos selected the doctrines of faith in this painstaking Book. Thus if you desire to smell the never-fading labours, behold the roses, behold the violets!

Culture and society in the eighteenth century

The eighteenth century was characterized by the centripetal trend of the expressions of intellectual life towards Cyprus, while the movement and creative activity of scholars in the diaspora continued, most notably with

Archimandrite Kyprianos. The trend for transferring expressions of intellectual life towards Cyprus raises the interpretive issue of the entwining of culture and society as a question about the means by which Cypriot society received and assimilated intellectual phenomena. The eighteenth century was a period of reconstruction for the Church of Cyprus, which under archbishops Silvestros, Philotheos, Paisios and Chrysanthos became the arc of education and culture on the island. Under their leadership a local version of the cultural phenomenon characterized by Nicolae Iorga as *Byzance après Byzance* took place in the Eastern Mediterranean.[36] One expression of this phenomenon was Cyprus's organic incorporation during that century in the cultural life of the Orthodox East with Ephraim the Athenian (Ephraim II, Patriarch of Jerusalem) and Seraphim of Pisidia as protagonists.

Archimandrite Kyprianos was the most typical proponent of Cyprus's incorporation into the culture of the Orthodox East through the publication, at the Greek printing establishments in Venice, of the commentaries of Theophilos Corydalleus and the special services in honour of Cypriot saints but especially through his *History*. This work, in which the Orthodox intellectual heritage of the Greek East meets the scientific spirit of the Enlightenment, effectively attempted to, and succeeded in, articulating the Orthodox response to the Western view of Cyprus's history proferred by Stefano Lusignan. From a long-term perspective, the emergence of Cypriot intellectual life during the three centuries of the island's early modern history can be seen as a mostly internal dialogue on Cyprus's historical identity. The relevant issues were initially raised by Stefano Lusignan in such a truly definitive manner that the majority of scholars who were aware of the land's historical heritage revolve and respond to them. Pietro and Giorgio Denores and especially, most characteristically Neophytos Rodinos in the seventeenth century as well as *skevophylax* Loizos of Lefkara, who translated Lusignan's *Chorograffia* into Greek, participate in the dialogue. This discourse continued in the eighteenth century with the participation of Archbishop Sylvester and the copier of the *skevophylax*'s translation, around 1734, but with Archimandrite Kyprianos Kouriokoritis, who effectively concludes the cycle of historical debate with the incorporation of Lusignan's historical legacy into an Orthodox framework. Through his landmark work, Kyprianos thus emerges as the decisive bearer and interpreter of the shaping of Cypriot society's self-awareness as a constituent of the Orthodox community in the Greek East.[37]

In the margins of the Enlightenment

Archimandrite Kyprianos finally closes the debate with the Renaissance but his work opens a new one — a dialogue with the Enlightenment. Some lesser scholars of the Cypriot diaspora participated in the culture of the Neo-Hellenic Enlightenment, but on the island, cultural contacts with the Enlightenment remained on a very limited scale — either as reflected through the Orthodox prism of Kyprianos's *History*, which had numerous subscribers on Cyprus,[38] or through initiatives aimed at modernizing education. Most important among these initiatives were certainly those introduced by Archbishop Kyprianos during the decade spanning 1810–1821.[39] Informed at the very least of the currents of the Neo-Hellenic Enlightenment which he had encountered during his stay in Moldavia, Archbishop Kyprianos emerges as the continuator of an older tradition of the Orthodox Church that becomes visible in the mid-eighteenth century when it opens education's gates to the currents of intellectual renewal in order to make learning and, literally, the civilizing of youth more effective.[40]

Here it is worth recalling Archbishop Kyprianos's thinking as expressed in the Foundation Charter of the Hellenic School of Nicosia in January 1812:[41]

> [...] having realized that the civic community of our island of Cyprus suffers from a great dryness of culture and lack of Hellenic lessons, which form the only means that can adorn the human mind and can make the human being in fact worthy of humanity [...] we have decided [...] to establish a Hellenic School in our homeland in order to benefit our compatriots to the extent possible [...] in order for the children of the community to be taught the faith of their forefathers [...] and to be educated at the same time in moral rectitude so as they mature to become men marked by piety, prudence, civility, rectitude, justice, love of homeland and of commerce [...] Our motivation in this was patriotic zeal but also all those countless public accusations against us Cypriots, which we heard with our own ears. Because everywhere we have been in other places and in foreign lands, we did not hear anything else but an incessant current of accusations against us Cypriots, to the effect that even the smallest islands and the smallest cities have established public schools, and the famous and splendid island of Cyprus has not been capable to establish a public higher school of letters for the youth of the community, so as to improve at least their barbaric tongue [...]

The founding of the Philological Gymnasium at Limassol could be considered the apex of the Enlightenment's expressions in Cyprus. The school, modelled on the Philological Gymnasium of Smyrna, had the support of both the church hierarchy and Cyprus's lay notables, especially the "beauty-loving merchants" of the island's two trading ports, Larnaca and Limassol.[42] Teaching duties were assigned to Dimitrios Themistoklis from Limassol, who was a graduate of the Philological Gymnasium of Smyrna, "where having completed his studies, he taught mathematics for a while".[43] Thus the widening of the network of higher education schools on Cyprus linked the island to the most advanced educational initiatives of the Modern Greek Enlightenment. The satisfaction and celebratory tone of the text with which the hierodeacon Hilarion of Cyprus announces this progress in the "illuminating of the homeland" in the pages of the periodical *Ermis o Logios* in 1820 appeared, therefore, justified.

The social basis of the reception of Enlightenment ideas in Cyprus can be traced from whatever information emerges from the study of the subscriber lists of Greek publications between 1750 and 1821. The quantitative approach in delineating intellectual phenomena, based on these data, allows the researcher to gauge the extent of the expressions of intellectual change in Cypriot society. The general impression from the consideration of this evidence on the circulation of modernist books in Cyprus during the Enlightenment[44] leaves little doubt that the phenomena of intellectual change, although tangible in some scholarly circles, especially in Larnaca and Limassol, remained marginal and were foreign to the mainstream of Cypriot society.[45] Yet at the same time, one could say that based on this scattered appeal of the Enlightenment in the Greek world's periphery in the Eastern Mediterranean, during this critical period, some form of receptivity could be noticed in Cyprus for the future intake of modernist ideas.

An inkling of the mechanisms by which modernist ideas were starting to penetrate Cypriot society during this period could be inferred from the data provided by the tables of subscribers to Greek books. The Greek edition of Rousseau's *Discourse on Inequality*, translated by Spyridon Valetas and published in Paris in 1818, has two Cypriot subscribers, both residents of Marseille—Georgios Bellias and the well-known scholar, editor of *The Iliad* and activist Nikolaos Theseus. The latter, who is listed as the representative of the merchant partnership Nikolaos Theseus and Company, prepurchased twenty copies of the book.[46] Should we assume that resourceful and indefatigable Theseus intended these books for recipients in Cyprus, thus bringing the merchants and scholars of Larnaca initially and perhaps also Limassol into contact with the social criticism of the radical Enlightenment? In any case, the social circles in these Cypriot port cities had, since the end of the 1790s, been exposed to the emotions propagated around Europe by French revolutionary ideas[47] and could potentially foster favourable predispositions for the reception of the radical Enlightenment. This is an alluring assumption which, nonetheless, must remain no more than a tantalizing hypothesis for the historical imagination.

Cyprus between national centres

The 1821 tragedy violently suspended the hesitant reception of Enlightenment ideas in Cyprus, disrupting, until the end of the island's Ottoman occupation, the tradition of modernist ideas initially traceable in that earlier period. Only after the arrival of the British administration in 1878, which reconnected the island with European culture, could one say that there was a revival of a type of "Cypriot Enlightenment",[48] albeit readapted to the circumstances of the late nineteenth century. Intellectual life in the last period of Ottoman administration, after the upheavals of the 1820s, preserved the evident features of earlier periods, mainly the primary importance of the diaspora as the setting for its expression. However, a new parameter was added to the island's international environment that was going to be of decisive importance for its intellectual life: the emergence from the liberation struggle of the 1820s and international recognition of the independent Greek state. The new Greece as an independent kingdom thus enters the foreground of the Mediterranean world's political history and assumes the role of a national reference point—that is a "national centre"[49]—for Cyprus as well as other Eastern Mediterranean territories inhabited by Greek populations.

The role of the national centre in the intellectual life of the Greek world in the nineteenth century was dual. This duality was characteristically illustrated by Cyprus through the examples of its scholars. On one hand, the national centre, with the university and related institutions of official intellectual life, tended to attract and absorb the periphery's most dynamic intellectual elements. A prominent example of the relationship between national centre and periphery is offered by the case of Nikolaos I. Saripolos, who "corrected" the family surname "Saripoglou" to a more Hellenized version and emerged, following his studies in Paris, as an eminent member of the national centre's intellectual, political and academic life.[50] On the other, the national centre projected its intellectual, scholarly and ideological priorities on the periphery—priorities that were largely dictated by the needs to consolidate its own social cohesion and collective identity. An example of this in relation to Cyprus is offered by the case of Athanasios Sakellarios, the outstanding educator from Kynouria in the Peloponnese, who laid the foundations for the Greek tradition of scholarly Cyprological research. This is, indeed, an excellent example because Athanasios Sakellarios's work does not easily lend itself to the reductionism of our contemporary approaches that like to "deconstruct" intellectual monuments without studying them. The breadth, depth and gravitas of the demand to understand and assess, in substance and not just ideology, the national centre's role in shaping the intellectual life of the periphery is illustrated in the case of Cyprus through the work of Athanasios Sakellarios and its importance for Cypriot society's self-awareness.[51]

The developing relationship between Cyprus and the national centre in Athens did not overshadow or annul the older and stronger bonds linking it to other great centres of Orthodoxy in the Greek nineteenth century. Through the end of the Ottoman period, Cypriot intellectual life remained oriented primarily towards Constantinople. Despite the new expectations and national emotions radiated from Athens, during this period of reconstruction for Cypriot society's intellectual forces, Constantinople never ceased to act as the cradle of the Orthodox community's traditions or the intellectual hearth of the established and familiar forms of collective self-definition. The Phanar Greek Orthodox College remained the educational palladium for Cypriots, and some of its Cypriot students served it later as teachers and even as scholarchs.[52] Cypriots turned to the Greek Philological Association of Constantinople for support and guidance in recovering the island's cultural tradition and found the expected responsiveness.[53] The Greek Philological Association of Constantinople's scholarly initiative for recording historical and cultural monuments of the Greek world did not omit Cyprus from the scope of its research purview.[54]

Jerusalem was another constant point of reference for Cypriot learning in the latter phase of the Ottoman occupation. The Cypriot intellectual diaspora in Palestine appears in the nineteenth century to possess an already centuries-old genealogy, and during this period it emerged as a very significant representative of Cypriot learning, including Neophytos Agiotaphitis, who is overlooked in the history of Cypriot letters but who could, without exaggeration, be considered one of the greatest Cypriot writers.[55] Since its founding in 1855, the Jerusalem Patriarchate's Theological School of the Cross attracted Cypriots instilled with a desire for a theological education. Its scholarchs include two Cypriot scholars, Ieronymos Myriantheus (1872–1874) and Epiphanios Matteos (1874–1875).[56]

Alexandria and Smyrna, two other important Greek centres in the Eastern Mediterranean, whose commercial activity propelled them into major centres of economic and cultural life in the nineteenth century, also formed points of reference for the Cypriot intellectual diaspora. The Greek printing houses and literary periodicals in these two cities, where Greek life was creatively enmeshed in the cosmopolitanism of the "age of progress", published the works of a new creative generation in the tradition of Cypriot learning that linked the island to the intellectual currents of Greek romanticism. G. N. Sivitanidis in Alexandria, Vassilis Michaelidis in Smyrna,[57] Theodoulos Constantinidis in Smyrna, Alexandria and Cairo linked Cyprus to Greek Romanticism, thus setting the preconditions for modern Cypriot literary creation to develop in conjunction with the broader currents and directions of Modern Greek literature.

The nineteenth century and the last phase of the Ottoman period maintained the dominant pattern of the expressions of Cypriot learning as a learning of the diaspora. During this period, Epameinondas Fragroudis may be seen as representing the quintessential intellectual of the diaspora with his presence in Corfu, Constantinople and Bucharest and his publications in Athens, Trieste and Smyrna.[58] However, N. I. Saripolos and Neophytos Agiotaphifitis can be considered the classic types of Cypriot scholars who illustrate the complexity and multifaceted but also constant regularities marking Cypriot learning after three centuries of fluctuations in the island's early modern history. Both imposing intellectual personalities thanks to the volume of their work, Saripolos represents the type of Cypriot scholar who was inducted into the national centre's life via the diaspora, symbolizing the dynamic of modernity and the recovery of the island's Western orientation, whereas Neophytos Agiotaphitis embodied the traditions and regularities of the Orthodox East thus emphatically recalling Cyprus's organic Middle Eastern ties.

These observations arise from the examination of precisely the last act of the drama of Cypriot learning during the period of 1571 to 1878. But perhaps they could be received as useful conclusionary reminders, not only of the breadth of the fluctuations of Cypriot learning in the period under review and the many levels on which its representatives moved, in the history of both Greek and broader European literature and scholarship, but mainly, and because of these sufficient reasons, as necessary methodological specifications for studying the subject in relation to multiple frameworks in recognition of its complexity and by eschewing one-sided and ideologically preordained interpretations.

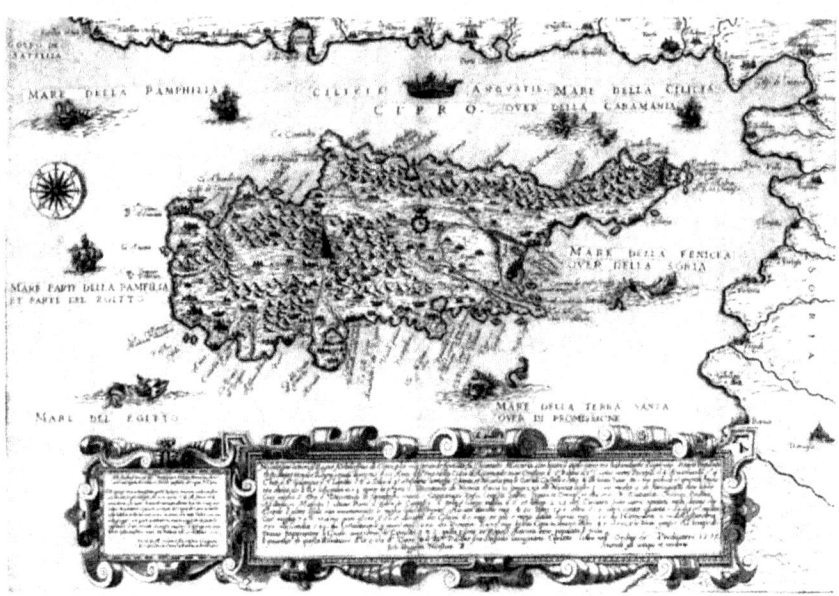

Figure 2.1 Steffano Lusignano, *Cipro* [Map of Cyprus] Padua 1575, dedicated to Filippo Mocenigo, Archbishop of Nicosia. Engraved by Giovanni Lango.

Notes

1 For the general historical backdrop, see Gianfranco Folena, *Culture e lingue nel Veneto medievale*, Padua: Editoriale Programma, 1990, pp. 256–262 and the classic evaluation of the phenomenon of cultural osmosis on Cyprus by Jean Richard, "Culture franque et culture grecque: le royaume de Chypre au XV siecle", *Byzantinische Forschungen* XI (1987), pp. 399–416. A detailed review of the literature and intellectual life during the medieval Kingdom and Venetian rule is offered, comprehensively and with insight, by Gilles Grivaud, *Entrelacs chiprois. Essai sur les letters et la vie intellectuelle dans le royaume de Chypre 1191–1570*, Nicosia: Moufflon Publications, 2009. For other aspects of this complex

historical issue, see Benjamin Arbel, "Resistance ou collaboration? Les Chypriotes sous la domination venitienne", *État et colonisation au Moyen Age et à la Renaissance*, M. Balard, ed., Lyons: La Manufacture, 1989, pp. 131–143 and with more specific reference to ecclesiastical issues, Z. N. Tsirpanlis, "Έλληνες και Φράγκοι στην Κύπρο και στη Ρόδο κατά τον όψιμο Μεσαίωνα. Συγκριτικό σχεδίασμα", *Βυζαντινά* 19 (1998), pp. 187–204.

2 The preeminent expression of Renaissance is found in sixteenth-century Cypriot literature, and specifically in a cycle of Petrarchan poetry transmitted by a single manuscript witness in codex Marc.gr.IX,32 at Marcian Library, Venice. The text, whose existence was first announced in 1873 by Constantinos Sathas, was published in 1881 by Legrand, but the critical edition was presented by Themis Siapkara-Pitsillidou, *Le Pétrarquisme en Chypre. Poèmes d'amour en dialecte chypriote, d'après un manuscrit du XVI siècle*, Athens: Collection de l'Institut Francais d'Athenes, 1952, and reprinted: Paris, 1975. The significance of the Cypriot petrarchan cycle can be seen in the extensive literary criticism that Pitsillidou's volume generated. Among the many contributions, see particularly the special studies by Kyriakos Hatziioannou, "Ο ποιητής των Κυπριακών ερωτικών ποιημάτων", *Κυπριακά Γράμματα* 21 (1956), pp. 159–163 [=*Η Μεσαιωνική Κύπρος;* Nicosia 1993, pp. 174–180]; Vincenzo Pecoraro, "Primi appunti sul canzoniere petrarchista di Cipro", *Miscellenea Neogrega. Atti del Convegno Nazionale di Studi Neogreci*, Palermo, 1976, pp. 97–127; Lucia Marcheselli Loukas, "Ρίμες αγάπης: Modelli ritmici dell'endecasillabo cipriota", *Θησαυρίσματα* 21 (1991), pp. 316–346; but especially the research of Elsie Mathiopoulou-Tornaritou, 'Lyrik der Spätrenaissance auf Zupern. Beobachtungen und Notizen zum Codex Marc. gr IX,31', *Follia Neohellenica* 7 (1985–1986), pp. 63–159 and 'Προτάσεις και παράμετροι για μια νέα έκδοση του κυπριακού "Αναγεννησιακού canzoniere της Μαρκιανής", *Αρχές της νεοελληνικής λογοτεχνίας. Πρακτικά του Δευτέρου Διεθνούς Συνεδρίου "Neogreca Medii Aevi"*, Venice, 1993, Vol. II, pp. 352–390. The latter codifies and critically examines all preceding bibliography and proposes the attractive hypothesis that Cyprus's Petrarchan poetry is the product of an entire circle of poets.

3 See Gilles Grivaud, "L'éveil de la nation chyproise (XIIe–XVe siècles)", *Sources Travaux Historiques* 43–44 (1995), pp. 105–106 and "Florio Bustron. Storico del Rinascimento Cipriota", introduction to the seminal text by Florio Bustron, *Historia overo Comentarii de Cipro* [Κυπριολογική Βιβλιοθήκη, N°. 8] Nicosia, 1998, pp. VII–XII.

4 See especially Giason Denores's speech on behalf of the Cypriot refugees to Sebastian Veniero in 1578, *Oratione di Iason Denores al Serenissimo Principe di Venetia Sebastian Veniero*, Padua, 1578, in which he lauds the patriotism of the Cypriot nobles who defended the island during the Ottoman invasion. The text is reproduced by N. M. Panagiotakis, *Ιάσων Δενόρες*, Athens, 1985 pp. 23–36.

5 See Gino Benzoni, "La fortuna, la vita, l'opera di Enrico Caterino Davila", *Studi Veneziani* XVI (1974), p. 313. The significance of Davila's work in the emergence of political thought in the Venetian state is lauded by W. J. Bowsma, "Venice and the political education of Europe", *Renaissance Venice*, ed. by J. R. Hale, London: Faber and Faber, 1974, pp. 445–466, esp. pp. 445, 449–451.

6 Etienne de Lusignan, *Description de toute l'Isle de Chypre*, Paris, 1580, folio 292. Also W. H. Rudt de Collenberg, "Les Litterae Hortatoriae accordées par les Papes en faveur de la rédemption des Chypriotes captifs des Turcs (1570–1597) d'après les fonds de l'Archivo Segreto Vaticano", *EKEE* XI (1981–1982), p. 51 and *Esclavage et rançons des Chrétiens en Méditerranée (1570–1600)*, Paris: Éditions Le Léopard d'or, 1987, p. 61.

7 Lusignan, *Description*, folio 291^v.

8 *Op. cit.*, folio 228^v.

9 [Aeneas Sylvius Piccolomini] Pius II, *Cosmographia*, Venice 1503. This work returned to the academic fore through the publication of Pius II's complete humanistic works, Basel 1551. Lusignan may have come across *Cosmographia* in this edition.

10 Strabo, Γεωγραφικά, Books V1, 2, 1; X, 3, 5; also, Claudius Ptolemy, Γεωγραφική Υφήγησις, I, A, 1–7. The trend towards a broader use of the term "chorograffia" in geographic literature at the time is indicative of the broader background to Lusignan's work. See for example Gaspar Barreiros, *Chorographia de alguns lugares que stam en hum caninho*, Coimbra, 1561.

11 Lusignan, *Chorograffia, e breve historia universale dell'isola di Cipro*, Bologna, 1573, folio 37.

12 Lusignan, *Description*, ff. 2^r, 67^r.

13 *Op. cit.*, f. 41^v, 97^v.

14 For a comparative analysis of the issue, see Chrysa A. Maltezou, "Η αρχαία κληρονομιά στην ιδεολογία του βενετοκρατούμενου ελληνισμού", *Τα Ιστορικά/ Historica*, no. 28–29 (June–December 1998), pp. 59–66.

15 Herbert Butterfield, "Historiography", *Dictionary of the History of Ideas*, Philip Wiener, ed., New York: Scribner, 1973, Vol. 11, pp. 484–486. Also R. G. Collingwood, *The Idea of History*, Oxford: Clarendon Press, 1947, pp. 57–58, but particularly D. R. Kelley, *Foundations of Modern Historical Scholarship: Language, Law and History in the French Renaissance*, New York and London: Columbia University Press, 1970, pp. 53–85, 129–141, 301–309.

16 See Fernand Braudel, *The Mediterranean and the Mediterranean World in the Age of Philip II*, translated by S. Reynolds, New York: Harper & Row, 1972, Vol. I, p. 152, footnote 187.

17 See Brunehilde Imhaus, "La minorité chypriote de Venise du XIVe siècle au début du XVIe siècle", *Chypre et la Méditerranée orientale*, edited by Y. Ioannou, F. Metral, M. Yon [TMO, no. 31], Lyons, 2000, pp. 33–41.

18 Biblioteca Marciana, Venice, Marc.gr.VII,16 (1080), f. 376^r.

19 See Aristeidis Stergelis, *Τα δημοσιεύματα των Ελλήνων σπουδαστών του Πανεπιστημίου της Πάδοβας τον 17ο και 18ο αιώνα*, Athens: Parnassos Literary Society, 1970, p. 45. For Cypriots' studies at Padua before Venice occupied Cyprus, see Bianca Betto, "Nuove ricerche sui studenti cipriotti all' Universita di Padova (1393–1489), *Θησαυρίσματα* 23 (1993), pp. 40–80 which supplements earlier information in G. Fabris, "Professori e scolari greci all'Università di Padova", *Archivo Veneto* 30 (1942), especially pp. 124–126. Of particular interest are B. Betto's observations about the Cypriot student association "Nazione Cipriota" at the medieval universities of Padua and Bologna, *op. cit.* pp. 69–79. See also Luigi Simeoni, *Storia della Università di Bologna*, Bologna, 1940 [reprinted 1987] I, pp. 150–158, Vol. II, pp. 63–67. In Bologna's *Archiginnasio*, in the year 1576 is recorded a "Nazione Sardegna e Cipro".

20 The Cypriots' presence at the Cottunian College can be observed through archives at the Archivio di Stato di Venezia [=ASV], *Riformatori dello Studio di Padova*, filza 498.

21 See Pietro Pompilio Rodotà, *Del rito greco in Italia* III (1763), Rome, p. 210; George Hill, *A History of Cyprus* IV, Cambridge: Cambridge University Press, 1952, p. 385.

22 ASV, *Riformatori dello Studio di Padova*, filza 498. Until the early eighteenth century, Hilarion Kigalas's portrait was also preserved at the Cottunian College according to records dated 1716 of the art works kept at the College.

23 Athanasios Karathanasis, *Η Φλαγγίνειος Σχολή της Βενετίας*, Thessaloniki: Adelfoi Kyriakidi, 1986, p. 52.
24 *Op. cit.*, pp. 60–64.
25 The text is published, *op. cit.* pp. 330–2 from Register Nº 20 of the Old Archive of the Hellenic Institute of Venice. See also ASV, *Riformatori dello Studio di Padova*, filza 505, where there are several copies of the estate and endowment of Bernardo Acris dated 20 August 1666.
26 Z. N. Tsirpanlis, *Το Ελληνικό Κολλέγιο της Ρώμης και οι μαθητές του (1576–1700)*, Thessaloniki, 1980, pp. 159–160.
27 *Op. cit.* 42–43 and other mentions, particularly J. Krajcar, S. J., *Cardinal Giulio Antonio Santoro and the Christian East. Santoro's Audiences and Consistorial Acts* [Orientalia Christiana Analecta, 177], Rome, 1966, pp. 126–127, 137, 158 and other mentions.
28 See Vittorio Peri, "Chiesa Latina e Chiesa Greca nell'Italia posttridentina (1564–1596)", *La Chiesa Greca in Italia dall' VIII al XVI secolo*, Padua: Antenore, 1973, [=Italia Sacra, no. 20–22], pp. 410–412. The extensive pertinent bibliography, which testifies to the Latin Church's historiographical interest in Germanos Kouskounaris can be seen at the entry [Consconari] by V. Peri, *Dizionario biografico degli Italiani [=DBI]*, Vol. 30 (1984), p. 510.
29 Biblioteca Nazionale, Napoli, Ms Branca c. I. B. 6, folios 450–451. The text of the confession, obviously an unsigned copy, is published by Vittorio Peri, "Inize e finalità ecumeniche del Collegio Greco in Roma", *Aevum* XLIV (1970), pp. 58–59 and in *Κυπριακή λογιοσύνη*, pp. 50–51.
30 Particularly by his modern-day editor and admirer, G. Valetas, editor of *Νεόφυτος Ροδινός. Κυπριακή δημοτική πεζογραφία. Λόγοι-δοκίμια-συναξάρια*, Athens, 1979. The historical context is described by the commentaries of Z. N. Tsirpanlis, *Το Ελληνικό Κολλέγιο της Ρώμης*, pp. 402–403. See also comments in N. B. Tomadakis, "Ο Νικηφόρος Πριλεγγεύς κατά Νεοφύτου Ροδινού περί του ιερού Φωτίου", *Ἐπετηρὶς Ἑταιρείας Βυζαντινῶν Σπουδῶν* 44 (1979–1980), p. 150.
31 See Biblioteca Apostolica Vaticana, codex Borg. gr. 17, folios 2–46ᵛ. The source of the vernacular adaptation of Rodinos was the biography of Saint Ignatius which is attributed to Niketas David Paphlagon and was first published in the early seventeenth century by M. Raderus and later by Severinus Binius. For related bibliographical data, see Fr. Halkin, *Biblioteca Hagiographica Graeca*, Brussels 1957, no. 817. The text is published with introduction and commentary in *Βίος ἡ μαρτύριον του εν Αγίοις πατρός ημών Ιγνατίου Αρχιεπισκόπου Κωνσταντινουπόλεως*, ed. by P. M. Kitromilides—Ch. Messis [National Hellenic Research Foundation, Πηγές της Κυπριακής Γραμματείας και Ιστορίας 1], Athens, 2008.
32 Leon Allatius, *Apes Urbanae sive de viris illustribus*, Rome, 1633, p. 198.
33 See Roberto Almagia, *L'opera geografica di Luca Holstenio* [Studi e Testi, no. 102], Città del Vaticano, 1942 (reprinted 1984), pp. 1–24 on the life and intellectual outlook of the man who inspired Neophytos Rodinos's epigrams. More specifically, on his position in the history of the Vatican Library, see Jeanne Bignami Odier, *La Bibliothèque Vaticane de Sixte IV à Pie IX. Recherches sur l'histoire des collections de manuscrits*, avec la collaboration de Jose Ruysschaert, Città de Vaticano: Biblioteca Apostolica Vaticana, 1973, pp. 137–139, 148–149.
34 Biblioteca Apostolica Vaticana, codex Barb. gr. 279, folios 311–312. See I. Mogenet, *Codices Barberiniani Graeci*, editor P. Canart, Biblioteca Apostolica Vaticana, 1989, Vol. II, pp. 139–140 with the epigrams' incipit and desinit. The two epigrams are published in *Κυπριακή λογιοσύνη*, pp. 52–53.
35 Biblioteca Apostolica Vaticana, codex Vat.gr. 1960, f. 3.
36 Nicolae Iorga, *Byzance après Byzance. Continuation de l'Histoire de la vie byzantine*, Bucharest, 1935. Especially worth noting are the references to Cyprus in

this most fertile text by the pre-eminent historian of Southeastern Europe. See especially pp. 40–41 and other mentions. In Iorga's terms, agents of the post-Byzantine spirit in Cyprus during the eighteenth century — aside from the senior clergy of the Autocephalous Church of Cyprus — could include the great interpreters, Christophakis Constantinou and Hadjiiosif, as implied by visual and other documentation of their political thought.

37 Paschalis M. Kitromilides, *Enlightenment and Revolution. The making of Greece,* Cambridge, MA. and London: Harvard University Press, 2013, pp. 84–87. The significance of Kyprianos's work was recognized by the thinkers of the modern Greek Enlightenment as evidenced by a relevant comment in the periodical *Ερμής ο Λόγιος* II (1812), pp. 73–74.

38 Archimandrite Kyprianos, *Ἱστορία Χρονολογικὴ τῆς Νήσου Κύπρου ἐρανισθεῖσα ἐκ διαφόρων ἱστορικῶν κα συντεθε σαι ἁπλῇ φράσει* [...] *ἀρχομένη ἀπὸ τοῦ Κατακλυσμοῦ μέχρι τοῦ παρόντος,* Venice, 1788, pp. 404–405. For attempts to identify some of these, see Paschalis M. Kitromilides, *Κοινωνικές σχέσεις και νοοτροπίες στην Κύπρο του 18ου αιώνα,* Nicosia: Popular Bank Cultural Centre, 1992, pp. 28, 37, 40, 42.

39 See L. Philipou, *Τα Ελληνικά Γράμματα εν Κύπρω κατά την περίοδον τῆς Τουρκοκρατίας* I, Nicosia, 1930, pp. 92–97 and also, *Η Εκκλησία Κύπρου επί Τουρκοκρατίας,* Nicosia, pp. 237–241 but particularly Benedict Englezakis, *Studies on the History of the Church of Cyprus, 4th–20th Centuries,* Aldershot: Variorum, 1995, pp. 257–278, 285–301.

40 Paschalis M. Kitromilides, "Initiatives of the Great Church in the mid-eighteenth century: hypotheses on the factors of Orthodox ecclesiastical strategy", *An Orthodox Commonwealth,* Aldershot: Ashgate/Variorum, 2007, Study Nᵒ V.

41 The text from Codex A of the Archdiocese of Cyprus is published by L. Philippou, *Τα Ελληνικά Γράμματα* I, pp. 93–97.

42 L. Philippou, *Τα Ελληνικά Γράμματα* I, pp. 234–240. Related documents are published in C. P. Kyrris, "Ανέκδοτα έγγραφα περί της Ελληνικής Σχολής Λεμεσού (1819, 1820)", *Κυπριακαί Σπουδαί* 42 (1978), pp. 85–106.

43 See Hilarion Cyprius, "Προς τον λόγιον κύριον Νικόλαον Θησέα", *Ερμής ο Λόγιος* X (1820), p. 521.

44 Among the books circulating through subscription during the period of the Enlightenment (1749–1821), only four have subscribers in Cyprus. One of these is Archimandrite Kyprianos's *Chronological History,* while none of the other three represent radical publishing initiatives. One is *Εκκλησιαστική Ιστορία* by Meletios of Athens, Vols. I and II, Vienna 1783, which both have three subscribers in Cyprus and much later Athanasios Stageiritis's *Ωγυγία,* Vol. V, Vienna 1820, that has forty-one subscribers in Cyprus. See Ph. Iliou, "Βιβλία με συνδρομητές. I. Τα χρόνια του Διαφωτισμού (1749–1821)", *Ο Ερανιστής,* Vol. 12 (1975), pp. 119–21, 160, 174. Based on these indications, it is estimated that a total of 205 copies of these four books circulated in Cyprus. An unpublished piece of information in a manuscript in Venice raises one concern with regard to the circulation of books in Cyprus as it provides the comparatively enormous figure of 16,000 copies sent from Venice to Syria and Cyprus between June 1748 and May 1749. See Museo Civico Correr/*Ms Dona delle Rose,* no. 342, Filza 10, Ins. 3, Fasc. III: *Decennio della quantitàt de' Libri à stampa usciti dalla Dominante* (1745–1755). This information, which is especially interesting, remains enigmatic with no means of speculating on the content of the books it documents for this specific year. Based on the records compiled by the note's signatory, Pietro Zampievetti, in the decade 1745–1755, the book trade between Venice, as exporter and Cyprus and Syria, as recipients, totalled 26,698 copies.

45 It is characteristic that during the period after the Enlightenment's peak and through 1832, the only book garnering the interest of subscribers from Cyprus appears to be Chourmouzios Chartophylax's *Αναστασιματάριον Νέον*, Constantinople, 1832, for which there were fourteen preorder subscribers, mainly clerics, from Kyrenia, Lapithos, Nicosia and the Kykkos and Machairas monasteries who ordered a total of twenty-four copies. See Ph. Iliou, 'Βιβλία με συνδρομητές II. Από τα χρόνια της Επανάστασης έως το 1832', *Ο Ερανιστής* 22 (1999), p. 229, 237. According to the data collected by Ph. Iliou through the 'Books with Subscribers 1749–1922' programme, in the years spanning 1749 to 1878, on Cyprus there were 3,205 subscribers to Greek books for a total of 4,476 copies.

46 Jean-Jacques Rousseau, *Λόγος περί αρχής και βάσεως της ανισότητας των ανθρώπων προς αλλήλους*, translated [...] by Dimitrios Aristomenous, Paris 1818, pp. [137–138]: unpaginated subscriber table. On Theseus's important Iliad project see Paschalis M. Kitromilides, "In Search of *litterae humaniores*. Presences and Absences in the Readership of the Biblioteca Laurenaziana", *San Lorenzo. A Florentine Church*, ed. by Robert W. Gaston and Louis A. Waldman, Florence: Villa I Tatti, 2017, pp. 679–697.

47 See Paschalis M. Kitromilides, *Η Γαλλική Επανάσταση και η Νοτιοανατολική Ευρώπη*, Athens: Poreia, 2000, p. 49.

48 See Theodore Papadopoullos, "Λογογραφία του Κυπριακού Διαφωτισμού", *Κυπριακαί Σπουδαί* 49 (1985), pp. 18–24 and *Σώμα εκπαιδευτικών εγγράφων*, Part I [Δημοσιεύματα της Εταιρείας Κυπριακών Σπουδών, αρ. 7], Nicosia, 1998, pp. iii–ix.

49 Paschalis M. Kitromilides, Κύπρος [1830–1878], *Ιστορία του Ελληνικού Έθνους*. 13, Athens, 1977, pp. 444–445 and "Το ελληνικό κράτος ως εθνικό κέντρο", *Ελληνισμός-ελληνικότητα. Ιδεολογικοί και βιωματικοί άξονες της νεοελληνικής κοινωνίας*, D. G. Tsaousis, ed., Athens: Estia, 1983, pp. 143–164.

50 *Κυπριακή λογιοσύνη*, pp. 240–245.

51 Ibid., pp. 234–237.

52 For details and important written documentation, see A. G. Mitsidis, *Οι Κύπριοι σχολάρχαι και διδάσκαλοι της εν Κωνσταντινουπόλει Μεγάλης του Γένους Σχολής*, Nicosia: Archbishop Makarios Foundation, 1983.

53 Cypriot education's debt to the Greek Philological Association of Constantinople is documented in the records of Nicosia's schools in the latter half of the nineteenth century, published by C. Papadopoulos, *Κυπριακαί Σπουδαί* 18 (1954), pp. ciii–clvii; 19 (1955), pp. 185–260; 20 (1956), pp. 173–207; 23 (1959), pp. 215–259.

54 Paul Schroeder (translated by K. Perdikidis), "Περί τινος κυπριακής επιγραφής", *Ο εν Κωνσταντινουπόλει Ελληνικός Φιλολογικός Σύλλογος [=ΕΦΣΚ]*, Archeological Annex XI (1878), pp. XXXI–XL. Also Dimitrios M. Saros, 'Παλαιογραφικός "Ερανος", *ΕΦΣΚ*, 13 (1914), pp. 94–6: "Κυπριακόν αρχείον" and "Κατάλογος χειρογράφων του εν Κωνστανινουπόλει Ελληνικού Φιλολογικού Συλλόγου"', *ΕΕΒΣ* 9 (1932), pp. 153–4, no. 118–120, p. 156, no. 128 and more recently Paul Moraux, *Bibliothèque de la Société Turque d'Histoire. Catalogue des manuscrits grecs (Fonds de Syllogos)*, Ankara: Turk Tarih Kurumuh, 1964, pp. 170–171 and 176–177.

55 *Κυπριακή λογιοσύνη*, pp. 209–210.

56 Chrysostomos A. Papadopoulos, *Ή Ιερὰ Μονὴ τοῦ Σταυροῦ καὶ ἡ ἐν αὐτῇ Θεολογικὴ Σχολή*, Jerusalem: Printing House of the Holy Community of the Holy Sepulchre, 1905, p. 119.

57 Vassilis Michaelidis (1849–1917), subsequently the national poet of Cyprus with his epic compositions in the Cypriot dialect, emerged in literature with the

satyrical poems "Χερσαίον και θαλάσσιον με έπλασεν η φύσις", "Μέγας είμαι! της απείρου φύσεως κεραυνοβόλως...", "Η τοκογλυφία", a text in which he first attempts the use of Cypriot dialect in his poems, and "Αηδόνια και κουκουβά-γιες" in the periodical *Πυθαγόρας της Σμύρνης*, issue 7 (March 1873), p. 54; 9 (May 1873), p. 66; and 15 (November 1873), p. 21 (Vassilis Michaelidis, *Απαντα*, P. Paraskevas, ed., Nicosia, 1987, pp. 13–18 and G. Katsouris, *Βασίλης Μιχαηλίδης, Η ζωή και το έργο του*, Nicosia, 1987, pp. 86–87).

58 *Κυπριακὴ λογιοσύνη*, pp. 266–268.

3   The patriotism of the expatriates

I am an expatriate. I belong to the diaspora of emigrants, exiles, strangers who have lived as displaced persons from the place they consider home. But am I a patriot? Many back home are sure I am not because the experience of exile has led me to question many of the comforting certainties around which the home society coheres. Maybe part of the blame is on me for failing to make the message of exile comprehensible. But again the blame for this failure in communication may not be entirely on the exile or on one's distance from one's homeland. The blame, at least partly, may belong to elements in the home society which want to protect vested interests, to monopolize benefits and profits, for which the comforting certainties I noted above serve very conveniently as the "pleasing illusions", whose important and necessary function for human society Edmund Burke was the first to point out. These comforting certainties or pleasing illusions as a rule include patriotism, the feeling of belonging, the love of country. For most ordinary people this is a genuine feeling, a part of their existence, a framework of meaning that lends life one of its purposes, besides self and family. And understandably people do not like to feel this framework of meaning disturbed or questioned because this creates confusion and discomfort. These ordinary patriots are genuine and sincere in their feeling and it is among them that heroes emerge, as happened in Cyprus for instance between 1955–1959. There are also those who preach about patriotism and develop militant rhetoric about it, a rhetoric that includes a considerable element of hatred against enemies, real or imaginary and especially against those among the expected patriots who do not fall in line, who ask questions, who may entertain a different conception of patriotism. We can more or less take it as a rule that the more militant the rhetoric the more questionable its motivations are. We can also take it as a rule that no heroes emerge from the ranks of rhetorical patriots. They want others to sacrifice themselves but they want to live on to enjoy the fruits of patriotism in the home society. It is these rhetorical patriots, whom we could also call "professional" patriots, who cannot recognize or tolerate a pluralist understanding of patriotism, remain adamant in the wish to ostracize all alternative views, including the patriotism of the expatriates and can be quite ruthless in stigmatizing the motives of all who disagree with them. This is the major reason for the failures in communication between the expatriates, who very often represent difference and alterity and the rhetorical traditions and conventional morality of the home society.

What I propose to do in the reflections that follow is to try to illustrate the form of patriotism associated with the experience of exile and offer a few hints concerning the failures in communication between the expatriate and the home society by looking at the political and historical thought of Cypriot exiles, who over the centuries have in fact developed an original and lively patriotism well before the home society could have any such notion at all. My main aspiration is to bring my readers into contact and make them aware of what in my judgement is a very significant chapter in the intellectual heritage of an important Mediterranean island. Furthermore, the subject possesses broader interest from a comparative perspective in that it invites reflection on processes of intellectual change generated by the interplay of a culture of exile with the collective conscience of the home society that could be uncovered in the experience not only of other Mediterranean islands, Crete, Sicily or Malta for example, but also of peripheral regions around the Mediterranean world in the early modern period. Despite its significance, the subject has been neglected by historical research for reasons having to do for the most part with the sociology of knowledge.

Since the early 1990s for almost twenty years now, I have worked and continue to work and reflect on the intellectual tradition of early modern Cyprus and I wish to share my impressions of its meaning and significance with the readers of these pages. What I want to stress, especially for the younger generation of researchers interested in the study of nationalism and patriotism, is that a dialogue with these earlier intellectual traditions will not only add a broader perspective but also intellectual depth and, I would dare to suggest, a more substantive understanding of the issues involved.

The phenomenon of migration and exile is not of marginal significance in the history of Cyprus. In the sources that have come down to us it is reflected as an important and recurring feature of the collective destiny of the island in the Medieval and Modern periods; through the centuries this movement of people took the form of migration mostly forced but also voluntary. On account of its geographical position Cyprus has been at the epicentre of movements of people throughout its history. In its ancient history the island had been primarily the recipient of incoming migrations, the earliest one of which (that of the Acheans) who brought with them the Greek language at the end of the second millennium BC, being the most important and the one with the most lasting consequences. By contrast the Medieval and modern history of the island have been marked mostly by outward movements of the islanders, forced or semi-forced migrations caused by incoming foreign conquerors or would-be conquerors like the Arabs in the seventh century, when the most important forced migration in Medieval Cyprus took place as we are reminded to this day by the official title of the Archbishop of Nova Justiniana and all of Cyprus.

The four centuries of the Medieval kingdom and Venetian rule were marked primarily by movements of people coming inward: Crusaders, knights errant, the Frankish settlers, Latin ecclesiastical and monastic orders, Venetian officials and military personnel, the settlement of the Maronites and other Christian population groups from the Near and Middle East. These, however, were not massive population movements. Under the conditions of feudalism the population of Cyprus remained mostly immobile and stable, tied to its land; yet there was a trickle of migration outward, Cypriots who left to study in the West and increasingly in the fifteenth and sixteenth centuries Cypriot emigrants who relocated to Venice and her empire.

The Ottoman conquest brought a major wave of forced migration. That early Turkish invasion and especially the fall of the island's two major cities, Nicosia and Famagusta, caused an exodus of refugees who sought refuge in Venice and her remaining domains in the Levant: Crete, Zante, Corfu. Venice eventually resettled many of the Cypriot refugees at the city of Pola in Istria. Thus a Cypriot diaspora of expatriates and exiles came into being in the early modern period. Their communities became points of contact and reception of a continuing stream of emigrants from the island in the centuries of Ottoman rule. This diaspora included many groups of people, among them scholars, writers and it was they who gave voice to the sense of patriotism of the expatriates, thus creating a prodigious literature of diaspora sensibility in Cypriot learning. It is to them we should turn in order to listen to the voice of expatriate patriotism.[1] I propose to converse with three authors, spanning early modern history, from the sixteenth to the eighteenth century. In order of appearance they are: Etienne de Lusignan from the sixteenth century, Neophytos Rodinos from the seventeenth and the Archimandrite Kyprianos from the eighteenth century. Together they form a paradigmatic model of the way diaspora thought and sensibility recovers, elaborates and recreates the sense of the distant motherland, which for them, under the conditions of emigration and exile of the period remained a lost motherland to which they knew they would never return.

Etienne de Lusignan or Brother Steffano Lusignano (1537–1590), as he originally recorded his name, was a Cypriot Dominican monk, scion of the Medieval royal dynasty of Cyprus. He became a refugee and a prolific author after the fall of Cyprus. In his first and most important book, his *Chorograffia*, he attempted a geographical, topographical and historical description of Cyprus. The historical outline included the pre-Christian past of the island, a clear reflection of the influence of Renaissance thought upon the author's interests.[2] The motivation of the work was to encourage the European powers and especially the king of France, to whom the work had been dedicated, to undertake military action to restore the island to Christian rule. This is clearly stated in the dedicatory address to Charles IX of France[3] and is supported by the detailed exposition of the history of the French Lusignan dynasty that had ruled the kingdom of Cyprus for three centuries. There is an inescapable impression, however, that beyond this geopolitical objective Lusignan is serving with his text another purpose as well. This transpires in the description of material life in Cyprus which closes his narrative. This section is significantly expanded in the French version of the work.[4]

In these closing chapters the exiled author tries to recall the natural environment and the material content of life in Cyprus. In the expanded French edition he begins with a description of the natural appearance of the inhabitants, in which he praises the beauty of the women of Cyprus, pointing out in particular that Paphian women surpass all others in sweetness and beauty probably, he says, because they lived in the same region inhabited by their ancestral gods.[5] He goes on to describe the various products of the island and the special varieties of food grown on it, fruits of the trees, aromatic and medicinal herbs, domestic animals and wildlife, listing with special care game birds, partridges, quails and the much sought after "vinebirds", to whose savoury taste he devotes several lines in his narrative.[6]

This section of Lusignan's narrative, after the long account of dynastic and feudal history, suddenly enlivens the text, it comes across as a living memory of the tastes, scents and fragrances of Cyprus, all those distinctive features and senses that make up the quality of life on the island. It would not be too much to claim that what he is painting in the isolation of the Dominican monastery in Naples and in the wanderings of exile is the image of a paradise lost, which he recalls with incurable nostalgia and wants to recapture and relive with his imagination. This material love of the lost homeland supplies the content of the patriotism of the expatriate.

There can be little doubt that the Dominican friar captured and articulated this feeling very accurately. This is attested by the widespread appeal of his work in the milieux of Cypriot exiles in Europe for many generations to come. In fact this part of his work became a matrix for the self-understanding of Cypriot identity in exile. It was widely imitated, translated, paraphrased and two centuries later provided the source of a similar attempt to elaborate a matrix of Cypriot identity by the Archimandrite Kyprianos.[7]

Lusignan remained the main interlocutor of the next Cypriot expatriate we will consider, Neophytos Rodinos (1576/7–1659). Born in the village of Potamiou in the highlands of Cyprus, Rodinos shortly after his twentieth birthday took the road of exile in pursuit of education. His life was an incessant peregrination that took him to many parts of Europe from Spain to Poland. He took monastic orders in the dependency of the Monastery of Sinai on Crete, studied at the Greek College of St Athanasius in Rome, converted to Catholicism, was ordained a Uniate priest and spent his life working as a proselytizer of Orthodox populations to Catholicism. Rodinos was a gifted author and he devoted his talents to works of catechism and religious polemic.[8] At the end of his life, nevertheless, he remembered his homeland which he had left at an early age never to return. In a gesture of remembrance and recovery of the lost homeland he composed his treatise on the historical, cultural and religious past of his native island, drawing extensively on Lusignan's account of the island's pagan heritage but adding his own original declaration of Cypriot patriotism. Published posthumously in 1659, and obviously written in the last years of his life, Rodinos's treatise is an explosively original work not only in the tradition of Cypriot learning but in Greek literature more generally[9]. Father Neophytos takes up his Dominican predecessor's recollections of Cyprus as a lost paradise of fragrances, tastes and material well-being and re-elaborates it theoretically into a doctrine of love of country. Let us listen to his own words:[10]

> Everyone must love and honour his homeland (πατρίδα) and ought to fight for her, because that old precept, which urges us saying "fight for your country" remains still a moral, essentially a law of nature for everyone to resist its enemies and defend his country, whether it is good and famous or insignificant, poor and unknown to the multitude.
> [...]
> One may change many faiths, thinking that one may be better than another, but one's homeland is never given up, it is never rejected nor hated and no one suffers it to be calumniated, even though he may be exiled or gone away from it; on the contrary he honours it and desires, like Odysseus to return to it.
> [...]

This love of country culminates in the nostalgia of return in a truly and dramatically existential sense:[11]

> A wise man says that people love their country when they are young but also in their old age. However they love it more when they are old and wiser than when they are young, because in old age the desire for the homeland increases and everyone wishes and craves to finish his days in his homeland, where his life had begun, there again to finish and leave his body in the land which had nurtured him and to be laid to rest in the graves of his forefathers.

Here Neophytos is recording his emotional autobiography, the story of his feelings in exile. It is obvious that it was the experience of displacement that had nurtured this lively craving for the lost homeland and for the identity that was felt to be at stake in the distance of exile.

In contrast with the cosmopolitan Dominican, who was ready to converse with princes and courtiers and obviously never lost the tastes of a bonviveur, for the dedicated Uniate missionary the lost paradise of the insular homeland was primarily a holy land, an island of saints and martyrs, including many women, virtuous bishops and scholars.[12] That was the homeland to which he craved to return in his declining years. He felt proud of his island, and wanted the world to know about it and about his devotion to it.

Our third diaspora author was Kyprianos [? –1805 (?)], the archimandrite of the archdiocese of Cyprus. He came from the village of Kilani in the highlands of Limassol, very close to Rodinos's own village, and in all likelihood took monastic orders in the monastery of Kykko. He entered the service of the arch-diocese of Cyprus and in 1777 was sent by Archbishop Chrysanthos to Venice to publish offices and special services in honour of Cypriot saints. Kyprianos lived in Italy for the rest of his life, studying in Padua, working as a proofreader and editor in the Greek printing workshops in Venice and as a teacher in Trieste.[13] Living in the diaspora he became homesick and he gave expression to his nostalgia by writing a history of Cyprus, published in Venice in 1788. This was and remains the most important historical work on Cyprus to appear in Greek and it is probably the most original historiographical expression of the Greek Enlightenment.[14] With this work Kyprianos provides an Orthodox response to Lusignan's conception of the history of the island, but at the same time he draws extensively on that earlier source not only in narrating the history of the Medieval kingdom but also in recording the island's natural, social and economic environment. In Kyprianos's pages we encounter the same attempt as in Lusignan's work to recover the sense of his lost homeland by recreating the material content of life on the island. Kyprianos updates and greatly enriches Lusignan's account, adding many details and making the lists of products longer, adding variety and colour to them. In the relevant section of his history the homeland's fragrances and tastes, including details about Cyprus's wines and cheeses, fruits and aromatic oils bring across the centuries a true cornucopia of material pleasures sought after through the imagination.[15] All this fortifies Kyprianos in his Cypriot identity and inspires him with a feeling of security in exile. He looks for this identity everywhere on the roads of diaspora and exile. He confides in his reader that he liked, while in Venice, to visit the church of San Giovanni in Bragora in order to venerate the relics of the Cypriot Saint John the Alms-giver.[16] Following Rodinos, Kyprianos likes to get across to his reader an account of Cyprus as an island of saints and martyrs, but also of virtuous lay people and scholars.[17] Thus like his Uniate predecessor on whom he relies extensively, the spokesman and historian of Cypriot Orthodoxy constructs a tradition of sainthood and learning defining the spiritual character of his island. He obviously feels heir to this tradition, which he records for posterity and bases his identity on it. In contrast with his Dominican and Uniate forerunners, however, Kyprianos primarily defines the identity of Cyprus by reference to a unique feature of its historical experience, its autocephalous Orthodox Church and its distinctive privileges which linked it integrally to the heritage of the eastern Roman Empire. In fact Kyprianos makes a point in publishing a report composed earlier in the eighteenth century by one of the most learned archbishops of Cyprus, Philotheos (1734–1759), on the autocephaly and privileges of the Church of Cyprus.[18]

We have come a long way from the mid-sixteenth century to the eve of the French Revolution tracing the construction of a Cypriot identity in exile, an identity expressed in a distinct variety of patriotism focusing on the island as a lost material and spiritual paradise. We should now pause briefly and reflect on how this prodigious articulation of Cypriot patriotism in exile and its exponents might have been received by the insular home society. It would not be an exaggeration to suppose that Etienne de Lusignan, despite his evocative recording of the charms and beauties of Cyprus, would be viewed with reservation and suspicion in the home society in subsequent centuries as a Catholic clergyman and a spokesman of the legitimacy of the Medieval kingdom, which for the modern-day Cypriot national conscience was a period of foreign rule by an alien dynasty which attempted to adulterate the Orthodox faith of the Cypriot people. In his turn Neophytos Rodinos, the Uniate missionary, would be viewed as a traitor to his ancestral faith and he would be condemned for his "negative services to enslaved Hellenism and to the Orthodox tradition of his homeland".[19] Yet it was this "traitor" who literally was the first to articulate with deep love, devotion and nostalgia a secular doctrine of patriotism focusing on his native island. Kyprianos, finally, a senior ecclesiastical dignitary and one of the best-educated Cypriots of his time, remained in Italy for more than thirty years, keeping safe distances from the ecclesiastical struggles and passions ignited in Cyprus in the opening years of the nineteenth century over the succession of his ageing patron Archbishop Chrysanthos. He did not seem to have ever contemplated the possibility of return to Cyprus, despite the longing and nostalgia that marks his account of conditions of life on the island in the closing pages of his history. Although he writes from an Orthodox perspective it is not clear that the openness to the Enlightenment that marks his historical thought would have made him particularly popular among ecclesiastical intellectuals in the Greek East and in Cyprus.

The foregoing are just some hints concerning the forms and sources of the failures in communication between the exponents of expatriate patriotism and the home society. Exile very often can function as a shield for the expatriate, protecting him from the consequences of such misunderstandings and failures in communication. Bitter disappointment can arise upon immediate contact, when the expatriate would discover at first hand that his patriotic nostalgia finds no receptivity, leaves the home society indifferent or even meets with hostility and suspicion. This is the point at which the expatriate can be perceived and treated as a heretic or be turned into an outcast. We see, therefore, that expatriate patriotism as a feeling of devotion and longing for the homeland and especially as a form of personal knowledge and interpretation of the lost homeland can be a quite different variety of cognition from patriotism as an ideology of social cohesion and conventional legitimacy in the home society. This cognitive difference can create serious forms of dissonance and ideological incompatibility. The extent and form the latter can take depend to a significant degree on the character of diaspora communities from which expatriate patriotism emanates. A closing reflection on the question of varieties of diaspora may therefore be in order.

Basing our judgement on the phenomena of Greek and Balkan diaspora in Central Europe, which historically functioned as a mechanism of mobility,

cultural change, openness to the world and in many instances personal liberation, we may be led to think that all diasporas fulfil similar functions. This is
not necessarily the case. Diaspora communities can be repressive for their
members, under tight controls by elders intent on preserving conventional
moral traditions and religious identities and thus hostile to openness to the
world around the diaspora community, xenophobic, introvert and intolerant of
those of their members who may be attracted by critical thought and promises
of emancipation from the multiple forms of traditionalist oppression. Spinoza
and his fate represents the experience of this kind of diaspora as do innumerable other dissenters who attempted to stand apart from the corporate structures and mentalities of many diaspora networks. The phenomenon of
repressive diasporas is not limited to the past nor is it associated with a specific
ethnic community. Many diasporas over time have been like that on many continents: fundamentalist Protestant communities in America, Asian diasporas of
diverse religious backgrounds in Africa and in Europe, Balkan diasporas in
Australia in our day are only a few of many more examples.

Each of the two kinds of diaspora, which we might call open and corporate respectively, is associated with a different kind of expatriate patriotism.
The expatriate patriotism connected with early modern Cypriot diaspora,
which we have surveyed above, mostly a diaspora of individuals and rather
small groups, belongs to the open diaspora variety and this can also explain
its potential difficulties in its encounters with the home society. Other forms
of expatriate patriotism, connected with corporate diasporas, can slide
towards extremism and even terrorism, an illustration being that of Irish
patriotism in America.

Let me draw all this up into some concluding reflections. I hope what has
been said so far has managed to bring forward the complex nature of
expatriate patriotism and to have dispelled any one-way or single-track
notions about its historical character. Studying it is useful because it illustrates the multiplicity of human phenomena and the difficulty of imposing
uniformity in their interpretation. On the subject of patriotism itself the
complexity and multiplicity we have noted makes plain, I think, the context-
ual nature of the phenomenon and thus supplies a serious methodological
pointer to its interpretation. Contextualism in its turn has its own pitfalls,
from which there is only one safeguard: staying close to the evidence of the
sources, evaluating and understanding each case on its own terms, accompanied by a healthy scepticism toward excessive theorization and especially
toward vacuous jargon that as a rule obfuscates rather than illuminates.
Beyond this the key to understanding is an imaginative and free of presup-
positions dialogue with the human population of history, with an attentive
ear to the polyphony of their voices. This will save us from Procrustean sim-
plifications and distortion in attempting to recover the meaning of an infin-
itely rich and varied human experience and its emotional expressions.

ΙΣΤΟΡΙΑ

ΧΡΟΝΟΛΟΓΙΚΗ ΤΗΣ ΝΗΣΟΥ

ΚΥΠΡΟΥ

ΕΡΑΝΙΣΘΕΙΣΑ ΕΚ ΔΙΑΦΟΡΩΝ ΙΣΤΟΡΙΚΩΝ

ΚΑΙ ΣΥΝΤΕΘΕΙΣΑ ΑΠΛΗ ΦΡΑΣΕΙ

Ὑπὸ τȣ,

ΤΗΣ ΑΓΙΩΤΑΤΗΣ ΑΡΧΙΕΠΙΣΚΟΠΗΣ

ΑΡΧΙΜΑΝΔΡΙΤΟΥ ΚΥΠΡΙΑΝΟΥ

ΑΡΧΟΜΕΝΗ ΑΠΟ ΤΟΥ ΚΑΤΑΚΛΥΣΜΟΥ ΜΕΧΡΙ ΤΟΥ ΠΑΡΟΝΤΟΣ

Ἐν ᾗ προσετέθη, καὶ ἡ περὶ τῆς Αὐτονομίας τῆς Ἱερᾶς
Ἐκκλησίας τῶ Κυπρίων Ἔκθεσις

ΤΟΥ ΑΟΙΔΗΜΟΥ ΑΡΧΙΕΠΙΣΚΟΠΟΥ ΚΥΡΙΟΥ

ΦΙΛΟΘΕΟΥ

Ἅμα ὲ περὶ ἐνδόξων Ἀνδρῶν, ὲ Ἁγίων Κυπρίων.

ΠΡΟΣ ΧΑΡΙΝ ΤΩΝ ΦΙΛΟΠΑΤΡΙΩΝ ΣΥΜΠΑΤΡΙΩΤΩΝ,

Ἤδη Πρῶτον δι᾽ ἰδίων Ἀναλωμάτων τυπωθεῖσα.

αψπή. ΕΝΕΤΙΗΣΙΝ. ΕΝ ΕΤΕΙ. 1788.

ΠΑΡΑ ΝΙΚΟΛΑΩ ΓΛΥΚΕΙ ΤΩ ΕΞ ΙΩΑΝΝΙΝΩΝ.
CON LICENZA DE' SUPERIORI, E PRIVILEGIO.

Figure 3.1 Title page of Archimandrite Kyprianos, *Chronological History of the Island of Cyprus*, Venice 1788.

Notes

1 Of cardinal importance on the subject is Z. N. Tsirpanlis, Ὁ κυπριακὸς ἑλληνισμὸς τῆς διασπορᾶς καὶ οἱ σχέσεις Κύπρου-Βατικανοῦ *(1571–1878)*, Thessaloniki, 2006. I have also devoted a few studies to this subject, which may be of interest to other scholars of diaspora and expatriate patriotism. They include the following titles: "Βιβλία και ανάγνωση στη Λευκωσία της Αναγέννησης", *Cipro-Venezia. Comuni sorti storiche*, ed. by Chryssa Maltezou, Venice: Istituto Ellenico di Studi Bizantini e Postbizantini, 2002, pp. 263–275; Κυπριακὴ λογιοσύνη *1571–1878. Προσωπογραφικὴ θεώρηση*, Nicosia: Cyprus Research Centre, 2002, esp. pp. 43–54; 'Esquisse d'une périodisation de la vie intellectuelle chypriote, 1571–1878', *Cahiers du Centre d'Etudes Chypriotes* 36 (2006), pp. 125–141, esp. pp. 127–133; "Κύπριοι στη Βενετία/Cypriots in Venice", *La Serenissima and La Nobilissima*, ed. by Angel Nicolaou-Konnari, Nicosia: Cultural Foundation of the Bank of Cyprus, 2009, pp. 207–217.
2 *Chorograffia et breve historia universale dell'isola di Cipro*, Bologna, 1573, new ed., Nicosia: Cultural Foundation of the Bank of Cyprus, 2004, pp. 6–17ᵛ. On the author and the composition of the work one may consult Gilles Grivaud, *Entrelacs Chiprois. Essai sur les lettres et la vie intellectuelle dans le royaume de Chypre 1191–1570*, Nicosia: Moufflon, 2009, pp. 287–299.
3 *Chorograffia*, pp. 23–27.
4 *Description de toute l'isle de Chypre*, Paris, 1580. Reprinted Nicosia: Cultural Foundation of the Bank of Cyprus, 2004, pp. 221–226.
5 Ibid., p. 219. Paphian women came from the region of Paphos in western Cyprus, an area associated in Greek mythology with the birth of Aphrodite, the goddess of love.
6 Ibid., p. 226. On the subject of "ucelli divigna" and its ecological connotations, see Benjamin Arbel, "Cypriot Wild life in Renaissance Writings", *Cyprus and the Renaissance (1450–1650)*, ed. by B. Arbel, Evelien Chayes, Harald Hendrix, Turnhout, Belgium: Brepols, 2012, pp. 321–344.
7 See Κυπριακὴ λογιοσύνη, p. 54.
8 The latest biographical profile appears in Neophytos Rodinos, Βίος ἢ μαρτύριον τοῦ ἐν Ἁγίοις πατρὸς ἡμῶν Ἰγνατίου ἀρχιεπισκόπου Κωνσταντινουπόλεως, ed. by P. M. Kitromilides and Charalambos Messis, Athens: Institute for Neohellenic Research, 2008, pp. 11–26. See also Tsirpanlis, *op. cit.*, pp. 153–170.
9 Neophytos Rodinos, Περὶ ἡρώων, στρατηγῶν, φιλοσόφων, ἁγίων καὶ ἄλλων ὀνομασ-τῶν ἀνθρώπων, ὁποῦ εὐγήκασιν ἀπὸ τὸ νησὶ τῆς Κύπρου, Rome, 1659, reprinted Nicosia, 2007.
10 Ibid., pp. 1–3.
11 Ibid., pp. 8–9.
12 Ibid., pp. 56–110. Holy women are listed on pp. 111–130.
13 Κυπριακὴ λογιοσύνη, pp. 174–177.
14 P. M. Kitromilides, *Enlightenment and Revolution. The Making of Modern Greece*, Cambridge, MA: Harvard University Press, 2013, pp. 84–87.
15 Archimandrite Kyprianos, Ἱστορία χρονολογικὴ τῆς νήσου Κύπρου, Venice, 1788, pp. 363–369. An English version of this part of the text appears in C. D. Cobham, *Excerpta Cypria*, Cambridge, 1908 (reprinted New York: Kraus, 1969), pp. 344–367.
16 Ibid., p. 349.
17 Ibid., pp. 333–344.
18 Ibid., pp. 370–390.
19 Th. Papadopoullos, "Ὁ Ροδινὸς ως διαφωτιστής", in Ροδινός, Περὶ ἡρώων, 2007 reprint, p. xl.

4 Repression and protest in traditional society

Cyprus 1764

The events of 1764 in Nicosia constitute a relatively well-known interlude in the history of a dark century. This is due to the fact that the episode is recorded in the leading eighteenth-century sources on the history of Cyprus, including the eyewitness account of the foremost Cypriot historian of the era, the Archimandrite Kyprianos, who preserved an echo of the affair that occurred at the seraglio in his narrative.[1] The Venetian consular report published here for the first time,[2] recounts the same events, confirming many pertinent details. Its major interest, however, does not consist in its vivid re-enactment of the drama but in the perspectives it opens for understanding its immediate political context. Some of the details supplied by the document allow us to penetrate into the dynamics of social repression and protest, especially the methods of the containment and diffusion of protest as they operated in Cypriot society under the conditions of Ottoman imperial decay. From this point of view the sequence and structure of events in the autumn of 1764 in Cyprus present in themselves considerable interest for the comparative analysis of the dynamics of social protest in traditional society.

Though not an eyewitness account—none of the sources speak of the presence of the European consuls in the episode—the report is partly a record of the impressions of Crutta, the chancellor of the British consulate in Larnaca who had been in Nicosia during the troubles. Its evidence, therefore, can be of use in the resolution of some minor issues which are disputed in the relevant historiography. It confirms for instance the fact of the sawing through of the supporting floor pillars on which the bishops stood and the concomitant intention of the governor to have them murdered. It was the revelation of this intention that finally triggered off the popular protest. This detail of the governor's scheme is recorded also by Giovanni Mariti and in the chronicle of the Oikonomos Ioakim, but disputed by Hill who makes an argument ex *silentio* based on Kyprianos.[3] The Venetian report also adds its own testimony concerning still another point of uncertainty, i.e. the exact level of the controversial tax which precipitated the fatal chain of events. To the figures recorded by Kyprianos, Ioakim and Mariti it adds a new one, putting the controversial levy at 42 1/2 piastres, thus suggesting an intermediate point between the figures given by Ioakim (40) and Mariti (44 1/2).[4]

As noted at the outset however, the document's primary importance consists in its depiction of the dynamics of oppression and revolt. It describes a tax rebellion, basically not dissimilar to those that punctuated the process of state building in modern Europe.[5] The 1764 outbreak illustrates the maximization of the potential of violent opposition to authority that was attained in Cypriot traditional society whenever tax extortions beyond normally acceptable levels burdened both ethnic elements. The historical experience of Cyprus under Ottoman rule suggests that this was the decisive precondition of revolt.[6] The consideration of the possible preconditions of revolt should also explore the probable connection of the revolt with a preceding harvest failure and the consequent population pressure on food resources which the sudden tax increase precipitated into violence.[7]

The revolt was effected through a typical outbreak of "traditional violence"[8] when institutional forms of protest such as the bishops' appeal to the Porte proved futile. The fear of popular resorts to violence in protest of excessive tax burdens was ever-present on the mind of the Orthodox hierarchy who occupied an intermediate position between the Christian subjects and the Ottoman power structure and often provided the first target to popular indignation. The pre-emption of such an eventuality appears clearly from the evidence of the report to have been the intention of their original action. The attempted appeal first through representatives and secondly in person to the central authority of the empire provided the institutionalized mechanism of protest which had traditionally been successful in defusing pressures from below by inducing the Porte to curb the arbitrary excesses of local potentates. The state of imperial decline in the eighteenth century was graphically reflected in the failure to utilize effectively this time-honoured mechanism of crisis defusion and the consequent escalation of the crisis to violence.

Of equal interest is the evidence of the report concerning the mechanisms of containment of traditional violence. In this connection the most notable aspect of the crisis was the intercession of the judicial institution through the actions of the Molla and the Ulema who acted as the exponents of political legitimacy by censuring and eventually declaring the oppressive measures of the local governor as a form of rebellion.[9] By means of this ideological device the resort to violence on the part of the populace could be sanctioned without damage to the concept of imperial sovereignty. In this manner traditional violence was co-opted into the maintenance mechanisms of the power structure. Besides the co-optation of violence through its judicial sanction, another method for the alleviation of popular discontent illustrated in this case, was the refund of taxes extracted by means that the imperial government came to acknowledge as tyrannical. This was the significance of the mission of the Vizir Choqadar who, in cooperation with the judicial institution, came to restore legitimacy by expounding the central authority's writ against the local governor who had turned rebel through tyranny.

The restoration of legitimacy however was not confined to the declaration of the tyrant as rebel and the consequent legitimization of the use of violence against him. In the intercession of the judicial institution and of the representative of central authority, equal stress was put on the symbolic aspect of submission on the part of the perpetrators of traditional violence. This was reflected in the demand for the return of the booty of the seraglio's plunder and in the imposition of an indemnity collected from the populace for the victims of the assault on the seraglio. The cycle of the restoration of order was complete with the eventual levy of a "forgiveness tax" by the next governor. This was willingly paid by the population according to Mariti,[10] probably out of the potent combination of fear and remorse typical of the psychology of traditional man. It was precisely this feeling that was captured in Kyprianos's comments over the terrible act of the breach of legitimacy.[11] Indeed the relevant passage in his *History* can be regarded as a classic description of the psychology of submission and fear nurtured by despotism in its subjects. Therefore only through the eventual gestures of submission by the population could the effects of disorder that comprised both the tyrant's rebellion and the popular resort to violence be undone and legitimacy considered restored.

The containment of violence and the restoration of legitimacy both on the power and the symbolic level makes the 1764 episode an integral part of the chain of "unfinished revolutions" described by Braudel as one of the endemic expressions of submerged social crisis in the Mediterranean world.[12] The violent eruptions of protest remained "unfinished revolutions" in that they never quite ran their full revolutionary course by effecting a change in the configuration of social conditions that originally precipitated them. The evidence in the historical record is ample that the "unfinished revolutions", originally located by Braudel in the sixteenth century, continued to highlight an increasingly intensified structural crisis in Ottoman society during the following two centuries. Continuing economic depression made unbearable by administrative decay, determined the shape of collective destinies in the Eastern Mediterranean and nurtured the muted despair of the masses beneath the symbolic acts of obedience and submission. Violence was the only channel available for the expression of this sense of collective malaise and depression. It was seized upon at moments of extreme desperation in order to make known the inchoate but profoundly felt will of the masses to survive. Violence was their way of breaking the silence of their historical destiny. The peasants of Cyprus in 1764 who joined their urban brethren for the feast and fair of Saint Demetrius, re-enacted, almost two centuries later, with the same desperation and basically for identical reasons, the violent remonstrance of the peasants of Villeneuve in Provence in protesting the cruel destiny of Mediterranean society through their unfinished revolution.[13]

VENETIAN CONSULAR REPORT ON THE NICOSIA RIOT OF NOVEMBER 5, 1764. (*)

1764, November 13

A.S.V. – Cinque Savii alla Mercanzia, *Lettere dei Consoli,* b. 648 (Cipro 1761–1769), unpaginated folios.

Abstract. A report by Venetian Consul in Larnaca Gerolimo Brigadi referring to the discontent caused in Cyprus by the rapacity of the governor Chill Osman. The bishops of the island attempted to alleviate the plight of the people by appealing to the Sublime Porte but they were arrested and imprisoned by the governor. The arrival of the Grand Vizir's Choqadar, sent to investigate the charges against the governor, set in motion a sequence of events which culminated in the assembly at the seraglio and the attempt of the governor to murder the bishops and his other critics by engineering a collapse of the part of the floor on which they stood. This triggered off the indignation of the populace who demanded and obtained the Molla's sanction for an assault on the palace. In this context the governor was killed and the palace set on fire. The report concludes with an account of the efforts to restore order following these events which took place on November 5, 1764,

> *Illustrissimi et Eccellentissimi Signori Signori e Patroni Colendissimi.*
>
> *Presentandosi incontro per Alessandria, ove si crede tutta via attrovarsi la nave del Capitano Antonio Francovich, onde m'approffitto dell' occasione per rassegnare a lume venerato di Vostre Eccellenze l'accaduta traggedia nella capitale di questo*

5 *Regno Nicosia il dì 5 del corrente, qual è come segue.*

> *Il tiranico governo del Mukassil Sellektar Zill Osman Agà, le di cui tiranie ed estorsioni tanto verso li Rajà, come alli Turchi, nel breve tempo del sua governo, giunsero a tal segno, che li quatro Vescovi del Regno, non potendole più tollerare le tante vessazioni al popolo, e tamendo loro di qualche sollevazione delli Rajà contro*

10 *se medemi, tentorono fuggire per Costantinopoli a portare li loro lamenti; ma penetrata la loro intenzione dal governatore li fece inseguire e fermare nell' atto della loro imbarcazione e li condussero in Nicosia, ove li tenne tutti quatro in arresto ben custoditi, ma loro non trascurando abbenche fermati spedirono quatro huomini Rajà del paese con i riccorsi necessarij alla Porta, da dove ottenero l'intento; spiccando*

15 *il supremo Vizir un suo Ciokadar con un commandamento fortissimo contro il Governatore, che debba astenersi da quatunque estorsion e tirania e che li Rajà non debbano pagare più di piastri 20 1/2 per testa giusto li preccedenti commandi, stante chelui prendeva piastri 42 1/2, onde che debba render conto, e restituir il di più che avesse rittirato sia per conto de drittio di estorsione.*

20 *Onde alli 4 del corrente giunto in Nicosia il detto Ciokadar del Vezir con due di quelli Rajà, che erano andati in Costantinopoli al riccorso e andò dirrettamentenel Mechemè dal Mullà ad alloggiare, con intenzione net giorno seguente di far comparire il detto Mukassil, con tutti li primati, e raddunar il Divano nel Mechemè per*

(*) The document is edited according to the standard diplomatic method.

far la lettura del commando reggio; però il Mukassil tentò ogni via e soddusse il Mullà

25 *e Vezir Ciokadar, acciò che segua il Divano nel di lui palazzo, invece del Mechemè, con scuse che temeva esponersi al popolo per andar al Mechemè, acciò non li venghi usata qualche insolenza per strada; cosi che il Mullà e Ciokadar del Vezir gli l'accordorono; e nel giorno seguente, che fù alli 5 detto, si raddunorono in Seraglio, cioè nel Palazzo, li quatro Vescovi, il Mullà e tutti li Aghà e primati del paese e li*

30 *Ullamà, cioè li leggisti suoi contrarij. Ma non fecce il Divano nel solito luogo pratticato bensi dentro un sallone nuovo da lui fabbricato, il quale era artiffiziato nel di sotto, avendo fatto siegare le collone di legno, che sostenevano la mettà di detto sal lone, come pure il gran travo, che era sostenuto dalle dette colonne; cosi che raddu nato che fù il Divano, fecce restore i quatro Vescovi e il Dragomano del Seraglio e*

35 *li Ullamà con li Rajà sopra la parte che erano le collone di sotto artiffiziate, e con corde ligate, e dalli suoi huomini guardate in attenzione de suoi ordini; onde letto che fù il commando reggio e lettera del Supremo Vizir dell'istesso tenore, principiò l'Arcivescovo e li Ullamà a rimproverarlo del suo tiranico governo, e lui sostentando il contrario, e loro chiamando per testimonij li Agà del Regno, li quali confermavano*

40 *il detto de Vescovi, in quello che si disputtava, lui fecce passare l'ordine alli suoi huo mini, ch'erano al disotto. Onde tutto ad un tratto tirando le corde, ch'erano legate le collone, fecce cadere in ruina la mettà della. camera con tutti li Vescovi, Dragomano, Ullamà e popolo Christiani e Turchi, che vi era di sopra, li quali chi si è rotta la gamba, chi il braccio, schiena, in somma tutti stroppiati, e l'idea sua era di farli strangollare*

45 *dalli suoi huomini in quella conffusione, però accorsi subito il Vezir Ciokadar, Mullà e Agani, li riccuperorono tutti e sortirono fuori del Seraglio. Rittornato che fù il Mullà nel suo Tribunale accorse tutto il popolo da lui, gridando vendetta contro il Governatore e che lo debba far comparire in di lui presenza per trattar la loro causa con il medemo e farlo render conto della sua azione traddittoria, che voleva truccidare*

50 *tanto popolo. (Accortosi anche il Vezir Ciokadar esser stato da lui avvelenato avanti che vaddunasse il Divano, stante che principiava a far l'effetto ma chiamò immediate un medico e presone contra velleno si riccuperò). Cosi che il Mullà mando a chiamarlo per due volte consecutive d'immediate comparire in giustizia a render*

55 *conto, perche il popolo era in sollevazione, ma lui non curandosi rispose con su periorità di non voler andare, nè sortire dal suo palazzo, anzi con strappazzi; il che rifferto al Mullà et inteso dal popolo esclamavano; il Mullà ciò vedendo li disse che siccome il Governatore è un tirano e ribelle alla giustizia et ai commandi reggij, che li diano l'assalto al suo palazzo e che lo ammazzino; ciò inteso dal*

60 *popolo accorse, e trovando le porte del palazzo serrate e pressidiate dalla sua ser vitù diedero fuoco alle porte, le quali arse che furono si gettò dentro la plehe arrabbiata, cosi pure anche dalle mura ruinate e passorono a fil di spada gran parte del la. di lui servitù, al numero di vinti sei, et incontratolo poi lui medemo, lo truccido rono; ma non contenti di questo diedero il sacco alle sue robbe e dennaro e di tutto*

65 *quello conteneva il palazzo, e lo lasciorono ardere, che si ruinò più della mettà, e spo gliatolo tottahnente, fino alle tavole portorono via. Il Mullà con li Agà procurorono calmare il popolo et acquieitarlo, stante che si attrovava la città molto popollata in quella giornata, essendo la fiera di Santo Dimitri, onde feccero sortire tutti li villani e foresti, girando in pattuglia tutti li Agà, con gran numero di gente armata, cosi che*

70 *a pocco alla volta acquiettorono ogni cosa, et il Mullà si è assunto del governo sin' ad altri ordini della Porta, già che non volsse nissun' Agà accettare il governo per esser cosi disordinato.*

Hanno rispedito in Costaniinopoli il Vezir Ciokadar con diversi altri Turchie Rajà, con l'esposizionie del successo alla Porta; onde tutti si attrovano in grand

75   *orghasmo in attenzione di quello sarà dalla Porta decciso, e come sarà tal azione intesa. Hanno scapullato diversi degl' huomini del Governatore, ma molti feriti, liquali vengono medicati da un certo Paolo Vondiziani medico Ceffaloniotto, che colàsi attrovò accidenitalmente.*

In ora tutto è quieto, e tranquillo il paese, giusto alla rellazione fattami dal cancelliere

80   *Crutta, che s'attrovava in Nicosia e nel successo, da dove rittornò ieri sera.*

Il Mullà doppo aver visto il popolo acquiettato, pubblicò con araldi dentro lacittà, che debbano restituire nel di lui Tribunale tutto quello saccheggiorono dal Sera-glio del Governatore, come robba attinente all' errario publico, onde giornalmentee di continuo trasportano robba nel Mechemè, che viene il tutto reggistratto con grand'

85   *esattezza, e fin' ora si è riccuperata molta robba, argentaria e dennaro.*

Mi è riuscito esimere in quest'anno li suddti dell'Isole a questa parte della contribuzione del karazo, che due anni sono mi ha convenuto superarla, mediante unregallo, stante che vi era un commandamento, stato dalla Porta spiccato sotto Cassum Agà predeccessore di quest'ultimo truccidato, che ancor questo aveva più volte già

90   *tentato farli pagare, e da me diffesi con tutto il fervore, che prego Iddio anche in seguito riuscirmi la loro esenzione.*

Questo è il quanto è la mia cognizione fin'ora, e che ho stimato di mio dovere parteciparlo all' Eccellenze Vostre, e quello seguirà in appresso non mancarò similmente avvanzarle le notizie_s nel mentre con tutto ossequio inchinandomi le baccio

95   *umilmente le vesti.*

Di Vostre Eccellenze

Umilissimo devotissimo et obbedientissimo servitore Gerolimo Brigadi, Console Veneto

Larnica di Cipro, adì 13 Novembre 1764

Commentary

V.8. *quatro vescovi.* The four bishops of the Orthodox Church of Cyprus at the time were the Archbishop Paisios (1759–1766), Chrysanthos of Paphos (1762–1767) and future successor to Paisios on the archiepiscopal throne (1767–1810), Makarios of Kition (1737–1776) and Chrysanthos of Kyrenia (1763–1773). On Paisios and his involvement in the incident, see John Hackett, *A History of the Orthodox Church of Cyprus*, London, 1901, pp. 218–222. See also, Parthenios Kirmitsis, "Ὁ Ἀρχιεπίσκοπος Κύπρου Παΐσιος καὶ ὁ ἰδιόχειρος αὐτοῦ κῶδιξ", *Κυπριακαὶ Σπουδαί*, vol. II (1938), pp. 1–30.

V.10. *tentorono fuggire.* The four bishops were apprehended near Liopetri, off the southeastern coast of the island, on their way to embark for Constantinople. According to Kyprianos, p. 319, they were given away because of an indiscretion of the bishop of Kition.

V.13. *quatro huomini Rajà.* The "Χρονικὸν Ἰωακείμ", records the name of one of the delegates, Haji Vassili of Mia Milia. See Myrianthopoulos, p. 54. There is some confusion in the Venetian Consul's information at this point. The four delegates had not been dispatched after the bishops' apprehension and confinement as implied by the report before. It was their delay in returning from Constantinople that prompted the bishops' own attempted flight.

V.15. *Ciokadar.* This official's name is recorded in the sources as Mechmet. See Hill, p. 81.

V.34. *Dragomano del Seraglio.* According to Kyprianos, p. 318, the post at the time was occupied by Haji Iossif. For more details see A. Indianos, "Δραγομανία καὶ δραγομάνοι στὴν Κύπρο", *Κυπριακαὶ Σπουδαί*, vol. II (1938), pp. 155–161. Kyprianos, p. 327, notes that later on the man became "almost a monarch" among Cypriot Christians.

V.63. *al numero vinti sei.* Kyprianos, p. 318, says eighteen dead besides the governor, a number recorded also by Mariti, p. 96.

V.68. *fiera di Santo Dimitri.* The discordance between the dates of the events given in the Venetian report, 4–5 November, and the traditional celebration of Saint Demetrios's day on 26 October is accounted for by the use of the Julian calendar followed by the Orthodox Church at the time. According to the "Χρονικὸν Ἰωακείμ", the riot of 1764 was the cause of the abolition of what apparently was a very important traditional fair at the opening of the winter season. See Myrianthopoulos, p. 55 and Kyprianos, p. 319. On the traditional fairs of Cyprus which survived into the twentieth century see C. D. Cobham, *The Churches and Saints of Cyprus*, London, 1910, pp. 26–29. On p. 28 three fairs of Saint Dimitrios are recorded in the villages of Leonarisso, Saint Dimitrios in Limassol district and Phyti in Paphos but none in Nicosia. A church of Saint Dimitrios is recorded in the Nicosia suburb of Agii Omologites and most probably the fair was held there until 1764. See p. 6, 34. A study of the traditional fairs of Cyprus, both those that survived into modern times and those, like the Nicosia fair of Saint Dimitrios, which disappeared under the pressures of political events and social changes is highly desirable. For a study of the historical development of the institution from antiquity through the Ottoman period, cf. Speros Vryonis, Jr., "The Panegyris of the Byzantine Saint: a Study in the Nature of a Medieval Institution, its Origins and Fate", in Sergei Hackel, ed., *The Byzantine Saint*, Sobornost Studies Supplement No 5 (1981), pp. 196–226. Braudel's comments are quite pertinent in this connection also in placing the subject in a broader context. See *The Mediterranean and the Mediterranean World*, vol. I, pp. 379–382 and passim.

V.77. *Paolo Vondiziani.* This is the earliest record of the presence of a member of this Cephalonian family in Cyprus. The Venetian consul was naturally keen in recording the presence of Vondiziani who was a subject of the Republic of Saint Mark as a native of the Venetian-held Ionian islands. For details on the family's settlement in Cyprus and their subsequent role in Cypriot social and political history, see A. L. Coudounaris, *Μερικαί παλαιαί οἰκογένειαι τῆς Κύπρου*, Nicosia, 1972, pp. 13–34. On Paolo Vondiziani see p. 31. The Venetian consuls reported regularly on the presence of Venetian subjects in Cyprus. For the earliest reports noted to date, see A. S. V., Cinque Savii alla Mercanzia, *Lettere dei Consoli*, b. 648: Cipro 1761–1769, documents dated 13 November and 20 December 1765, both of which give details on natives of the Ionian islands living in Larnaca and Limassol. See also ibid., b. 652: Cipro, 1785–1790 for multiple references.

V.80. *cancelliere Crutta*. Drummond refers to Doctor Crutta, "chancellor and first dragoman" on the British consul's staff, during his visit to Cyprus in 1745. Signor Crutta, "chief dragoman of the British nation" reappears in the same traveller's narrative of his second visit in 1750. See Cobham, *Excerpta Cyprta*, pp. 284, 304. Apparently Dr Crutta occupied the same position in 1764. He must have been by then a senior and well respected member of the European colony in Larnaca, on whose impressions the Venetian consul obviously felt he could safely rely.

V.85. *è riccuperata molta robba*. This quite unequivocal statement is important in documenting the population's resubmission to authority after the outburst of traditional violence. As a historical detail it is interesting in view of Hill's claim that very little of the loot was recovered. See *A History of Cyprus*, vol. IV, p. 83.

V.86. *esimere li sudditi dell' Isole*. This statement can be explained as a reference to the practice of the capitulations whereby the European consuls could intervene on behalf of their nationals and achieve various exemptions and privileges for them in the Ottoman domains. Apparently the Venetian consul refers here to a tax exemption he managed to secure for the Venetian subjects from the Ionian islands living at the time in Cyprus. Cf. on the subject the 1575 capitulations treaty between Venice and the Ottoman empire in *Treaties between Turkey and Foreign Powers, 1535–1855*, London, 1855, pp. 713–724, reprinted in Theodoros Papadopoullos, ed., *Προξενικὰ Ἔγγραφα τοῦ ΙΘ΄ αἰῶνος*, Nicosia, 1980, pp. 470–476. See especially p. 474, on the exemptions of Venetian subjects from the capitation tax.

V.98. *Gerolimo Brigadi*. The presence of Gerolimo Brigadi as Venetian consul in Larnaca can be documented between the years 1748 and 1764. His signature as "Console Generale per la Serenissima Repubblica di Venezia in questo Regno di Cipro" appears in a letter dated 27 July 1748. See A. S.V., Cinque Savii all Merchanzia, *Lettere dei Consoli*, b. 647. The correspondence for the year 1765 in b. 648 shows the position of Venetian consul in Larnaca occupied by Bernardo Caprara.

Notes

1 Archimandrite Kyprianos, Ἰστορία χρονολογικὴ τῆς νήσου Κύπρου, Venice, 1788, pp. 318–321. For an English language version see C. D. Cobham, *Excerpta Cypria*, Cambridge, 1908, pp. 356–362, reprinted in Harry Luke, *Cyprus under the Turks 1571–1878*, Oxford, 1921, pp. 39–45. References to Kyprianos are to the original 1788 edition. Giovanni Mariti, *Travels in the Island of Cyprus*, London, 1909, pp. 94–97 and "Χρονικὸν Ἰωακείμ" in Constantinos Myriantho-poulos, Χατζηγεωργάκης Κορνέσιος, Nicosia, 1934, pp. 54–55. See also Sir George Hill, *A History of Cyprus* IV, Cambridge, 1952, pp. 80–84, Wilhelm H. Engel, *Kypros. Eine Monographie*, Berlin, 1841, Vol. I, pp. 770–771, Philios Zannetos, Ἰστορία τῆς νήσου Κύπρου, Larnaca, 1910, pp. 1116–1121, Philippos Georghiou, Εἰδήσεις ἱστορικαὶ περὶ τῆς Ἐκκλησίας Κύπρου, Nicosia, 1875, pp. 105–109, Loizos Philippou, Ἡ ἐκκλησία τῆς Κύπρου ἐπὶ Τουρκοκρατίας, Nicosia, 1975, pp. 188–190, H. Fikret Alasya, *Kıbrıs Tarihi*, Nicosia, 1939, pp. 99–101. The earliest reference to the incident I could trace in a published Greek source is in Ἰστορία τοῦ παρόν-τος πολέμου ἀναμεταξὺ Ρουσίας καὶ τῆς Ὀθωμανικῆς Πόρτας, translated. by Spyri-don Papadopoulos, Venice, 1770, Vol. I, pp. 371–372.
2 Archivio di Stato di Venezia (A.S.V.), Cinque Savii alla Mercanzia, *Lettere dei Consoli*, b. 648: Cipro 1761–1769, 13 November 1764, report of Venetian Consul Gerolimo Brigadi from Larnaca, unpaginated ff. 1–7. The research on which this chapter is based was carried out during a residence at the Istituto Ellenico di Studi Bizantini e Postbizantini in Venice in the Spring-Summer 1976. I am grateful to the Director of the Institute Professor M. I. Manoussakas for his hospitality and advice and to Anastasia Papadia for help in the preparation of this chapter. Mary Constantoudaki-Kitromilides has rendered substantial assistance throughout.
3 Hill, *op. cit.*, pp. 81–82.
4 Kyprianos, *op. cit.*, p. 318, Mariti, *op. cit.*, p. 94, Myrianthopoulos, *op. cit.*, p. 54.
5 Cf. Charles Tilly, ed., *The Formation of National States in Western Europe*, Princeton, 1975, pp. 61, 71 and passim.
6 See P. M. Kitromilides, "From Coexistence to Confrontation: The Dynamics of Ethnic Conflict in Cyprus", in this collection, Chapter 9.
7 Cf. Robert Foster and Jack P. Green, eds., *Preconditions of Revolution in Early Modern Europe*, Baltimore and London, 1970, p. 110.
8 The term has been coined by Eric Hobsbawm, *Revolutionaries*, New York, 1973, p. 212.
9 On the role of the Ulema as ideologists and guardians of legitimacy in the Islamic state cf. Manfred Halpern, *The Politics of Social Change in the Middle East and North Africa*, Princeton; Princeton University Press, 1963, pp. 15–18.
10 Mariti, *op. cit.*, p. 97.
11 Kyprianos, *op. cit.*, p. 320.
12 Fernand Braudel, *The Mediterranean and the Mediterranean World in the Age of Philip II II (1972)*, New York, pp. 735–738.
13 Ibid., p. 736.

Appendix

The French Consul's report

Archives Nationales/Série Affaires Étrangères/ *Larnaca AE BI 639*

The uprising of October 1764 was extensively covered at the time in consular correspondence from Cyprus. The French Consul André-Benoît Astier[1] gives a detailed account of the events in his report of 18 November 1764 to the Duke de Praslin, Minister of the Navy of the Kingdom of France. Consul Astier's presence in Larnaca and the importance of his role on the island is recorded by the historian of Cyprus, Archimandrite Kyprianos,[2] who also publishes in Greek translation a report by Astier on an earlier uprising, based on the oral testimony of two elderly eyewitnesses, one Turk and one Greek.[3]

Astier's report on the 1764 rising, written only five days after Consul Brigadi's report, largely corroborates his evidence.

BENOÎT ASTIER, CONSUL DE FRANCE À CHYPRE, AU DUC DE PRASLIN, MINISTRE DE LA MARINE, LARNACA, 18 NOVEMBRE 1764.

J'ai l'honneur de donner information à votre Grandeur d'un soulèvement général qui a eu lieu le 5 de ce mois à Nicosie, dans lequel Chil Osman aga, gouverneur de l'île, fut privé de la vie avec environ 30 de ses *tchoccadars*. Ce musselim, qui se trouvait en place depuis la nouvelle lune de juin dernier, et qui avait été annoncé comme un favori des plus accrédités du Grand Vizir, avait débuté par des actes de justice et d'équité qui faisait espérer que le bon ordre se rétablirait en Chypre pendant l'année de son gouvernement, et que l'on y jouirait du repos et de la tranquillité; mais l'on fut bientôt déçu de ces espérances et l'on s'aperçut au second mois de son installation, que ses opérations ne tendaient qu'à extorquer par la crainte de son crédit et la terreur de son nom, les argents qu'il ne pouvait prétendre en vertu des commandements qui fixent la perception des droits du *miry,* et qui n'étaient pas auprès de lui, comme ils l'étaient auprès des gouverneurs passés, un frein à son excessive et insatiable avidité.

Au lieu de 20 piastres ½ pour droits de *karatch,* et autres, auxquels le Grand Seigneur a soumis par tête les *rayas,* il en prétendit 42 de premier abord, et en fit exiger une partie par la force de son autorité, sans qu'aucune fixation préalable eut été faite dans les assemblées par les évêques, suivant les règles et l'usage, défendant même de livrer des billets, l'argent étant perçu. Il doubla jusqu'à la taxe de 5 piastres à laquelle sont tenus les *Garibs* (Turcs tant indigènes qu'étrangers ne vivant point de la profession des armes) et il fixa la vente des denrées et du produit des arts à un prix bien au-dessous de leur valeur, ce qui lit disparaître les marchandises des magasins, au grand préjudice des vendeurs et du public.

Dans le même temps, les officiers en place n'étaient occupés sur toute l'île qu'à faire des avanies sous les moindres prétextes, et sans aucune formalité de justice, et il suffisait d'être censé avoir quelque chose pour être imputé: aussitôt l'accusé était mis en prison et sous le bâton, et il se voyait contraint, pour éviter de périr sous les coups, d'accorder l'argent demandé ou de donner des sûretés.

Toutes ces violences, de comptes faits, avaient déjà produit en *jérémés* au gouverneur de 3 à 400 bourses, sans y comprendre les sommes payées pour les droits du Prince. Les quatre évêques de l'île, qui sont les cautions du *miry* auprès du Grand Seigneur, connaissant le pays dans l'impossibilité de subvenir à toutes ces levées, craignant même de n'être taxés de connivence par les *rayas,* et voyant que toutes ces extorsions réduisaient les familles dans la plus affreuse misère, et rendaient toujours plus l'île déserte, les *rayas* restants devant payer pour ceux qui s'expatriaient, ils firent parvenir dans le mois de septembre leurs plaintes à La Porte, et, en attendant de savoir ce qui en résulterait, ils avaient projeté de s'enfuir eux-même à Beyrouth dans l'espoir que leur absence suspendrait l'oppression de Chil Osman aga. Mais ils furent découverts et saisis dans les premiers jours du mois dernier au moment de leur embarquement; et ce gouverneur les faisait garder à vue à Nicosie, et il ne voulait point absolument les mettre en liberté qu'ils n'eussent consenti à la levée des 42 piastres de sa prétention, sur l'exemple du fameux Ali aga que le feu Grand Vizir Raguib Pacha avait placé en Chypre en l'appuyant de sa faveur, et qui fut étranglé après la mort de son patron.

Les choses en étaient restées là lorsque le 4 de ce mois un vizir *tchoccadar* arriva de Constantinople à Nicosie, à l'ouverture de la foire unique et générale de la Saint Dimitri, qui se tient pour cette fête toutes les années pendant 3 jours dans cette capitale, et qui y attire de tous les endroits de l'île environ 12 000 personnes. Il était chargé d'un commandement adressé au *molla* portant ordre de réduire le gouverneur à ne percevoir que 20 piastres ½ par *raya,* suivant les anciens commandements, et de procéder juridiquement aux enquêtes de tout ce qu'il avait exigé de plus, ou extorqué injustement, pour lui en faire la restitution. Chil Osma aga envoya au devant de cet officier pour le complimenter et l'inviter d'aller loger chez lui; mais il s'en excusa sur ce qu'il avait ordre d'aller au Mékémé. Il fut cependant souper chez le gouverneur.

Le lendemain 5 le *molla,* contre l'avis du vizir *tchoccadar,* accorda au musselim, à l'insistance même des évêques, la politesse d'aller faire chez lui la lecture du commandement, et à cet effet il se rendit au sérail vers les 8 heures du matin avec le Grand officier de La Porte ; les *ulémas* (gens de la loi), les évêques, et quantité de peuple turc et raya, et Chil Osman aga les reçut en compagnie des agas qui formaient son Divan. Cependant ce gouverneur ayant prévu dès l'arrivée du *tchoccadar* que les enquêtes ordonnées par le commandement apporté ne pouvaient que le jeter dans le plus grand embarras, il forma pour sortir de ce labyrinthe le projet infernal de se défaire en même temps, et tout à la fois, du vizir *tchoccadar,* des évêques, et de tous ses autres accusateurs.

Les lettres de Nicosie, dont le contenu a été attesté et certifié de tous ceux qui furent ensuite examiner occulairement le lieu nous apprirent généralement et constamment qu'il avait fait donner par deux fois du poison au vizir *tchoccadar* dans du café, et qu'il avait fait affaiblir pendant la nuit et scier par moitié les solives et les appuis de la partie de la salle de son Divan, où se devaient tenir les évêques et le peuple, et qu'il y avait fait attacher des cordes pour les faire crouler à un signal. Le fait est que dans le temps que le gouverneur et les évêques, soutenus du vizir *tchoccadar* et des ulémas, en étaient aux invectives au sujet des plaintes portées par le commandement, l'on sentit une secousse et le plancher de la salle s'affaissa et s'abattit du côté du peuple, entraînant après soi dans sa chute les évêques avec environ 300 personnes turques et *rayas,* dont quelques unes furent estropiées et d'autres perdirent la vie; et chacun s'enfuit et se retira où il put.

Mais le peuple et quelques ulémas estropiés coururent en foule au Mékémé, demandant à hauts cris justice du gouverneur, et attribuant à sa méchanceté ce croulement que je croirais plutôt l'effet de la vétusté de l'appartement, comme il se peut que les vomissements du vizir *tchoccadar,* attribués au poison contre lequel il prit des remèdes, aient été causé par la surprise de l'émeute soudaine et imprévue d'un peuple qui s'irrite.

Le *molla,* le vizir *tchoccadar* et le *mufty* sommèrent par trois fois le gouverneur de comparaître mais ce fut inutilement. A ce refus les cris du peuple redoublèrent et ces officiers craignant d'être insultés eux-mêmes, ils déclarèrent que Chil Osman aga était un rebelle au Grand Seigneur et à la justice. Dans l'instant, la populace courut aux armes, au nombre de 7 à 800 hommes, et fut investir le sérail dont les portes furent fermées; mais un coup de fusil qui en fut tiré et dont un Turc perdit la vie, fut comme le signal de l'assaut. Le feu fut mis aux portes, et l'on entra de tout côté avec fureur dans le palais, faisant main basse sur tout ce qui se rencontra. L'on courut de chambre en chambre, et l'on fouilla partout jusqu'à ce que l'on eut trouvé le gouverneur. On le surprit lorsqu'il cherchait à se cacher avec ses trésors, et il fut tué par un nègre, dont il ne put obtenir quartier, et qui lui répondit que deux mois auparavant, recevant par son ordre trois cents coups de bâton il n'avait point voulu lui en faire.

Il y a eu 30 de ces *tchoccadars* tués et blessés, et les autres avec les agas se sauvèrent dans la mêlée au moyen des amis qu'ils y trouvèrent. Tout fut pillé, argents, nippes, meubles, ustensiles, harnais et jusqu'aux provisions les plus communes, et le feu qui, de la porte cochère, se communiqua à la partie fenestre des habitations qui sont à l'entrée de la cour, ne cessa que le jour suivant après les avoir consummées, ne laissant que les quatre murailles.

Pendant cette émeute, les agas chypriotes du gouverneur, qui méritaient de participer à son sort parce qu'ils étaient les moteurs de toutes les avanies, se réfugièrent au Mékémé, et ils n'osèrent que dans la nuit se mettre à la tête de leur troupe pour faire les rondes et les patrouilles. Mais ce désordre, qui n'avait été occasionné que par la chute de la salle du Divan, et par le refus avec mépris du gouverneur de se rendre à la justice pour y répondre aux accusations du peuple sur ce fait, n'a pas eu d'autres suites. Tout fut tranquille après la mort de ce musselim, et lorsque son sérail eut été, à 5 heures du soir, entièrement saccagé.

Ce sont les Turcs étrangers, pour la plupart Caramaniotes, venus à l'occasion de la foire qui fut ensuite prohibée, qui mirent en train ce soulèvement, excités principalement par les ulémas. Grâce à Dieu il ne s'est point communiqué à Larnaca comme il y avait grande apparence [...]. L'île se trouve actuellement gouvernée par le *molla* de Nicosie et par les cadis, attendant les ordres du Grand Seigneur [...].

Tout ce que je puis observer c'est que la faute principale du gouverneur dans son administration, relativement à lui-même, a été son obstination à vouloir tout engloutir et à ne faire aucun cas des ministres de la justice. Ses prédécesseurs percevaient également les droits au-delà de la fixation prescrite par les commandements ; mais ils avaient la politique d'intéresser dans cette perception les évêques et les chefs des contrées, qui sont les vrais tyrans du peuple, et ils n'entreprenaient aucune affaire qu'avec le concours des *naibs* et des cadis.

Chil Osman aga ne favorisait que ses officiers chypriotes qui lui désignaient les Turcs et les rayas qui pouvaient supporter quelque avanie. On lui impute encore le projet formé de vouloir faire périr les principaux habitants de l'île pour mieux envahir leur argent et leur bien, et qu'il devait ensuite se réfugier au Caire auprès de l'un de ses frères qui y est *Bey*.

L'on dit même que les Francs étaient réservés pour la bonne bouche. Cependant, ceux-ci n'avaient eu à se plaindre que d'un déni de justice qu'il fit à tous les consuls [France, Angleterre, Venise], dans les premiers jours du mois dernier parce qu'ils lui demandaient la punition de son *deidaban* de Larnaca qui était son âme damnée. Ce *deidaban* m'avait demandé à parler à M. Lenoir ; mais ce premier drogman se trouvait dans ce moment en empêchement, je lui envoyais le second pour savoir ce qu'il souhaitait. Il lui donna pour toute réponse un soufflet et des coups de bâton. Cette insulte offensant toute l'Echelle, je fus au Mékémé pour la constater et pour obliger cet homme à venir y rendre compte de sa conduite. Les consuls d'Angleterre et de Venise, qui voulurent prendre part dans cette affaire pour la sûreté commune des nations franques, y envoyèrent en même temps leur drogman.

Mais ce *tchoccadar* refusa de comparaître sur trois sommations du cadi. Je déclarais alors à ce *naib,* et les drogmans d'Angleterre et de Venise le déclarèrent au nom de leurs consuls, que nous ne traiterions plus à l'avenir avec un pareil homme qui méprisait et se rendait rebelle à la justice, et que lorsqu'il y aurait quelque affaire à discuter avec nous, nous les porterions au Mékémé si le gouverneur ne nous donnait satisfaction. Il nous la refusa, et ne voulut pas même répondre à aucun de nous : chaque consul lui avait porté ses plaintes séparément [...].

ARCHIVES NATIONALES
Série Affaires Étrangères
Larnaca AE BI 639

Notes

1 Ministère des Affaires Étrangères, Centre des Archives Diplomatiques de Nantes, *Ambassade de France à Constantinople. Série D: Larnaca 1751–1912,* Nantes, 2005, p. 107. See also Amaury Faivre d'Arcier, *Les oubliés de la liberté. Négociants, consuls et missionnaires français au Levant pendant la Révolution (1784–1798),* Frankfurt: Peter Lang, 2007, p. 212 and passim.
2 Archimandrite Kyprianos, Ἱστορία χρονολογικὴ τῆς νήσου Κύπρου, Venice, 1788, p. 309.
3 Ibid., pp. 310–311.

5 The anonymity of a prominent woman in eighteenth-century Cyprus

Our knowledge concerning the dragoman of Cyprus, Christophakis Constantinou, was until fairly recently limited to two allusions in eighteenth-century historical sources to his violent death on Easter 1750, and to the pictorial evidence of his sponsorship of the construction and decoration with wall paintings of the chapel of Saint George on the estate of Arpera near the village Tersefanou in the borough of Larnaca. The first record of Christophakis's death on 15 April 1750 is by the archimandrite Kyprianos, who mentions the event in his narrative of the misdeeds of Hadji-Bakki, the one-eyed Ottoman tyrant of Cyprus.[1] The other, more dramatic record comes from the chronicle of the monastery of Pallouriotissa's chancellor, Ioakim:[2]

> *The late Dragoman Christophakis*
> *was killed by the Ottomans on Holy Sunday*
> *as he made his way to the holy church*
> *in order to hear the good news; half way*
> *they hit him and he died.*

The wall painting of the donors of the church of Arpera (Figure 5.1) is more eloquent than the written testimonies. It presents Christophakis offering the church to Saint George with the members of his large family, eight people in all, by his side. The accompanying inscriptions reveal to us that the family was even larger, because they also mention the names of children who had died at a young age, but whose names were subsequently given to their younger siblings. The wall painting, the work of the well-known Cypriot iconographer Philaretos,[3] is the most impressive depiction of donors in Cypriot art of the eighteenth century. It was noticed quite early on by David Talbot Rice and Tamara Rice[4] and published by Andreas and Judith Stylianou in their study on the church of Saint George of Arpera.[5] Andreas and Judith Stylianou also publish the inscriptions which accompany the wall painting of the donors. From these we learn that Christophakis "built the church himself from its foundations and decorated it at personal expense" in 1745, in order to thank Saint George, who was his "tireless helper" and "ever-ready deliverer from exile".

Figure 5.1 Dragoman Christophakis Constantinou and his family.
Fresco in the Church of Saint George of Arpera. (author's photograph).

Another inscription, which accompanies the wall painting of the donors, repeats the gratitude to Saint George for Christophakis's deliverance from exile and begs him to intercede on his behalf:

> *INTERCEDE FOR ME, BEING YOUR WRETCHED SERVANT*
> *CHRISTOPHAKIS CONSTANTINOU, FOR MY PARENTS*
> *AND FOR MY CHILDREN*

At the prothesis of the church another inscription, on a scroll held by an angel, gives us the names of all these supplicants to Saint George, living and dead, clarifying that they are indeed Christophakis and his children; mentioned are sixteen living and nine deceased. The observer of the dedicators's wall painting and reader of the inscription at the prothesis is struck by the unexplained absence of any mention of Christophakis's wife. The benefactor prays on behalf of himself, his children, living and deceased and his parents, but mentions nothing of his wife. This silence makes an impression on Andreas and Judith Stylianou, who hypothesize that the elder woman who appears in the wall painting in between the younger girls could be identified with Christophakis's mother or sister and suppose that, since a spouse is not mentioned, perhaps she had already died.

This was the general picture of Christophakis and his family in the bibliography of eighteenth-century Cypriot history.[6] The first well-known dragoman of the eighteenth century remained a somewhat distant and tragic figure; a figure, however, with whom the great era of Cypriot dragomany essentially begins, an era that was chiefly marked by the actions of Christophakis's successors, the all-powerful Hatziyosif, "almost a monarch to the Greeks",[7] and the famed Hatzigeorgakis Kornesios, who also fell victim to the tyrannical violence of the authorities.[8]

The enigmatic figure of Christophakis should now be enabled to emerge from the shadows of the church of Arpera and become somewhat more discernible as an historical actor, after many years of research in pursuit of his sparse historical traces and his activities in Cypriot society during the first half of the eighteenth century. This research, which began in 1976[9] with the exploration of the records of the Venetian consulate at Larnaca (records deposited in the State Archive of Venice), continued over the following decades in archives in France and Britain and has produced a much more complete picture of the first of the great Cypriot dragomans of the eighteenth century, his economic transactions, as well as his political activities. This information, which is constantly being enriched, will hopefully in the end be compiled into a biography of Christophakis.

Among the documentation uncovered by this research is a letter dated 20 April 1750,[10] written in other words five days after the murder of Christophakis. This letter may be considered the tragic epilogue of the dragoman's life. It is addressed to the consul of Ragusa in Cyprus, Giovanni Garmougliezi,[11] and reads as follows:

Illustrious, most glorious, and most capable lord and signore Giovani Garmougliezi, consul of Araouza and our master and benefactor,

We humbly prostrate ourselves before Your Gloriousness and greet you in awe, beseeching the Lord of All Christ our God to preserve You in health, happiness and the highest good fortune, for many years to come, amen.

We are sure that Your Gloriousness has heard of the events, which befell us wretched ones. Today Your envoy Andreas came, bearing the records of my ill-fated husband; as it seems, they are true, and are from all of your accounts, and conform to what he always told us and occupied himself with. The amount of one of the bills is twenty thousand piastres and the other is for three thousand piastres. Minus two thousand five hundred which he told us that he received; the rest he did not receive. One way or the other we are sure that you would never want to harm his orphaned children, who have been left miserable and wretched; and I, ill-fated woman, who have been made more wretched than everyone, since I have lost my life, my light, my comfort, have nowhere to turn for refuge and no way to manage my affairs, since I have lost him and all that I had. And so, I have no other hope than first, our Lord God and second, Your Gloriousness. And I am sure that the love you had for my husband you will now show in even greater measure to me and to our children. And that you will help us with all your heart and soul.

For this reason we beg of Your Gloriousness to send us this money, as much as you have received. Because for the time, all of his records and receipts are sealed and closed to us; and we do not know anything else but what he told us, but that of my brother Petrakis, who had taken it on himself, and from whom you were to take four thousand piastres; and from the bishop of Kyrenia two thousand five hundred; and from Antonis Tzohias one thousand five hundred, since he gave You a bill, if indeed this is a debt to the deceased, since he asked him to lend it to him. There is also some wheat and cotton and silk that he gave to you. For all this we beg of You to make a record of the amount that you took, so that we may know how much remains of his debt, that they can make a record of it in the City, to confirm it and for the reimbursement to come, as the deceased told us that he was to give you twenty one purses. If you take three more, it becomes twenty four.

Page 2.

So he told us and so we knew. Now, more or less, Your Gloriousness you knew the accounts, what he gave you. And we hope that no injustice will be done to us, since you are an extremely Christian man, and you do not want to harm us, us being so wretched that even the stones pity us in our unhappiness and misfortune. And so, we are sure that you will not ignore our tears and sighs. And we wish to be from today on your servants, and suppliants to God to reward you in his heavenly kingdom. This for the present, and may Your years be plentiful and full of happiness.

> *April 20, 1750.*
> *Of Your Gloriousness,*
> *The wretched wife of luckless Christophakis,*
> *And his sons Konstantinos, Nikolaos,*
> *And the rest remain at Your command.*

Somewhat strangely, the letter of the "wretched wife of luckless Christophakis" to the brutal moneylender and businessman who acted as Ragusa's consul in Larnaca, offers a perspective for the interpretation of the wall painting of the donors of Arpera. First, it offers us documentation so that we may test the hypothesis that was proffered by the church's first systematic researchers, Andreas and Judith Stylianou, regarding the absence of any mention of the benefactor wife in the church's inscriptions. The letter dated 20 April 1750 makes it clear that their hypothesis about the possible early death of Christophakis's wife cannot stand. The woman, mother of so many children, outlived her powerful husband. And after his violent death she appears, in the midst of her despair, to take on the responsibilities of the enterprising dragoman's many and varied businesses.

Since, then, Christophakis's wife was living when the wall painting was made in 1745, she must appear as one of the three women who are represented there. But which one could she be? It would be reasonable to identify her with the eldest woman wearing the dark-coloured head covering, who Andreas and Judith Stylianou considered to be possibly Christophakis's mother or older sister. She could, however, be one of the younger women who are depicted in the wall painting with a much more well-groomed appearance, wearing brightly coloured clothes, jewellery and head coverings that differ from those of traditional Cypriot clothing. While the elderly woman's figure in Figure 5.1 presents clothing within the traditional realm of Cypriot fashion, the two young women are probably displaying the characteristics of fashionable urban dress of the period.[12]

Could the anonymous wife of Christophakis, then, be the female figure directly by his side in the wall painting or the other woman who stands at the other end of the painting among the children? The question cannot be answered. The wife remains unidentified and anonymous, as the couple's daughters remain unidentified, even if we know their names, at least, from the inscription in the prothesis.[13] On the contrary, the two eldest sons, Konstantinos and Nikolaos, who sign the letter of 20 April 1750 together with their mother, can be identified in the wall painting with exactitude.

Thus, in the end, the wall painting of the donors of St George of Arpera reveals to us much more about Cypriot society in the mid-eighteenth century than what the benefactor intended. It primarily reveals to us the structures of inequality that were deeply ingrained in the mentality of the time and required, by means of a powerfully symbolic anonymity, the submission and disappearance of the woman's personality and her transformation, even in terms of personal appellation, into merely a complement of the man. This manifold levelling of the woman appears in an almost classic form in the case of Christophakis's wife. We have her portrait, without being able to identify her with precision amidst her large family; we have the letter she signs, without knowing her name; she makes a fleeting appearance on the stage of Cypriot social history, remaining insistently silent about herself in the midst of her distress. And yet, from what the reader of the letter can tell, this lady of Nicosia society, in a way the first lady among the Greeks of Cyprus until 15 April 1750, quite possibly came from one of the most distinguished families of the educated urban class of the island, if her brother Petrakis, mentioned in the letter, can be identified with the well-known personality of Nicosia, Petrakis Karydis.[14]

The letter also allows for the appearance of a personality marked by decisiveness and initiative, that does not seem disposed, five days after the sudden tragedy that befell her, to give herself up to fatalism and to accept stultification: she asserts her and her children's rights against her husband's debtors, among whom is included a prelate of the Church of Cyprus, "the holy man of Kyrenia", who may be identifiable with Metropolitan Nikiforos of Kyrenia.[15] However, within the normative climate of the mentality of the time, this lady of eminent Cypriot society of the mid-eighteenth century, under the additional weight placed upon women by unbending and ideologically inescapable hierarchical structures, as happened everywhere in early modern European society,[16] and, despite the attempt that shows in her letter to rearrange in a moment of tragic tribulation the margin to which the structure of reality forcefully confined her,[17] remains anonymous and comes down to us, through the chiaroscuros of time and records, simply as "the wretched wife of luckless Christophakis".

Notes

1 Archimandrite Kyprianos Kouriokourenios, *Ἱστορία χρονολογική τῆς νήσου Κύπρου*, Venice, 1788, p. 327: 'The bloodthirsty tyrant had his men seize Dragoman Christophakis and murder him at dawn on Easter Sunday, 1750'.
2 K. I. Myrianthopoulos, *Χατζηγεωργάκις Κορνέσιος ὁ Διερμηνεὺς τῆς Κύπρου, 1779–1804*, Nicosia, 1934, p. 52.
3 M. Hatzidakis—Evgenia Drakopoulou, *Ἕλληνες ζωγράφοι μετά την ἅλωση (1450–1830)* 2, Athens, 1997, pp. 443–444. The two painters mentioned as Philaretos are probably the same person.
4 D. Talbot Rice, *Icons of Cyprus*, London, 1937, p. 136 and table 16 facing p. 112.
5 Andreas and Judith Stylianou, "The Historic Church of St George of Arpera", *Κυπριακαὶ Σπουδαί* 36 (1972), pp. 149–164; *eidem, The Painted Churches of Cyprus*, Nicosia, 1997, pp. 440–446. See also N. Gkioles, *Η χριστιανική τέχνη στην Κύπρο*, Nicosia, 2003, pp. 263, 267–268.
6 Antonis K. Intianos collects the sporadic references to Christophakis in his "Dragomany and dragomans in Cyprus", *Κυπριακαὶ Σπουδαί* 2 (1938), pp. 153–155. See also George Hill, *A History of Cyprus, IV: The Ottoman Province, the British Colony*, edited by Harry Luke, Cambridge, 1952, pp. 94–95. P.M. Kitromilides, *Κοινωνικές σχέσεις και νοοτροπίες στην Κύπρο του δεκάτου ογδόου αιώνα*, Nicosia, 1992, pp. 19–21.
7 Archimandrite Kyprianos, p. 327.
8 Myrianthopoulos, pp. 78–144.
9 M. I. Manousakas sets out a synopsis of the first discoveries in "Ekthesi pepragmenon Ellinikou Institoutou Byzantinon kai Metabyzantinon Spoudon Venetias", *Θησαυρίσματα* 13 (1976), pp. 333–334.
10 Archivo di Stato di Venezia/Lettere dei Consoli, *Consolato Veneto di Cipro*, b. 20: Atti e Lettere Greche 1703–1797, no. 75. See also *Archivio del Consolato Veneto a Cipro (fine sec. XVII-inizio XIX)*, ed. Giustiniana Migliardi O'Riordan, Venice, 1993, 73 (summary listing by A. Pardos).
11 Concerning this: Kitromilides, *Κοινωνικές σχέσεις και νοοτροπίες*, pp. 15–18, 24–25.
12 Evphrosyni Rizopoulou-Igoumenidou, *Η αστική ενδυμασία της Κύπρου κατά τον 18ᵒ και 19ᵒ αιώνα*, Nicosia, 1996, pp. 67–69.

13 Stylianou, p. 153.
14 P. M. Kitromilides, *Κυπριακὴ Λογιοσύνη 1571–1878. Προσωπογραφικὴ θεώρηση*, Nicosia: Cyprus Research Centre, 2002, p. 164, and in greater detail G. Papacharalampous, "Ὁ Πετράκης Καρύδης, τὸ χειρόγραφον καὶ ἡ οἰκογένειὰ του", *Κυπριακαὶ Σπουδαὶ* 29 (1965), pp. 183–209. "The most educated Mr. Petrakis Karidis" also appears among the subscribers of Archimandrite Kyprianos, *Ἱστορία χρονολογικὴ*, p. 404.
15 J. Hackett—C. I. Papaioannou, *Ἱστορία τῆς Ὀρθοδόξου Ἐκκλησίας τῆς Κύπρου* II, Piraeus, 1927, p. 100. This is apparently Metropolitan Nikiforos III of Kyrenia, about whom there are references for the years 1741–1743, 1753, 1754, 1759, 1764.
16 See Natalie Zemon Davis, *Women on the Margins. Three Seventeenth-century Lives*, Cambridge, MA: Harvard University Press, 1995, p. 203.
17 See Davis, pp. 209–212.

6   A Moldavian connection to the introduction of the Enlightenment in Cyprus

The contribution of Archbishop Kyprianos (1810–1821)

For Cypriots Archbishop Kyprianos has been and remains a legendary and tragic figure, literally and symbolically the historical embodiment of the bearer of the cross of the martyrdoms of their island throughout its history. His historical figure is perceived by means of the symbolism of his monuments, the unaffected bust in front of Nicosia's cathedral of Saint John the Evangelist and the evocative mausoleum of the ethnomartyrs of 9 July 1821 in the courtyard of the Phaneromeni church. The foremost channel of transmission of Kyprianos's mystique to Cypriot sensibility through the generations remains, nevertheless, the epic poetry about the drama of the 9th of July, composed in Cypriot Greek in the late nineteenth century by Vassilis Michaelidis, Cyprus's national poet.[1] There can be little doubt that this work, its symbolic language and the collective feelings it evokes constitutes one of the major factors in Cypriot self-awareness. Archbishop Kyprianos is a major presence in all this and thus he forms an integral part of the way Cypriot collective conscience understands and defines itself.

If we attempt to move this epic presence from legend to history in order to attempt an appraisal, on the basis of the standards of academic analysis, of its position in the historical destinies of Cyprus, we will discover that the Thucydidean judgement that Athens, "alone among her contemporaries, when put to the test, proves superior to the report of her" (Thucyd., II, 41), applies fully to the case of Kyprianos. If we examine carefully and impartially the data on Kyprianos's life and activity we will have to concur with Thucydides that his prominence as a leader and as a hero "is no mere boast […] but actual truth".

In order to transact the task of this appraisal it is necessary to go through the motions of academic judgement on a succession of levels of analysis. First we have to critically appraise the information that is available on Archbishop Kyprianos, his life and work. Secondly we must reflect critically on earlier attempts to evaluate Kyprianos and his standing in the history of Cyprus. Finally we must attempt to recover from available—and accessible—sources the historicity of Kyprianos's own witness in the context of his contemporary secular and ecclesiastical politics.

Let's begin with an appraisal of available knowledge. Kyprianos was born in 1756 in Strovolos, at the time a village in the outskirts of Nicosia. At an early age he entered Machairas monastery in the highlands south of his native village as a novice. His entry into the ranks of Orthodox monasticism must have taken place sometime in the mid-to-late 1760s. In 1783 he was ordained deacon by Archbishop Chrysanthos of Cyprus (1767–1810). This is about all that is known of Kyprianos's early life.[2] The best documented, and consequently best known, phase in the biography of Archbishop Kyprianos is the period of his tenure of the archiepiscopal throne of Cyprus in the years 1810–1821. Conversely the most serious lacuna in Kyprianos's biography concerns the period of his residence in the Danubian principalities of Moldavia and Wallachia in the years 1783–1802. If we take into account that this twenty-year period is exactly twice as long by comparison with the relatively better known last phase of Kyprianos's life, we will be able to appreciate the seriousness of the methodological problem concerning the writing of the biography of a personality of such critical importance in the history of Cyprus. The problem is illustrated by the fact that the distinguished historian of Greek-Romanian intellectual ties, Ariadna Camariano-Cioran, in her exhaustive study of Cyprus's ties with the Danubian principalities, could neither add any novel information nor document with any precision various hypotheses and received information on Kyprianos's extensive residence in the region. It is also characteristic of the absence of historical documentation on this period of Kyprianos's life that in her monumental work on the princely academies of Bucharest and Jassy Ariadna Camariano could not locate the slightest indication of any relationship of the monk from the Machairas monastery with those two top academic institutions in Southeastern Europe. Thus Ariadna Camariano had only just repeated the received opinion of earlier sources that during his residence in Jassy Kyprianos he could have attended courses at the local princely academy.[3] When exactly this attendance took place remains entirely unspecified.

Historical method, nevertheless, as a method of critical enquiry and reappraisal of sources, supplies other possibilities for approaching the past. On the basis of the information that Kyprianos lived in the principalities from 1783 onward we could attempt at least to recreate the context within which he reached intellectual maturity and to recover a sense of the political and intellectual influences he absorbed and under which he formed his judgement about the condition of the Orthodox community under Ottoman rule. The sources insist that Kyprianos met and was attached to the retinue of prince Michael Soutzos, who appreciated the abilities of the Cypriot Hierodeacon and took care of his ordination as a priest and subsequently appointed him as a chaplain of the chapel of the princely palace. Where and when all these important biographical steps were taken remains unclear. Cypriot sources mention that the acquaintance of the young Kyprianos with Michael Soutzos took place in Jassy. When the alms-collecting mission of Machairas Monastery, composed of the archimandrite Charalambos and his nephew Kyprianos, reached the principalities in 1783–1784, Michael Soutzos was prince of Wallachia in Bucharest, a position he held precisely in the years 1783–1786. During the same period the princely throne of Moldavia was occupied by Alexander Mavrocordatos (1782–1785, 1785–1786). Michael Soutzos returned to the throne of Wallachia in 1791–1793, following the Austrian occupation of the country, moving to the Moldavian throne in 1793–1795.[4] When and where, then, was Kyprianos acquainted with Michael Soutzos, which prelate ordained him as a priest and in which princely palace he became a chaplain, in Bucharest or Jassy? All this remains a matter of conjecture—and this is typical of almost any attempt to appraise biographical evidence in the history of Cyprus and of the Greek world under Ottoman rule more broadly through the early nineteenth century. I refer to these methodological difficulties, which arise from the practical problems created by fragmentary evidence and insufficient documentation even for recent periods such as the eighteenth or the early nineteenth centuries in the history of the Greek world in order to point to the endemic epistemological issue of uncritically accepting and repeating inaccuracies or legends from older sources, a practice that plagues even contemporary Cypriot historiography to a noteworthy degree.

On the basis of available information we can at least attempt to bring some precision into Kyprianos's biography by suggesting that his residence in Jassy might be chronologically located in the years 1793–1795, during the tenure of the Moldavian throne by Michael Soutzos.[5] The 1790s was a period of revolutionary ferment in the principalities caused by the influences of the French Revolution, which were propagated by agents of revolutionary France, Greek Enlightenment intellectuals and Polish refugees taking refuge there after the partition of Poland.[6] All this must have influenced the formation of Kyprianos's ideas.

Beyond the influences of the Enlightenment we may more safely assume that Kyprianos's outlook must have sustained the impact of ecclesiastical culture in Moldavia and Wallachia, which during the period of his residence was going through a phase of vigorous intellectual and educational activity under the leadership of metropolitans Gregorios and Dositheos in the diocese of Ungrowallachia in Bucharest and Gabriel and Iakovos in the diocese of Modavia in Jassy. These senior prelates took the lead not only in the construction of churches and monasteries, but especially in a vigorous publishing activity aimed at the spiritual guidance of clergy and laity alike. The distinguished historian of the Orthodox Church of Romania Mircea Pacurariu has described this period a "splendid page" in the history of the cultural and intellectual contribution of the Church in the Romanian lands.[7] Gabriel of Moldavia in particular, whom probably Kyprianos met in person during his residence in Jassy, had attracted the respect and admiration of important exponents of the Balkan Enlightenment like Iosipos Moisiodax and Dositej Obradović.[8]

It is my argument that Kyprianos's ideas were shaped in this intellectual environment, which supplied him with models for his future leadership of the Church of Cyprus. Kyprianos's activity in Cyprus, following his return in 1802, is a much better known period of his biography. A personal detail that is certainly interesting and might be revealing of the new mentality he espoused in the principalities is the fact that he brought back with him a portrait of himself, which still survives at Machairas monastery. It shows Kyprianos as a young clergyman with very lively eyes, which suggest great intelligence.[9] Following his return Kyprianos was given the position of steward (οικονόμος) of his monastery's dependency at Strovolos, his own native village just outside Nicosia. Very soon, however, he was called to the service of the archdiocese of Cyprus in the same capacity, being charged with the management of the financial affairs of the Church. In March 1804 during an uprising of the Muslim population of the city motivated by the scarcity of wheat, Kyprianos had an opportunity to show his leadership qualities. The young steward of the archdiocese, who also had a good command of Turkish, managed to ward off the mob that was threatening to set the building of the archbishopric on fire. Talking on behalf of the ageing and ailing archbishop Chrysanthos Steward Kyprianos contributed to the defusing of the crisis.[10] It is reported that on this occasion he appealed both to the mediation of European consuls in Larnaca but also came to an understanding with the agas of the island, whereby public opinion and social attitudes in the city of Nicosia were pacified. From then onward the affairs of the archbishopric passed almost entirely into Kyprianos's hands, despite the presence of other more senior clergymen in the entourage of the elderly archbishop.

Kyprianos's moment came in 1810. Under conditions that have remained unclear, but obviously through the intervention of powerful supporters who were looking for a new and dynamic archbishop, in the late spring and early summer of 1810, a new crisis in the Church of Cyprus led to the expulsion of archbishop Chrysanthos by edict of the Sublime Porte and his replacement by Kyprianos. The old and ailing archbishop Chrysanthos, and his nephew and namesake metropolitan of Kition, were expelled from their sees and banished from Cyprus to the island of Euboia. Kyprianos was named archbishop by the Porte and the archimandrite Meletios was named metropolitan of Kition.[11] For the change on the archiepiscopal throne to be completed, however, the intervention of the secular authority had to be sanctioned by ecclesiastical election and ordination. The remaining hierarchy in Cyprus, Chrysanthos of Paphos and Evgenios of Kyrenia along with other senior clergymen and lay dignitaries appealed to Constantinople for guidance with a detailed report dated 28 June 1810.[12] Patriarch Jeremiah III with a letter of 15 July 1810 responded by charging the Archbishop of Sinai Constantios, who happened to be in Cyprus at the time, to proceed to the ordination of

Kyprianos and Meletios.[13] Constantios however, hesitated on canonical grounds since the old archbishop was still alive and had not tendered in his resignation. The solution was provided by the death of archbishop Chrysanthos on 1 September 1810 in Chalkis. This removed the canonical obstacles and Kyprianos was duly ordained on 29 October 1810.[14] Thus begins the last and best documented phase in Kyprianos's biography.

Kyprianos's tenure of the archiepiscopal throne of Cyprus is a relatively brief period, just a decade compared to the almost half a century tenure of his predecessor (1766–1810). Despite its brevity it was a period of critical significance in the history of the Church of Cyprus because under Kyprianos Cyprus and its Church were exposed to the influence of what might be described "ecclesiastical Enlightenment". With this admittedly imperfect term I attempt to describe the noteworthy phenomenon of the openness shown by the Orthodox Church since the mid-eighteenth century to the exponents of the culture of the Enlightenment in the Greek world. This attitude expressed the realization on the part of the leadership of the Church that the scholars of the Enlightenment possessed better training and superior learning by comparison with the exponents of traditional culture and could, therefore, serve move effectively the pastoral work of the Church in the educational domain. This attitude characterized the options of several ecumenical patriarchs and senior Orthodox prelates and was expressed for instance in the initiative of the Ecumenical Patriarchate to entrust the reform of the Athonite Academy to Evgenios Voulgaris 1753 and of the Patriarchal Academy in Constantinople to the same controversial Enlightenment scholar in 1759. It was further expressed by employing a succession of important and articulate exponents of modern scientific learning at the helm of the school of the patriarchate repeatedly until the early nineteenth century.[15] Major representatives of the "ecclesiastical Enlightenment" included the Ecumenical Patriarchs Cyril V, Seraphim II and Cyril VI and senior metropolitans such as Dionysios and Meletios of Ephesus, Dorotheos of Adrianople and Ignatius of Ungrowallachia. Kyprianos of Cyprus could be added to this group. How else could one interpret the founding document he issued for the establishment of the "Hellenic School" in Nicosia, which he inaugurated on 1 January 1812? This document was in fact, in the Cypriot cultural context, a manifesto of the Enlightenment. The archbishop, in drafting the charter of his new school, expresses his expectation that its pupils and future graduates will become "men marked by piety, prudence, civility, rectitude, justice, love of country, love of commerce".[16] An even more daring manifesto of the Enlightenment was Kyprianos's other foundation document of 18 August 1819, whereby he gives his blessing to the initiative of community leaders in Limassol to establish a second Hellenic School in that city also and to appoint as its head a well-known Cypriot exponent of Enlightenment culture, Dimitrios Themistocles, whose character is praised by the archbishop who calls him "a philhellene and patriot".[17] The school of Limassol, which the archbishop so full-heartedly endorsed, transferred to Cyprus the spirit of the Enlightenment on the model of the foremost such institution in the Greek world at the time, the Philological Gymnasium of Smyrna, where Dimitrios Themistocles had been trained and later taught.

Kyprianos's initiatives in the domain of education were neither isolated nor the product of conjuncture. They in fact represented the apex of a long-term strategy of the Church of Cyprus, a strategy that is discernible already in the sources at the time of Archbishop Philotheos (1734–1759). This strategy aimed at the revival of the tradition of Greek letters on the island as a factor that would strengthen the Christian faith but also the historical self-awareness of the flock of the Church. Philotheos's intentions transpired in the invitation he extended to one of the foremost scholars of his time, Ephraim the Athenian, to come to Cyprus from Patmos where he taught, in order to lead the revival of Greek learning on the island. Philotheos's strategy was carried on and expanded by Archbishop Chrysanthos, Kyprianos's immediate predecessor. Archbishop Chrysanthos, although of rather limited education himself, was a great renovator of Cypriot ecclesiastical life: this is attested by his extensive project of restoration of churches and monasteries, his sponsorship of the publication of books, some of which veritable "chartered texts" for the Church of Cyprus, his initiative for the revival in Nicosia of Philotheos's old school.[18]

The final stage in the unfolding of this strategy came with the initiatives of Kyprianos. Although by his actions he was continuing an earlier tradition, in fact his educational projects, as noted above, were marked by a distinctly modernizing purpose which aimed at the introduction of a new "civility" in the island, the culture of the Enlightenment. This is made plain by what he says in his foundation document for the Hellenic School in Nicosia, quoted above, but more affirmatively in what he writes in his blessing for the Philological School of Limassol, which he expected to cultivate the faith obviously but also civility, "right policy".[19] All this is particularly important because Kyprianos's commitment to the Enlightenment remains unwavering at a time when elsewhere in the Greek world, a marked change is observable in the attitude of the Church toward the Enlightenment, as ideological tensions and conflicts escalated on the eve of the Revolution. In Cyprus, however, at the distant eastern periphery of the Greek world, the Enlightenment was introduced by the Church. These initiatives attracted the enthusiasm and admiration expressed by Constantine Oikonomos in 1816 for Archbishop Kyprianos as a pillar of the culture of the Enlightenment.[20]

This I would like to suggest is the appropriate context for the interpretation and appraisal of Archbishop Kyprianos's historical presence. Obviously complex historical personalities like Kyprianos should be understood in connection with multiple contexts, taking into account the many levels upon which their activity extended. In the case of Kyprianos, besides the ecclesiastical Enlightenment outlined above as the primarily pertinent context within which his archiepiscopal strategy should be interpreted, two other contexts should also be considered. One is the context of his pastoral activity as head of the autocephalous Orthodox Church of Cyprus and another is the context of power relations in the Ottoman empire and the ways these power relations affected the collective life of Cypriot society.

In considering Kyprianos's pastoral work we might comment upon the density of his activities in the traditional domains of ecclesiastical life: his concern for his flock, as shown in the part of his correspondence which has survived, his active interest and support of monastic foundations, including his own monastery of Machairas but also other important monastic foundations under his jurisdiction, Kykko, St Neophytos and St Barnabas.[21] A considerable part of this work was of an economic nature and given the nature of available evidence this component of the prelate's activity is extensively documented: transactions over property transfers on behalf of ecclesiastical institutions, loans to cover the needs of the flock, constant care to secure the financial interests of the Church vis-à-vis its creditors. Two initiatives of Kyprianos are of particular interest: on 2 February 1815 he issued an encyclical addressed to the bishop of Kition in Larnaca warning against the suspect religious views of Freemasons.[22] This is an interesting document in that it confirms Kyprianos's place within the ecclesiastical Enlightenment, whose limits are delineated neatly by this initiative. In 1820 Kyprianos issued another encyclical advising his flock to exterminate locust as a "destructive beast" and urging then to divest themselves of superstitious fears and prejudices that were acting as hindrances in this task.[23]

The other context of Kyprianos's activity as archbishop, that of Ottoman power relations and their specific configuration in Cyprus, has been reconstructed in considerable detail in recent scholarship and there is very little that needs to be added here.[24] What should perhaps be pointed out in this connection is the fact that Ottoman power relations formed the inescapable and repressive historical framework within which the strategy of the Church for the survival of its flock had to be elaborated. This framework involved compulsions which were by definition unjust and often violent and the Church had to conform by devising adjustments and by looking for outlets which required compromises justifiable only in terms of the economy of necessity. This approach, however, which was dictated by the material necessities of worldly power cannot and should not be the only variable in interpreting the activity and attitudes of the Church, detaching them from the canonical conscience, the sense of pastoral responsibility and from the code of Christian values which define the Church as an institution and inform its mission. This framework provides the pertinent context of interpretation and meaningful criticism.

The final act in Kyprianos's life is made up of the tragedy of the year 1821 in Cyprus. The news of the Greek Revolution and the panic it caused in the wielders of Ottoman power, combined with suspicions about a possible implication of Kyprianos in the revolutionary cause, provided the Ottoman governor of Cyprus at the time, Kuchuk Mehmet, with the pretext he was seeking for a showdown with the Church with the intention to eliminate its power. The particular details of the escalation of the confrontation during the first half of 1821 have been extensively and in great detail reconstructed in other sources and it is unnecessary to repeat them here.[25] Let it be noted first of all that the suspicions of the Ottoman governor concerning a possible involvement of Kyprianos with the politics and plans of the Greek war of independence were never confirmed by any form of evidence. Naturally this hypothesis has proved particularly appealing to the nationalist mind and it has been supported by argument but not by conclusive evidence in pertinent writing in Greek and Cypriot historiography.

By contrast to such interpretations which stretch and overextend rather meagre and completely circumstantial and conjectural evidence, Kyprianos's own record and other testimonies of this period convey an impressive and moving picture of the deep sense of responsibility and awareness of the lurking dangers for his flock, which motivated the archbishop's actions. What we possess in terms of documents from the months preceding Kyprianos's martyrdom are two pastoral letters addressed to his flock, urging them to surrender their arms to the authorities and to show submissiveness and loyalty to their masters in order to avoid reprisals and persecution for any form of behaviour that could be considered subversive or simply disrespectful of authority. The tone of these two letters, one addressed to the inhabitants of Nicosia, the other to the rural folk of the administrative unit of Kythrea[26] is deeply moving. The two texts are full of foreboding but also of calm determination, dignity and faith. They reflect Kyprianos in his hour of trial. In counselling submission and prudence, Kyprianos makes plain his deep sense of responsibility for the safety and survival of his flock.

This is the sense of responsibility that distinguishes a true leader, who exercises his authority and his options with full cognizance of their consequences, which would not affect only him personally but the collective destiny of the people whose guardianship has been entrusted in him. There can be little doubt that this "ethic of responsibility" was also a source of moral courage, which enabled Kyprianos to choose the road of martyrdom when he felt called upon to do so. He walked to his martyrdom with dignity and self-assurance. We possess an invaluable relevant testimony from an English visitor to Cyprus at the time, John Carne, fellow of Queen's College Cambridge. John Carne had met Kyprianos during a visit to Nicosia in June 1821 and was deeply impressed by him and his attitude to the storm that was brewing at the moment. He recorded in detail their meetings and Kyprianos's words and feelings.[27] I think the more appropriate way to conclude this sketch of Kyprianos's personality and place in the history of Cyprus, could be provided by quoting Carne's appraisal[28]:

Highly eminent for his learning and piety, as well as for his unshaken fortitude, Cyprian was the last rallying point of the wretched Greeks; and his frequent remonstrances and reproaches had rendered him very obnoxious to the Turkish authorities. He often shed tears when he spoke to us of the slaughter of his countrymen. We asked him why, in the midst of such dangers, he did not seek his own safety, and leave the island; but he declared he would remain to afford his people all the protection in his power to the last, and would perish with them.

[...]

Cyprian, in this trying moment, behaved with uncommon courage and dignity: he demanded of the Governor what crime these ill-fated men were guilty of, that they should suffer so dreadful a fate; recounted the spoliations and insults they had already endured, declared their entire innocence, and that, if nothing but blood would satisfy the Governor's cruelty, he was ready to shed his own rather than they should perish.

Figure 6.1 Archbishop Kyprianos

Notes

1 For an English version see *Poems of Cyprus: a selection from the work of Vassilis Michaelides and Dimitris Lipertis*, translated by Athan Anagnostopoulos, introduction by Costas Proussis, Nicosia, 1970, pp. 1–21. Kyprianos's martyrdom as described by G.I. Kipiades, Ἀπομνημονεύματα τῶν κατά τὸ 1821 ἐν τῇ νήσῳ Κύπρῳ τραγικῶν σκηνῶν, Alexandria, 1888 and reprints, is the locus classicus of the perception of the events in Cypriot conscience.

2 See Ἀρχιεπίσκοπος Κύπρου Κυπριανός: Ἀρχεῖον κειμένων, Machairas Monastery, Cyprus, 2009, pp. 31–33. This is an exhaustive collection of all documentary evidence surviving by and on Archbishop Kyprianos and provides invaluable help to his biographer. Other sources on Kyprianos include Sir George Hill, *A History of Cyprus IV: The Turkish Province, the British Colony*, ed. by Sir Harry Luke, Cambridge, 1952, pp. 119–122, 127–129, 360–363 and passim, who writes unsympathetically but drawing on all earlier sources; Loizos Philippou, Ἡ Ἐκκλησία Κύπρου ἐπί Τουρκοκρατίας, ed. by A. Phylaktou, Nicosia, 1975, pp. 135–142 and most recently the detailed survey by Andreas Mitsides, "Ἡ Ἐκκλησία Κύπρου επί Τουρκοκρατίας", Ἱστορία τῆς Κύπρου VI: Τουρκοκρατία, ed. by Th. Papadopoullos, Nicosia, 2011, pp. 698–722. Also Michael N. Michael, Ἡ Ἐκκλησία της Κύπρου κατὰ τὴν Ὀθωμανικὴ περίοδο (1571–1878). Ἡ σταδιακὴ συγκρότησή της σὲ θεσμὸ πολιτικῆς ἐξουσίας, Nicosia, 2005, pp. 218–240. On Kyprianos as an intellectual personality P. M. Kitromilides, Κυπριακὴ λογιοσύνη 1571–1878, Nicosia, 2002, pp. 55–56, 177–180.

3 See Ariadna Camariano-Cioran, "Contributions aux relations roumano-chypriotes", *Revue des études Sud-Est européennes XV* (1977), pp. 493–508, esp. pp. 506–508.

4 See Metropolitan Ieronymos of Rodopolis, Φαναριῶται, Athens, 1987, pp. 22–23.

5 In favour of this chronological specification one might also cite the chrysobul issued by Michael Soutzos as prince of Moldavia for the benefit of Machairas monastery in 1795. See Ἀρχεῖον κειμένων, pp. 130–131.

6 On the relevant cultural background see Andrei Pippidi, "L'accueil de la philosophie française du XVIIIe siècle dans les principautés roumaines", *Byzantins, Ottomans, Roumains. Le Sud-Est européen entre l'héritage impérial et les influences occidentales*, Paris: Champion, 2006, pp. 289–338.

7 Mircea Pacurariu, *Istoria Biserici Ortodoxe Române* II (2006), Jassy, pp. 349 and 355.

8 See P. M. Kitromilides, *The Enlightenment as Social Criticism. Iosipos Moisiodax and Greek Culture in the Eighteenth Century*, Princeton: Princeton University Press, 1992, p. 70˙ *The Life and Adventures of Dositej Obradovic*, translated by George Rappal Noyes, Berkeley, 1953, p. 281.

9 The portrait is reproduced in Ἀρχιεπίσκοπος Κύπρου Κυπριανός, Machairas Monastery, 2008, p. 45.

10 See the report of the Spanish traveller don Domingo Badia y Leyblich writing under the pseudonym Ali Bey in C. D. Cobham, ed., *Excerpta Cypria*, Cambridge 1908, pp. 391–412. The references to stewart Kyprianos as "the guardian angel of his community", on p. 395. On the events of 1804 see also the eyewitness account of a famous Cretan icon painter active in Cyprus at the time, Ioannis Cornaros, published by E. Rizopoulou-Igoumenidou, Νέα εικόνα και ιστορική μαρτυρία Ιωάννου Κορνάρου του Κρητός, Nicosia, 2000, p. 18. On the 1804 revolt see also M. N. Michael, "Local authorities and conflict in an Ottoman island at the beginning of the nineteenth century", *Turkish Historical Review* 2 (2011), pp. 57–77. See esp. p. 68 on the role of Kyprianos.

11 See Mitsides, op.cit., pp. 699–702.

12 Archimandrite Kallinikos Delikanis, ed., Τὰ ἐν τοῖς κώδιξι τοῦ πατριαρχικοῦ ἀρχειοφυλακείου [...] ἔγγραφα [...] πρὸς τὰς Ἐκκλησίας Ἀλεξανδρείας, Ἀντιοχείας, Ἱεροσολύμων καί Κύπρου, Constantinople, 1904, pp. 602–604.

13 Ibid., pp. 605–606.
14 Ἀρχεῖον κειμένων, pp. 173–174. On the canonical issues see Benedict Englezakis, *Studies on the History of the Church of Cyprus*, Aldershot: Variorum, 1995, pp. 279–283.
15 See P. M. Kitromilides, "Orthodoxy and the West. Reformation to Enlightenment", *The Cambridge History of Christianity V: Eastern Christianity*, ed. by Michael Angold, Cambridge, 2006, pp. 202–205, 208–209.
16 The full text in Ἀρχεῖον κειμένων, pp. 181–189.
17 Ibid., pp. 261–262. On Dimitrios Themistocles see *Κυπριακὴ λογιοσύνη*, pp. 140–141.
18 For more details P. M. Kitromilides, "Ἡ παράδοση τῶν ἑλληνικῶν γραμμάτων καὶ ἡ κυπριακὴ λογιοσύνη τῆς Ὀθωμανικῆς περιόδου", *Ἰστορία τῆς Κύπρου VI: Τουρκοκρατία*, ed. by Th. Papadopoullos, Nicosia, 2011, pp. 509–511.
19 See note 15 above.
20 See Ἀρχεῖον κειμένων, pp. 240–243. For Kyprianos as an exponent of the spirit of the Enlightenment see Benedict Englezakis, *Studies on the History of the Church of Cyprus*, pp. 257–278.
21 See Ἀρχεῖον κειμένων, pp. 187–189, 212–216, 233, 237.
22 Ibid., pp. 228–232.
23 Ibid., pp. 289–293.
24 Michael N. Michael, *op. cit.* (note 2 above).
25 Most recently and in great detail by Andreas Mitsides, *op. cit.*, pp. 710–722. The pertinent documentary record is collected in Ἀρχεῖον κειμένων, pp. 309–375.
26 The texts in Ἀρχεῖον κειμένων, pp. 303–307. For commentary see Englezakis, *Studies*, pp. 285–301.
27 John Carne, *Letters from the East written during a recent tour through Turkey, Egypt, Arabia, the Holy Land, Syria and Greece* II (1830), London, pp. 162–165.
28 Ibid., pp. 166 and 178.

7 Cyprus in 1821 a report to the Levant Company and the layers of historical memory

On 31 December 1821, Antonio Vondiziano, representative of the Levant Company in Larnaca, Cyprus sat at his desk in the comfortable surroundings of his house, nicely furnished with imported European furniture, to write his report to their magnificences, the Governors of the Company. The British Vice Counsul must have felt relief. A terrible year for the island was drawing to its unhappy end. He also must have felt slightly embarrassed. He had not written to the Company for two whole years, since 31 December 1819. Business had been slow, British ships or ships under British protection only very rarely called at Cyprus's only port at Larnaca. There had been neither business news nor profits worth reporting. So the Counsul had remained silent for two years.

Antonio Vondiziano belonged to a Cephalonian family that had settled in Larnaca toward the middle of the eighteenth century.[1] Around that time, Antonio's father Paul or Paolo Vondiziano, a well-known physician, had moved to the island and became quite successful by virtue of his professional expertise. He had risen to prominence thanks to his services in taking care of the wounded following the rising of the Christians and Muslims of the island against the rapacity of the governor Chill Osman in October 1764.[2] Paul Vondiziano's son Antonio was born in 1755. He was said to have been trained in foreign languages in Paris and in law in London but this is doubtful on the evidence of the quality of his French in the report published below. He is also said to have served in the British Embassy to the Sublime Porte and later until 1799 he served at the chancery of the British Consulate in Larnaca.[3] In that year he was appointed Vice Counsul of the Levant Company and exercised these functions until his death in 1838.

A glimpse into the social world of Antonio Vondiziano and of the consular corps in Larnaca, which included the consuls of France, Russia, Austria and Spain, is provided in the account of his 1815 visit to Cyprus by William Turner. Having been formerly attached to the British ambassador in Constantinople, Sir Robert Liston, Turner arrived in Larnaca with a letter of introduction to the local British Consul and stayed at Vondiziano's house[4]:

I went to the house of the English consul to whom I delivered des-
patches from Mr. Liston, and who received me with the greatest
hospitality, and put me into a very neat room, where I soon forgot
the fatigues of my voyage in a good bed, which was the more
acceptable, as I had slept on boards in the boat without pulling off
my clothes. Mr Vondiziano, my host, is a man in easy circumstances
(a native of Cephalonia), whose family consists of a wife and five
daughters.

[...] When I rose in the morning I was happy to find myself in the
house of a British consul, who keeps up the dignity of his character. He
has the King's Arms over the door of his house, at which two janizaries
are stationed.

[...] Mr Vondiziano, with all the expenses of the consulate, a wife and
five children, a large house, six servants, two janizaries, a carriage, horse
and mule, spends only 5000 piastres a year [....]

In the morning I went with Signor Vondiziano (who put himself in
grand state, with a large cocked hat which he always wears, even in the
house, a gold-headed cane, and proceeded by a janizary) to visit the Austrian consul, who lived in a good house near us [...]

Through their lifestyle and social comportment Antonio Vondiziano and his
wife acquired a considerable reputation which extended beyond Cyprus and
was recorded in a most characteristic way by Lady Hester Stanhope. After
noting that as a rule the conduct of British Vice-Consuls in the Levant had
been the worst possible she added: "must make an exception in favour of
the Consul in Cyprus. I do not know him personally, but from what I hear
of him and his wife, they are two most honourable and estimable people".[5]

All of a sudden this world of dignity, comfort and meticulously observed
convention appeared to come under serious threat. Such had been the
worry that motivated the report composed by Consul Vondiziano on
31 December 1821. Not only had business declined by comparison with
a few years earlier, when he had reported to Turner about a much more
active commercial transit in Larnaca,[6] but a serious political upheaval had
hit the island during that year. The Consul was an experienced man. In
writing to their magnificences he knew he could not allow his emotion to
get the better of him. He begins his report with business, he makes sure to
insert his requests concerning his own share of the proceeds in the Company's accounts and then he turns to the tragedy of the year that was drawing to a close that evening.

There had been an insurrection in Greece earlier in the year he writes,
but the Greeks of Cyprus had no intention of joining the rebels:

*Les Grecs de Chypre ont toujours témoigné la plus
parfaite soumission envers leurs maîtres et sans avoir
dans aucune occasion laissé de soupçonner de leur fidelité.*

They had been perfectly loyal and submissive to their masters, paid their taxes and when called upon, on the occasion of the Greek rising, to turn in their arms, they promptly did so in order to continue to at least enjoy *"au milieu d'une vie malheureuse leur tranquilité"*. The malignity of the local Ottoman governor, nevertheless, would not be satisfied. He obviously saw the occasion of the uprising in Greece as an opportunity to settle once and for all his accounts with his main rivals in the control over the population and resources of the island, the hierarchy of the Orthodox Church of Cyprus. The rivalry had been the main issue in the politics of Cyprus for a long time. It had been noted and commented upon by William Turner in 1815 and by many others.[7]

In fact it had been the backbone of local politics since the mid-eighteenth century and it had given occasion to many upheavals, including the uprising of 1764, described by the Levant Company Consul Timothy Turner as "a great rebellion".[8] It was the occasion that allowed the rise to prominence of Antonio's father Paul Vondiziano. Despite the heavy costs unfailingly incurred, the prelates usually won the contest with the local governors by appealing directly to the Sublime Porte, very often with the support of the Consuls at Larnaca.[9] This time, however, the Governor out-manoeuvred the prelates. Through false reports to the Porte he misled his superiors that the Greeks of Cyprus were on the verge of revolt: *"ne manqua pas de dépeindre pas ses dépêches à Constantinople que ces infor-turés insulaires Grecs entretenaient une correspondance avec les Rebelles du Grand Seigneur, et qu'ils avaient toute la bonne disposition de les imiter, énorme accusation et fausseté!"* By means of this deception the pasha obtained authorization to execute all those suspected of being implicated in the revolutionary project. Thus the tragedy of the year 1821 set in.

The Consul goes on to give a general account of the tragic events, with-out too many details and practically without names. He was too experi-enced to know that the authorities of the Levant Company would not be particularly interested. He does mention the events of 9 July 1821 without recording the exact date: the execution of Archbishop Kyprianos[10]—the only name among the victims recorded in his account—and the three bishops of the island, Chrysanthos of Paphos, Meletios of Kition and Lav-rentios of Kyrenia, who are mentioned only by the titles of their dioceses, not by name. He adds that an additional number of up to one hundred and fifty senior ecclesiastics and prominent laymen were executed. Obviously the governor was trying by this carnage to totally decapitate the subject Chris-tian population by eradicating its leadership. This was not all: the properties of the executed were confiscated and their families, formerly the most pros-perous part of the population, reduced to misery and mendicity.

The European colony in Larnaca did not suffer casualties but was exposed to the direct consequences of the tragedy: they were the main cred-itors of the archbishop. In addition, many of the other victims and the ruin of the Cypriot elite were threatening to bring about their own ruin as well:

they were left without recourse as to how to recover their money and this reduced them to desperation.[11] Furthermore the European colony and the Consuls were exposed to threats and insults by the troops transferred to Cyprus from Syria and Asia Minor on the alleged pretext of staving off the supposed pending revolt of the Greeks. The Consuls appealed to their superiors, the European ministers in Constantinople and they in turn secured an order from the Grand Vezir to the governor of Cyprus ordering him to respect and protect the Europeans *"qui y sont amis de la Sublime Porte"*. When the order was received, with considerable delay it is true on the basis of other accounts,[12] things for the European colony improved. The British Consul mentions with gratitude a particular measure taken by the British Ambassador, whose name he misspells as Lord Stangford,[13] who secured a special Vezirial order for the more effective protection of British subjects as outstanding friends of the Porte. These are details that come to light from Consul Vondiziano's account.

Following these measures things gradually moved back to a more normal pace. After outlining the crisis and its consequences the Consul could finish his report by returning to business as usual: reporting on the movement of ships in Cyprus waters and recording political and military news reaching the island from the Near East. An incident of piracy in November 1821 is also recorded, especially drawing attention to the anxiety and uneasiness it caused to the Turks of Cyprus.

The full text of Antonio Vondiziano's report[14] is published diplomatically below:

à Larnaca en Chypre
le 31 Décembre 1821

   A son Excellence
   My Lord Gouverneur et aux Nobles Membres
   de la Vénérable Compagnie du Levant
   à Londres

   My Lord et Messieurs
   Depuis mes derniers respects du 31 Décembre de l'année 1819, je n'ai plus osé d'écrire à vôtre Excellence, My Lord et Messieurs, faute de matière qui pouvoit intéresser sa Seigneurie; j'ai maintenant la gloire d'humilier ma présente et y transmettre en même tems trois différens comptes de quelque petites perceptions Consulaires sur trois navires Aglo-Maltois qui se sont fait voir dernièrement en Chypre. Ces Entrées réunies ne forment qu'en petit objet de Piastres 360 38/40 dont j'ai enregistré au crédit de leurs Seigneuries, et par contre crédité moi même de p[iastres] 103 04/40 de deux Septièmes. Sur ces mêmes Entrées dont leur Magnificence m'allouent, extrêmement fâché de voir continuer en Chypre depuis assés de tems la cessation des moyens qui me privent du doux plaisir à y être de quelque utilité aux intérêts de leurs Seigneuries ainsi que j'ai eu la satisfaction de l'être

ci-devant, et pendant que la Marine marchande des autres nations, surtout des français, Autrichiens et Sardes qui est bien nombreuse et dont leur abord est fréquent en Chypre et qu'ils importent et exportent beaucoup de Marchandises, il y aura très peu à s' attendre des marins Maltois dont le// nombre de navires diminuea considérablement et leur navigation dans les Mers du Levant devint insignifiant à l'exception d'Alexandrie en Egypte où quelqu'uns de leurs Bâtimens vont changer de Comestibles pour compte du Gouvernment de Malte.

J'ose par ma présente très humble lettre de rappeller au gracieux Souvenir de vôtre Excellence, My Lord et Messieurs, et d'en Supplier humblement afin qu'elle Se daigne d'ordonner au Trésorier à Constantinople de me reconnoître de la dernière Balance qui en résulte en ma faveur appert l'Extrait du Compte Courant du 31 Décembre 1819.

Je me crois en devoir de ne pas laisser ignorer à vôtre Excellence, My Lord et Messieurs, des événemens malheureux qui ont eu lieu en Chypre en Juillet dernier à la suite de l'insurrection des Grecs en Turquie, ou pour mieux dire par méchanceté du Gouverneur de Chypre qui, à peine eut-il connoissance de cette insurrection ne manqua pas de dépeindre par Ses dépêches à Constantinople que ces infortunés insulaires Grecs entretenaient une correspondance avec les Rebelles du Grand Seigneur, et qu'ils avoient toute la bonne disposition de les imiter, énorme accusation et fausseté! puisque les Grecs de Chypre ont toujours témoigné la plus parfaite Soumission envers leurs maîtres et sans avoir dans aucune//occasion laissé de soupçonner de leur fidélité. Supportant patiemment à des impôts qui les abyment et pour preuve évidente de la docilité des Rayas Grecs de Chypre et de leur Sentimens pacifiques, ayant été sommés au commencement du Soulèvement de leurs Patriotes de se dégarnir de toute espèce d'armes à feu etc., ils s'empressèrent tout aussitôt sans la moindre répugnace de les remettre entre les mains des préposés du Gouvernement; se flattant que n'ayant rien à se repprocher ils continueroient de jouir du moins au milieu d'une vie malheureuse leur tranquillité, mais tout cela n'a rien valu, et malheureusement pour eux à la suite des rapports dé-favorables à leur égard du Gouverneur de Chypre, reçut celui-ci un Firman du Grand Seigneur l'autorisant de faire subir la peine capitale à tous ceux qu'il reconnoitroit le mériter il n'en fallut que cela au Gouverneur pour mettre en exécution Ses exécrables desseins commençant par faire pendre l'archevêque Cyprien et ses trois Suffragans, les Evêques de Paphos, Cytium et Cerygne dont on leur trancha la tête, on fit subir le même Sort et presqu'en même tems à plusieurs Ecclésiastiques et les plus qualifiées parmi les Grecs au nombre de Cent Cinquante par la confiscation de leurs maisons, propriétés etc. et sans se soucier de tant de familles, réduites au désespoir et à la mendicité, ces térribles exécutions jointes aux persécutions contre ces//malheureux habitans Chrétiens ont ruiné de fond en comble l'île de Chypre, les Européens même établis en Chypre exerçant leur commerce, et créanciers de beaucoup du ci-devant Archevêque, de ceux qui ont été mis à mort et de beaucoup d'autres fugitifs Grecs ne savent pas comment se faire payer; et toute démarche de tous les Consuls réunis auprès de ce Gouverneur à cet égard a été inutile, ce ne sera que Messieurs les Ministres à Constantinople à qui ils s'adressèrent qui leur feront faire justice et sans permettre que nous soyons sacrifiés de la sorte, ces mêmes Européens ont été plusieures fois exposés à des attaques et insultes des troupes étrangères dont on fit venir de Syrie et Caraman sous pretexte de défendre l'île des attaques des ennemis du dehors et pour contenir en Sujetion les habitans Grecs, le Gouverneur de son côté au lieu de reprimer l'audace de ces insolantes troupes les encouragoit en certaine façon et sans faire attention aux plaintes des Consuls, qui se virent obligés de recourir à leurs Ministres respectifs à Constantinople en leur représentant le procédé indigne du Gouverneur de Chypre à leur égard, et qu'ils s'empressèrent d'obtenir et remettre des lettres du Grand Visir ordonnant à ce Gouverneur de rentrer dans ses devoirs en respectant et en protégeant les Européens qui y sont amis de la Sublime Porte et de prendre bien garde d'agir différemment et qu'il y seroit responsable à de nouvelles plaintes qu'on pourroit faire passer contre lui, ces corrections produisirent//tout le bon effet dont on s'attendoit, et ce fier Gouverneur dut assitôt changer de conduite en faveur des Consuls qu'il s'efforça de leurs témoigner de l'amitié la plus cordiale et en s'acquittant très exactement d'accueillir favorablement les affaires nationales dont on lui expose, ayant moi même reçu une lettre Visiriele que S[on] E[xcellence] Lord Srangford voulut bien m'adresser conçue d'une manière très énergique en faveur de la nation et protégés Britanniques en Chypre et dans un sens différent de celles reçu par les autres Consuls. S'apperçut le Gouverneur du grand cas dont on fait pour les Anglois, et c'est en quoi qu'il épuise tous les moyens pour me rendre content afin d'obtenir de moi une lettre pour la dite Excellence de Son comportement à mon égard et de Ses protestations à ne pas donner le moindre sujet de plaintes, il faut d'ailleurs convenir que nous jouissons maintenant de tranquillité, et les Européens assés bien respectés.

De vaisseaux de guerre françois se font souvent voir en Chypre venant de l'Archipel et Smyrne ceux de Sa Majesté croisent toujours aux parages de Smyrne, il ne vint ici le 30 Septembre dernier que le seul Sloop Racehorse Mr Abbot Capitaine, rien que pour m'apporter le Pli de Mr l'ambassadeur, il reprit le large après trois jours pour repasser à Smyrne.

En Novembre dernier et pour la première fois l'on//vit croiser sur ces parages quelques corsaires insurgés, ayant même capturé de Navires et Bateaux Ottomans dont les équipages ont été débarqués sur quelque points de l'île et sans avoir été maltraités, ce qui a beaucoup rejoui les Turcs de Chypre de cet acte d'humanité de la part de leurs ennemis, d'un autre côté l'approche des insurgés causa aux habitans Turcs de grandes inquiétudes, ils y sont extrêmement alarmés veillant toutes les nuits et parcourant les endroits maritimes les plus accessibles dans la crainte de quelque descente des ennemis.

Par de nouvelles certaines d'Alep l'on sait que les Perssans remporterent une victoire complette contre le Basha de Bagdat poussant toujours en avant leurs avantages du côté du Kurdistan.

J'implore très humblement, My Lord et Messieurs, la continuation de vos bienfaits et haute protection, ne cessant toujours pénétré de la plus vive reconnoissance d'avoir l'honneur d'être avec le plus profond respect et la plus parfaite soumission
My Lord
de vôtre Excellence

Le très humble, très obéissant,
très dévoué et très soumis
Serviteur
Ant[onio] Vondiziano

The British Consul's report to the Levant Company does not supply radically new information on the events of the year 1821 in Cyprus. It does corroborate the well-known drama that unfolded in the summer of that year on the island as a consequence of the outbreak of the Greek war of independence and it supplies a few details, deemed worthwhile to record by the British Consul. The main value of the report as a source of evidence consists in enhancing the perspective on the events, which in their details have been mostly known through the French Consul's account.[15] By enhancing the documentary evidence Vondiziano's report adds nuance and texture to our knowledge of a critical and tragic episode in the history of the island, an episode of great symbolic significance in subsequent historiography.

The Consul writes with remarkable calm and phlegm as it befits a servant of the British crown. He remains silent on his own personal activities during that year of tragedy and pain for the Christian population of Cyprus. The main Greek source on the events, however, supplies details on his active support of the victims and his strenuous efforts while the events were unfolding to do whatever he could to alleviate the pain caused by the catastrophe: he sheltered proscribed victims and their families in his residence and arranged their escape on European boats anchoring in the port of Larnaca.[16] He also saved the plate of the church of Chrysopolitissa in Larnaca, whereas elsewhere churches and monasteries were plundered.[17]

We cannot know whether the Consul exhibited the same reticence in connection with his activities on behalf of the victims in his conversations in his domestic environment. Prudence may have counselled a total silence in those dangerous times but again as often happens in domestic environments legends grow and are transmitted within the family. We will never know. The Consul died in 1838, lauded with the esteem and respect of the whole island. He was buried in his official uniform and cocked hat he so much liked to wear according to the evidence of his guest William Turner.

In 1847 his nephew and namesake Antonio Vondiziano (1815–1885), the son of his younger brother Andreas, appears among the subscribers of a historical novel by Epaminondas Frangoudis.[18] The work in question, entitled *Thersandros*, was published in Athens and it is the romantic story of the ill-fated love of two young people from Larnaca. The main scene of the story is located in Larnaca in the years 1821 to 1823. The chronological framework gives the Cypriot author the chance to include in his narrative, in the form of a long explanatory footnote in the very early part of the novel, a dramatic account of the tragedy of 9 July 1821.[19] It would be very interesting to know what subscriber Antonio Vondiziano felt and thought in reading these lines. In 1821 he was six years old and he probably remembered very little of what had taken place during that year of terror and bloodshed. He could have heard stories about the sorrow and the pathos of those years from his uncle and from his father. How did these stories compare with Frangoudis's account, which so powerfully records the crystallization of collective memory around that critical moment that was destined to form the kernel of Cyprus's modern self-conception, supplying the terms of epic and tragedy necessary for this purpose? We will never know the answers to these questions, as it is as a rule the case in connection with the way the dramatic events in the foreground of the theatre of history are experienced in the personal life of people. Reflecting on the diverse fragments of evidence presented here we are made at least aware of the unanswered questions concerning the layers of memory that form the content of collective consciousness and also supply the raw material of historical narrative.

Notes

1 The main source on Antonio Vondiziano as British Vice-Consul is Sir Harry Luke, *Cyprus under the Turks 1571–1878. A Record based on the Archives of the English Consulate in Cyprus under the Levant Company and After*, London, 1969, pp. 7, 99, 104, 118, 128, 146, 153, 176. See also A. C. Wood, *A History of the Levant Company*, London, 1964, p. 196. For a biographical sketch see A. Coudounaris, Μερικαί παλαιαί οικογένειαι της Κύπρου, Nicosia, 1972, p. 13.

2 See P. M. Kitromilides, 'Repression and Protest in Traditional Society. Cyprus 1764', *in* this collection. See also *idem, Κοινωνικές σχέσεις και νοοτροπίες στην Κύπρο του δεκάτου ογδόου αιώνα*, Nicosia, 1992, pp. 26 and 28.

3 Luke, *Cyprus under the Turks*, p. 118.

4 From William B. Turner, *Journal of a Tour in the Levant* II (1820), London, pp. 31–52, 528–594 as excerpted in C. D. Cobham, *Excerpta Cypria*, Cambridge, 1908, pp. 424–450. See especially pp. 424–425, 427. Another English guest who enjoyed Vondiziano's hospitality six years later was John Carne of Queen's College Cambridge. See John Carne, *Letters from the East*, Third edition, London, 1830, Vol. II, p. 140.

5 Luke, *op. cit.*, p. 153.

6 *Excerpta Cypria*, p. 449.

7 Ibid., pp. 436–437, 447–448. For a general survey and appraisal see Sir George Hill, *A History of Cyprus* IV: *The Ottoman Province, the British Colony*

1571–1948, ed. by Sir Harry Luke, Cambridge, 1952, pp. 100–123. See also L. Philippou, *Η Εκκλησία Κύπρου επί Τουρκοκρατίας*, Nicosia, 1975, pp. 183–202 and more recently M. N. Michael, *Ἡ Ἐκκλησία τῆς Κύπρου κατὰ τὴν Ὀθωμανικὴ περίοδο (1571–1878)*, Nicosia, 2005, pp. 137–140, 157–162, and A. N. Mitsides, "*Ἡ Ἐκκλησία Κύπρου ἐπὶ Τουρκοκρατίας*", *Ἱστορία τῆς Κύπρου* VI (2011), ed. by Th. Papadopoullos, Nicosia, pp. 698–709.

8 The National Archives of the United Kingdom, SP 105/119, p. 130.

9 For a survey of the period immediately preceding the events of 1821 see John Koumoulides, *Cyprus and the Greek War of Independence 1821–1829*, London, 1974, pp. 27–39.

10 Kyprianos's last days, his character and overall attitude amidst the tragedy are described with great admiration by John Carne, *op. cit.*, II, pp. 162–170. See pp. 177–179 on Kyprianos's execution. See also Mitsides, *op. cit.*, pp. 710–722. A complete documentary record on Kyprianos is collected in *Ἀρχιεπίσκοπος Κύπρου Κυπριανός. Ἀρχεῖον Κειμένων*, published by Machairas Monastery, Cyprus, 2009.

11 On Vondiziano and the other consuls as creditors of the archbishop and other prelates and monasteries see Hill, *op. cit.*, p. 111 and Michael, *op. cit.*, pp. 199, 283–285.

12 Hill, *op. cit.*, p. 143.

13 His Majesty's ambassador to the Sublime Porte was Stratford Canning, Lord Stratford de Redcliffe.

14 The National Archives of the United Kingdom, SP 105.139, ff. 359–361v.

15 Consul Méchain's letters were translated by N. Kyriazis and published in *Κυπριακὰ Χρονικὰ* VII (1930), pp. 55–75 and are Hill's primary source in the narrative of the events. See *A History of Cyprus*, IV, pp. 132–136, 142–145. See also Koumoulides, *op. cit.*, pp. 40–65.

16 G. Kipiades, *Ἀπομνημονεύματα τῶν κατὰ τὸ 1821 ἐν τῇ νήσῳ Κύπρῳ τραγικῶν σκηνῶν*, Alexandria, 1888 (reprinted Nicosia, 1972), p. 28. Also Hill, *op. cit.*, pp. 129–130. See also Carne, *Letters from the East* II, p. 150.

17 Kipiades, *op. cit.*, p. 24. Solomon Nicolaides, Cypriot, as he styles himself, also a victim of the events of 1821, records in his chronology of world history the tragic events of 9 July 1821 in his native island noting in particular the refuge supplied by European consuls and merchants in Larnaca to some of the victims. See S. Nicolaides Cypriot, *Χρονολογικὸς Πίναξ*, Aegina, 1833, pp. 154–155.

18 Epaminondas I. Frangoudis, *Ο Θέρσανδρος*, Athens, 1847, p. 121. The list of subscribers is omitted in the new edition of the work, Athens, 2002.

19 See E. I. Frangoudis, *Ο Θέρσανδρος και άλλα αφηγήματα*, ed. by L. Papaleontiou, Athens, 2002, pp. 42–45.

8 Collective consciousness and poetry three moments in the literary tradition of modern Cyprus[1]

The purpose of this brief essay is not to provide a historical survey of the development of modern Cypriot literature. To be sure, such a project is greatly needed, in order to fill a serious lacuna in the literary history of Cyprus. My objective here, however, is no more than to suggest how the study of modern Cypriot literature might be approached in order to place it in the wider context of the political and cultural history of Cypriot society. The following observations, therefore, can be considered hints at a research design that might be useful in setting some guidelines for such a literary history of Cyprus. Inevitably, the focus of the following remarks will be on poetry, which, in terms of volume of production in successive historical periods and in terms of expressive significance as an outlet of collective yearnings and aspirations typical of Cypriot culture, has been unquestionably the most important form of literary expression.

I.

Between the period that produced the exquisite Renaissance lyric poetry of Cyprus[2] and the era that witnessed the birth of a modern literary tradition on the island stretch three dark centuries. This was the era of Ottoman rule, which not only stamped out all intellectual life but repeatedly placed in jeopardy the very survival of Hellenism in Cyprus. The literary monuments surviving from this period are mostly folk songs. The works of a number of Cypriot intellectuals who appeared in this period, mostly at the time of the neo-Hellenic Enlightenment, are typical not of the extinguished intellectual life of Cyprus but of the wider cultural currents of the Tourkokratia, into which some Cypriots were integrated. The only personal poetry that could be identified in this period are a few narrative poems inspired by such dramatic occurrences of the time as the Ottoman conquest in 1570–1571 or subsequent uprisings against social oppression. Although important as historical sources, these narrative poems have little to recommend them as far as literary merit is concerned[3]—in contrast to the remarkable poetic virtues of other Cypriot folk songs.

It is within this heritage of restricted intellectual life that one must trace the development of a modern literary tradition in Cyprus.

The first moment I would like to identify is what can be considered as the historical origins of the modern Cypriot literary tradition. I am referring to a small group of poets and playwrights who toward the end of the Ottoman period became the exponents of nineteenth-century neo-Hellenic romanticism in Cyprus. Poets and dramatists, these people cannot be described as forming a literary school and are considered as a group only for analytical purposes. They shared, in any case, certain common cultural characteristics.[4] Cypriots by origin and by birth, they moved between their native island and the great centres of Hellenism in the Eastern Mediterranean: Smyrna, Alexandria, Cairo, Jerusalem. In those cities they were imbued with the cultural outlook of Greek romanticism. They wrote in the purist katharevousa and, following the romantic pattern, they derived their inspiration and their themes from the historical past of Cyprus. In this way, they responded to the ideological needs of nineteenth-century Greek national historicism, which was extended to the Greek periphery—including Cyprus—in the middle and late decades of the century. In the intellectual history of Cyprus, this was the period of the foundation of the systematic study of the Hellenic character of Cypriot civilization.[5]

In the absence of printing presses in Cyprus before 1878, the productions of these early poets were published outside the island. Thus, G. N. Sivitanidis published the drama *Cyprus and the Knights Templar* in Alexandria in 1869. Theodoulos Constantinidis published the play *Two More Victims of Love* in Smyrna in 1873 and *Peter the First, King of Cyprus and Jerusalem* in Cairo in 1874. After the British occupation and the establishment of printing presses in Cyprus, he published the play *Kuchuk Mehmet or 1821 in Cyprus* in Nicosia in 1895. (This was the time that Vassilis Michaelidis was working on his classic *The Ninth of July*). The most distinguished of this first generation of Cypriot poets was Themistocles Theocharidis, whose play *Peter Synglitikos* was awarded second prize (έπαινος) in the Voutsineos poetry competition conducted by the University of Athens in 1875.[6] He continued his literary production during the early years of British rule, publishing a novel and lyric poetry.

The cultural activity of this first group of poets, in the closing years of the Ottoman and the early years of British rule, already marks the emergence of a basic pattern that would determine the nature of the Cypriot poetic and more generally, literary production. Cypriot intellectuals would transmit to Cyprus the literary and intellectual currents prevalent in the major centres of modern Greek culture, and they would use this cultural language as the medium of expression of their poetic sensibilities, along with their preoccupations with the past and present and their aspirations for the future of Cyprus.

II.

Out of this literary climate emerged two poets destined to produce the classics, in every sense of the word, of modern Cypriot literature. Actually, the end of the first moment in the modern tradition of Cypriot poetry and the beginning of the second, the moment of the classics, was marked by the publication of the early romantic poetry of Vassilis Michaelidis and Dimitris Lipertis. They both made their first appearance with poems in katharevousa published toward the end of the nineteenth century, but soon transcended this phase. From the artificial katharevousa of latter-day Greek romanticism they moved to composition in the Cypriot dialect.

In studies, critical or historical, of the Cypriot literary tradition, Michaelidis and Lipertis are always treated together, due to the coincidence that they both used the dialectical form of Cypriot Greek as their medium of expression. But their substantive similarity ends more or less at this point. What they have in common is neither style, poetic themes and subject matter nor even sources of inspiration, but the fact that in their work Cypriot culture attains self-consciousness. The use of dialectical language in their great works constitutes only one element of this attainment of self-consciousness. What must be made clear in connection with their use of the language is that, although they used the full range of traditional Cypriot diction, there is nothing folk about their language. In both cases, they used a distilled language which drew on the complete wealth of vocabulary and forms of speech of Cypriot Greek but which was, nonetheless, beyond any doubt the poets' own creation, according to the needs of their respective art. Their linguistic achievement is all the more significant for Cypriot self-consciousness in that it showed that what was considered a peripheral and indeed semibarbaric Greek dialect possessed remarkable poetic powers and could provide a medium for great art.

Their art differs. In Vassilis Michaelidis's great narrative poems, "The Ninth of July 1821 in Nicosia" and "The Woman of Chios", Cypriot culture and Cypriot sensibility are led through the epic recreation of history to national self-consciousness. The two epics capture with superb artistic power the most tragic moments of Cypriot history in the grand drama of the hero's vision and sacrifice and in the profound anguish which historical storms bring to the life of anonymous individuals. The elevation of history to the epic of collective self-awareness makes Vassilis Michaelides the national poet of Cyprus. His gifts as an epic poet are comparable to those of any great craftsman of the genre.

Consider in the following excerpts from "The Ninth of July 1821" how the epic sense is gradually built up to set the scene for the emergence of the hero:

When the secret winds began their blowing
And the clouds in secret gathered over Turkey

Until the weather started mounting
Then Cyprus had, as others had, her secret-
She had her share of the impending storm ...
....
A night in July, a night of utter silence,
A Friday night when stars by the millions shone...
A breeze so faint, and not even a sapling stirred...[7]
....
The night was stretching thin across the sky
The east was turning to a rosy rue
And as the Saturday began its bitter dawn
The sounding of the wooden gong was heard
In his great grief, Kyprianos left the house.
He entered the church...
....
And stood there sadly, deep in meditation...
Unmoving, sorrowful, with folded arms...[8]

The human drama begins at this point with the hero's declaration to his awed captors:

My heart's like stone—don't waste your pity.[9]

The impending tragedy finds its catharsis in the inspiration and unwavering faith in a vision which is articulated in response to the tyrant's threat, "I will, if I can, rid Cyprus of the Greeks":

The race of the Greeks was born when the world
was born;
No one has ever been able to root it up.
God shelters it from the heights; it cannot die.
Not till the whole world ends will the Greek race
vanish!
You may kill us till our blood becomes a torrent...
But when an ancient poplar is cut down
Three hundred offshoots sprout and grow round it.[10]

Past and future, bitter experience and hopeful aspiration, history and faith are woven together into a determined collective consciousness that consoles those experiencing the predicament of the present:

... whoever sees me, pities me
because the path I walk to reach you
is full of thorns.[11]

In Lipertis's poetry, Cypriot culture reaches self-awareness in a different way. Here the moral wisdom of traditional society, the ethic of personal decency and the characteristic sense of Cypriot aesthetics find expression in a lyric didacticism which, in the four volumes of Lipertis's *Τζυπριώτικα Τραούδκια* (Cypriot Songs),[12] reaches great poetic perfection. Lipertis is a great master of the art of genuine lyricism. Consider these examples:

> Do you see the narcissus that sways and quivers
> When the wind blows sweetly, sweetly from the
> valley?
> It seems to be listening to secrets that make it
> happy—
> Maybe the wind, seduced, sings songs of its own
> making,
> Touching and caressing it as it comes and goes,
> Till it gives off abundant, resurrecting fragrance.[13]

Sensitivity to natural beauty is always enriched with human feeling. The human presence is always united with nature; it is underlined by a full awareness of the natural and social surroundings, as in the poem "Sunset":

> Tomorrow when the four pallbearers come to take me
> in the midst of the turmoil,
> please come to church too,
> don't be ashamed.
> I loved you with all my soul and they'll blame you for
> it
> ....
> After sunset, when the dusk is growing deep,
> when the paths become empty
> and no creature passes
> who might startle you,
> Then come to my grave and light a candle from the
> Sacred Tomb in the little pitcher,
> and burn the incense, maiden,
> and call my name and weep.[14]

Lipertis's great achievement consists in capturing and translating into poetry all the physical beauties of the Cypriot landscape and the moral beauties of the world of traditional human relations still intact in Cyprus at his time:

> A tree is not held to the ground by its branches.
> Nor by its offshoots or its wide, spreading boughs.
> For without the roots, a tree will never flower—
> If it blooms at all, it still will bear no fruit.

> A parent needs respect as a tree needs water
> To support its branches, its boughs and blossoms.[15]

In doing this he combined the love of what was beautiful in the Cypriot experience with the basic sense of dignity that derives from a consciousness of the beauty of what is one's own. It is precisely in this sense of dignity that Lipertis's lyric didacticism finds the moral inspiration to proceed with an articulation of the national aspirations of the Cypriots:

> When a river has been blocked with dams for years
> By those who would divert and steal its waters,
> It still does not entirely dry up,
> Nor does running water turn stagnant.
> It will rush back to its own bed one day,
> Breaking temporary dams, overflowing barriers.
> We, too, have set our course to where our blood
> flows,
> To where our minds run naturally night and day,
> Where people talk about us and care about us
> There, in the bosom of our dear mother.[16]

Or,

> We have become a slingshot, the plaything of
> sorrow,
> Can a stranger's children prosper near a stepmother?
> Can they live by facing in two directions?
> Her bosom is cold as marble, her breath stone-hard...
> ....
> Our guts are consumed by a ranging fire.
> As a cataract cannot keep silent or be diverted,
> So a slave never closes his eyes or finds peace,
> Day and night his mind circles, turning to his
> mother,
> As steadfast as the sun in its orbits.[17]

The classic moment in the literary tradition of modern Cyprus culminated precisely in the expression of the yearning for national redemption and the expectation of freedom:

> Dear Greece, for your sake we suffer in silence—
> Your memory, mother, is our greatest treasure.
> A dawn is coming that will dissolve the night,
> Though we are wracked on the cross and on the
> gallows.[18]

The moment of the classics brought out what was best in Cypriot cultural exceptionalism in the context of neo-Hellenic civilization. At the same time, with the achievements of Michaelidis and Lipertis, Cypriot cultural exceptionalism reached its limits. The basic pattern marking Cypriot intellectual history, i.e., the integration of Cypriot themes into wider modern Greek literary currents which were transmitted to Cyprus, was thus necessarily resumed.

III.

The classic moment was followed by a period covering the interwar and immediate postwar decades, which witnessed the mature flowering of Cypriot poetry. This phase was marked by the emergence of the generation of the most distinguished contemporary Cypriot poets, who followed faithfully the literary currents of metropolitan Greek culture. Many of them have remarkable poetic achievements to their credit.[19] Although Cyprus was a British colony in this period, English cultural influences remained negligible. Indeed, Cypriot literature became one of the main vehicles of resistance to British rule and was one of the decisive spiritual influences in the intellectual preparation of the liberation revolt of the 1950s. There is a dimension of the poetic production of this generation to which I would like to draw attention as the third moment in the development of the Cypriot literary tradition. For some of the best poets of this generation, poetry, always animated by unfulfilled national aspirations, became in addition a medium of social criticism.

The importance of this moment of social criticism cannot be adequately emphasized. I have tried to explain elsewhere how the nationalist ideological orthodoxy that came to prevail in Cypriot society excluded, as it did in Greece, social criticism from the universe of socially acceptable modes of consciousness.[20] As it happened in Greece as well, social criticism, inspired by a vision of a better society and directed at social and political ills, found refuge in poetry. The engaged poets of Cyprus became the exponents of social criticism as an articulate intellectual outlook. Three names can be mentioned in this connection: Glafkos Alithersis, and most notably Tefkros Anthias and Thodossis Pierides. Beginning from the distinctively Cypriot basis of lyricism that constitutes the shared substratum of the poetry of Cyprus, they raised their voices to the level of social and political protest.[21] By articulating an alternative vision of society, Anthias and Pierides achieved two things: they provided the yearning for freedom animating Cypriot literature with its proper social content; and beyond this they rescued Cypriot literature from a disembodied idealism and an aestheticism that was becoming increasingly misguided and, after the Second World War, alarmingly reactionary. If the undoubted quality of Anthias's poetry was at some points damaged by his need to get his political commitments across, Pierides combined in his work the most authentic traditions of Cypriot lyricism with a refreshingly lively human vision and a noble sense of the poetry of life, which make him one of the prominent poets in his generation. Among all Cypriot poets, Thodossis Pierides is the one who most integrally belongs to the poetic school of the Left in twentieth-century modern Greek literature. He managed very effectively to replace, both in the ideological content and in the style of his poetry, the parochialism of local concerns that occasionally fetters Cypriot poetry with a convincing sense of their wider human and aesthetic relevance.

There are other poets of distinction in this generation who, however, do not belong to the moment of social criticism.[22] And there is a later, very recent moment in the literary tradition of Cyprus, embodied in the work of the younger generation of poets who appeared and matured on the cultural scene of independent Cyprus. Drawing on the remarkable poetic heritage of the previous generation, on the great achievements of modern Greek poetry, especially of the generation of the 1930s and broadening their inspiration by following the orientations of contemporary European and American poetry, this was indeed the moment of great promise. The recognized quality of the writing of some of its best representatives, such as Kyriakos Charalambides,[23] brought Cypriot lyricism to new heights of achievement. The hopes of a new synthesis in Cypriot civilization that this moment represented during the period of Cyprus's independent statehood were submerged by the tragedy of 1974. The new synthesis in Cypriot poetry has been pre-empted by the anguish of lost expectations and profound human grief. The poetry of Cyprus has been transformed from the poetry of hope into a literature of painful soul searching and human protest, a poetry of mourning and distress.[24]

Notes

1 This chapter is a revised version of a paper originally presented at the annual convention of the Modern Languages Association, New York, 26 December 1976. I am grateful to Valerie Kaires for her editorial suggestions.
2 See Themis Siapkaras-Pitsillides, *Le Pétrarquisme en Chypre: Poèmes d'amour en dialecte chypriote*, 2nd ed. (Athens, 1975).
3 For an evaluation see Costas M. Proussis, "Τά ιστορικά Κυπριακά τραγούδια" [Historical Cypriot Folksongs], *Κυπριακαὶ Σπουδαὶ* 7 (1943): 21–46.
4 For biographical details, see Loizos Philippou, *Τά Ελληνικά Γράμματα ἐν Κύπρῳ κατά τήν περίοδον τῆς Τουρκοκρατίας, 1571–1878*, Nicosia, 1930, 2, pp. 128–155.
5 For details on the social and cultural background, see the survey of the period, "Κύπρος 1830–1878", in *Ιστορία του Ελληνικού Έθνους*, Athens, 1977, Vol. 13, pp. 437–445.
6 See *Κρίσις Βουτσιναίου Ποιητικού Αγώνος 1875 υπό του εισηγητού Θ. Αφεντούλη*, Athens, 1875, pp. 46–48, 61–62.
7 *From Poems of Cyprus: A Selection from the Work of Vassilis Michaelides and Dimitris Lipertis*, translated by Athan. Anagnostopoulos, Kinereth Gensler and Ruth Whitman, with an introduction by Costas M. Proussis, Nicosia, 1970, p. 1.
8 Ibid., p. 4.
9 Ibid.

10 Ibid., p. 7.
11 Ibid., p. 37, from the poem "Cyprus to her Mother".
12 Published in Nicosia in 1923, 1930, 1934 and 1937.
13 *Poems of Cyprus*, p. 62, from the poem "The Womanly Graces".
14 Ibid., pp. 71–72.
15 Ibid., p. 86, from the poem "The affected Mother".
16 Ibid., p. 79, from the poem "Welcome to the Greek Athletes".
17 Ibid., p. 80, from the poem "Welcome—Blessed Be Your Coming".
18 Ibid., p. 120, from the poem "October 1931".
19 For an appraisal, see Costas M. Proussis, "Σύγχρονοι Κύπριοι Ποιητές", Ἑλληνικὴ *Δημιουργία* 4 (1949), Athens, pp. 860–870.
20 See my "The Dialectic of Intolerance: Ideological Dimensions of Ethnic Conflicts", *Journal of the Hellenic Diaspora* 4:4 (Winter, 1979), pp. 5–30.
21 The name of a poetess, Eugenia Paleologou-Petronda, should be added to the moment of social criticism. Like Pierides, she belongs to the Greek cultural tradition that flowered in Egypt in the twentieth century, as well as to Cypriot literature. Although her poetry tends to be homiletic, she is, again like Pierides, one of the most effective links of the poetry of Cyprus with the main currents of modern Greek poetry.
22 Among them one could mention Nikos Kranidiotis, Manos Kralis, Kypros Chrysanthis and most notably Costas Montis, the only poet in the literary tradition of modern Cyprus who can be said to have created a school of lyric poetry to which younger poets have been attracted.
23 See the appraisal by G. P. Savidis, *Εφήμερον Σπέρμα*, Athens, 1978, pp. 166–172.
24 For a sensitive and moving survey of the poetry of catastrophe, see Kyriakos Charalambides, "Η σύγχρονη ποιητική μας παραγωγή και η σχέση της με την Κυπριακή τραγωδία", *Χρονικό '75*, Athens, 1975, pp. 365–369.

Part Two

The politics of the Cyprus question

9   From coexistence to confrontation

The dynamics of ethnic conflict
in Cyprus

I.

Although the Cyprus Question has been treated as a regional problem in world politics and the focus of those concerned with it has been mostly on interaction at the international level, I believe that in order to fully appreciate the impact of international pressures, it is necessary to round up the examination of foreign policies with a consideration of domestic developments at the receiving end. The distinction between domestic politics and international relations is only an analytical one; foreign policies do not operate in a vacuum but are conditioned by the domestic realities of the states involved. As covert and overt forms of foreign intervention are increasingly becoming a core element of the foreign policies of major powers today, the mystique of a neoimperialism tends to obscure the fact that intervention and imperialism in their subtle contemporary forms are possible to a considerable extent because domestic conditions in the "host" country provide the needed opportunities. There is no doubt, of course, that the dynamics of domestic politics are manipulated and distorted by foreign interference in directions that facilitate the objectives of intervention, but to attribute all developments within a country to outside manipulation without looking at domestic structures would amount not only to oversimplification but also to a mystification of such notions as foreign penetration and imperialism—a mystification that ultimately undermines the possibility of a critical social science.

It is for these reasons that I propose to discuss the nature of ethnic strife in Cyprus by identifying the factors, domestic as well as external, that went into the making of the conflict. By looking at the dynamic of social and political change domestically and at the impact of outside factors, I hope to convey a sense of the dialectic between endogenous and exogenous forces which constitutes the essence of every political situation. Indeed, I would like to suggest that a systematic examination of domestic developments in all their complexity constitutes the best foundation of a full appreciation of the effects and real proportions of external influences, manipulation and intervention. It is only in this way, I think, that one can become fully aware of alternative possibilities in the development of events, potential choices and lost opportunities on which meaningful social and political criticism can be based.

This brief chapter seeks to conceptualize the issues arising out of the history of ethnic relations in Cyprus in the light of the theoretical perspectives offered by the study of social change. What I attempt here is not a history but an interpretative essay, and all I hope to accomplish is to touch upon and identify the many issues and problems that need to be studied in order to attain a full understanding of the nature of ethnic conflict in Cyprus.

The research problems I would like to address could be stated in terms of Fernand Braudel's conceptualization of the historical destiny of the insular Mediterranean on the basis of a contrast which, according to the great French historian, marks the fate of the Mediterranean islands. The contradiction runs between the "precarious, restricted and threatened" internal life of the islands and their external life, "the role they have played in the forefront of history ... The events of history often lead to the islands", Braudel observes, but he immediately adds "it would be more accurate to say that they make use of them."[1] These are precisely the topics with which my research project is concerned: an examination of the threatened internal life of Cyprus and the uses that the events of history have made of the ethnic differences that have marked Cypriot society.

II.

In considering the problem of the origins and the processes leading up to conflict, the natural starting point is the historical and social situation in which conflict is absent. This, of course, is the stable context of traditional society in which ethnic and social groups do not question their station in life but go about following deeply entrenched patterns of behaviour and thus have no occasion to come to blows.

In Cypriot traditional society we encounter a remarkable phenomenon of ethnic coexistence which represents an extension to Cyprus of the pattern of Greek-Turkish, or more accurately Christian Orthodox Muslim symbiosis that had characterized the rural life of Ottoman Asia Minor from the late Middle Ages until the expulsion of Asia Minor Greeks in 1922–1924.

Coexistence in traditional society was founded on a shared folk piety and a common life style conditioned by the agricultural cycle of rural life. The most eloquent testimony to this pattern of coexistence has been the ethnic geography of Cyprus which, before its violent subversion by the Turkish invasion in 1974, was marked by interspersion of Greek and Turkish settlements all over the island and the existence, in addition, of many ethnically mixed communities. No predictable geographic pattern of ethnic settlement existed largely because a great part of the Muslim rural population was created by the Islamization over time of Christian village communities. This was a common practice in Ottoman years and was either the product of outright coercion or forced choice in view of escape from the capitation tax that came with conversion to Islam.[2] The names of Christian Saints borne by several Turkish Cypriot villages, especially in the Paphos and the Karpass regions, offer a convincing indication of these cases of Islamization.[3]

It should be made clear in this connection that this sort of evidence is not cited here in order to question the Turkish Cypriots' Turkishness—which, as is the case with modern national identity generally, has to do more with states of consciousness and less with the "purity" of ethnic origins. All that is intended is to suggest a concrete explanation for the phenomenon of traditional coexistence which was essentially the product of the common provenance of the religious groups composing the population of Cyprus. "Voluntary" or coerced conversions might involve a change in religious practices and perhaps beliefs, but did not fundamentally alter the character of traditional rural society: therefore people in different quarters of the same community or in neighbouring villages continued to behave and deal with each other as they did before.

A remarkable indication of the shared social and cultural identity of traditional Cypriot religious groups is offered by their common participation in the commercial and religious fairs organized in the towns and villages of Cyprus on the day of their patron saint. In the folk narrative poetry that sprang from these social congregations we find references to Christian and Muslim pilgrims and traders sharing in the worship and exchange occasioned on such days. The most important testimony of the shared cultural content of premodern life has been offered by the discovery among illiterate Muslim peasants in the Paphos countryside of folk Akritic ballads in fuller versions than those which were recorded by folklore field researchers from recitations of Greek peasants.[4] This suggests graphically both the community of culture and the greater attachment of the Muslim population to tradition.

Since conversion was essentially an act of economic necessity it is not surprising that acceptance of Islam did not involve radical social and cultural change. Especially since the Christians—as well as the Jews—were considered "people of the book" by Islamic sacred law and thus they were decisively distinguished from pagan heathens, their incorporation into the body of the faithful did not require any fundamental changes in their mode of existence. This naturally secured their continuing symbiosis with their former coreligionists. For the same reason, forms of religious syncretism were not only possible but to a certain degree tolerable to the popular practice of Near Eastern Islam which accepts Christian Saints and their miracles in its hagiology.

A case in point is offered by the borderline sect of *Linobambakoi* (linen cottons), the Cryptochristians of Cyprus. As suggested by their name, they partook of two entities, practised the rites of both Islam (publicly) and Orthodox Christianity (covertly) and their double identity was characteristically expressed in the fact that each person used to have a Christian and Muslim name.[5] Evidence is also available indicating that intermarriage between Muslims and Christians was practised in the past, especially under the Ottomans, without a requirement of religious conversion.[6] This practice continued to be encountered with increasing infrequency down to the recent past.

These phenomena of syncretism and symbiosis can be understood in the broader context of the civilization of the Middle East. In this great meeting ground of faiths, religion, after the consolidation of Islamic rule, has not traditionally been a source of conflict but on the contrary it fostered other social needs like coexistence of different elements in the same historical space. Religion became a pretext of conflict only whenever it was politically manipulated to that end. Even then, as the tragic experience of the Lebanon in the mid-1970s suggests, it is no more than a cover for other forces working to subvert the *modus vivendi* achieved by the peoples of the area.

The aforementioned are just a few examples of traditional interethnic coexistence which have persisted down to our own time (i.e., well after the ethnic differentiation of the two Cypriot communities and the development of Greek and Turkish nationalism on the island) in the form of agricultural co-operation and social intercourse in the context of the integrated village unit of rural Cyprus. Therefore, it seems that the first cluster of research problems facing the student of the history of ethnic relations in Cyprus will involve the exploration in systematic detail of the forms of ethnic coexistence in traditional society. A model of such an examination is offered by Speros Vryonis in his study of Christian-Muslim symbiosis in Asia Minor following the Islamization of the peninsula from the eleventh through the fifteenth centuries.[7]

These phenomena which pointed towards the emergence of an integrated Cypriot society, were essentially the product of shared conditions of existence and the basic needs of survival set by the land-bound pattern of life in traditional society. There could be no more real source of the pattern of coexistence. This can also explain the depth, tenacity and resilience of the phenomena of interethnic coexistence despite the sharp distinctions on the level of formal ideology between the two religions and the deontological requirements that derived therefrom. These requirements aspired to keep the faithful of each religion apart and formed the basis of formal institutional arrangements in Ottoman society, designed precisely to actualize this separation. This of course was conditioned by socio-economic needs and the social division of labour among the nationalities of the Ottoman Empire. Some observers deduce from the incompatibility of formal Islamic and Orthodox doctrine and its institutional consequences, the impossibility of social coexistence between members of the two religions at the grassroots. Despite the institutional and deontological obstacles, however, coexistence at the grassroots was nurtured by socio-economic needs which fostered also a relevant cultural climate. As it will be shown in a moment, the context of formal institutions and violence from above disrupted these integrative potentialities from time to time and historical developments blocked their further evolution.

The foregoing analysis of the nature of ethnic coexistence is not meant to suggest that everything was peaceful and idyllic in the traditional society of Ottoman Cyprus. The previous sociological observations should be understood against the background of certain important facts of history: in short that the Ottomans not only came and settled in Cyprus by means of a violent conquest[8] but that their rule was very oppressive, arbitrary and often violent; that this period was punctuated by internal conflicts and repeated insurrections of Christians and Muslims and that on one occasion (1821) the Turks killed the prelates and scores of lay Christian notables ostensibly because a revolution had broken out in Greece. These events must be explained for the arguments about traditional coexistence to make full sense.

The conception of traditional coexistence presented here, derives essentially from an analysis of the social structure and the nature of social relations in Ottoman Cyprus. In a basically agrarian society Christian Orthodox and Muslim peasants were respectively at the basis of two systems of social control. According to the millet principle of Ottoman law,[9] membership in each power structure was determined on the basis of formal religious identity regardless of the character of actual religious practices and beliefs at the grassroots which were stamped throughout by extensive syncretism. In each structure ultimate control lay in the hands of the Ottoman pasha and the aghas, and the Orthodox hierarchy respectively. A careful scrutiny of the available historical sources clearly suggests that in all those occasions (1665, 1680, 1712, 1764–1765, 1783, 1804)[10] that troubles and outbreaks of various forms of violence are recorded, conflicts came as either violent protests from below (in which Christian and Muslim peasants joint forces) against oppression from above (usually excessive rapacity and tax exactions), or power struggles within the local Ottoman structure or between the powerful groups heading the two *millets* on the island. The latter contests arose whenever either group tried to monopolize authority on the island. Since the Turks controlled the material means of coercive power they had a definite advantage in these power struggles (as proved to be the case in 1821) except when the prelates managed to appeal successfully to the Sublime Porte. It follows that in none of these cases does it make sense to talk of ethnic violence: methodologically this would mean interpreting events out of their historical and social context by projecting subsequent social situations into the past. To insist to see ethnic violence even in the dramatic events of 1821 in Cyprus, is not just a misreading of history but it is a projection into historical explanation of the interpretative theses of nationalist historiography which capitalized on the powerful symbolism of that tragedy.

In the Ottoman social context oppression from above in fact consolidated the conditions of coexistence at the grassroots: it stimulated common protests in various forms (risings, appeals to the Porte) in which formal religious distinctions subsided before shared claims to the right of survival, thus setting in the social experience of the Cypriot religious groups valuable precedents of common action. Also by forcing upon Christian peasants the choice of mass conversion (of which there is evidence as late as 1825–1828)[11] to escape the rapacity of the tax collectors, it corroded ethnic differences and extended the social basis of coexistence as it has been explained above.[12]

Indeed the dynamic of coexistence nurtured by these conditions could work itself out unobstructed when an extended period of tranquillity and order was made possible in Cyprus in the last fifty years of Ottoman rule in the nineteenth century. A British consular report (dated 1862) on the condition of the island in this period, states that "the Muslims live in peace with their Christian neighbours in town and country".[13] The continuation of tranquillity and order in the several decades following the British occupation in 1878 allowed this harmony to survive down to the third quarter of the twentieth century despite the vicissitudes of nationalism and the process of ethnic differentiation at work in this period.

III.

Against the background of coexistence in traditional society one should try to trace the process of ethnic differentiation that culminated in communal conflict. This transformation began with the gradual growth of Greek irredentist nationalism in Cyprus. The first stirrings of nationalism were felt on the island early in the nineteenth century, with Cyprus's responses to the Greek War of Independence and the first formal expression of the desire for union with Greece, *enosis*, in an appeal of the Cypriot prelates and lay notables to John Capodistria in 1827.[14] The nationalist movement for *enosis* was to be intensified later in the nineteenth and twentieth centuries, and it essentially represented an extension to Cyprus of the same historical phenomenon that elsewhere in Europe took the form of the Italian Risorgimento, the movement for German unification and the irredentist movements of the Balkan nations. In Cyprus the elite nationalism of the early nineteenth century spread and took hold among the urban population by the middle decades of the century.[15] From 1878 onwards, under the British, the movement gained momentum partly because the Ottoman regime was replaced by a more tolerant administration.[16]

Economic change and social mobilization, slow but steady during the first decades of British rule, were the preconditions of the intensification of nationalist demands.[17] The penetration of nationalism from the cities to the rural areas through the channels of church, school and political and economic patronage provided the mass basis for the development of the *enosis* movement into a potent political force in the politics of Cyprus.[18] All available evidence suggests that by the 1920s Greek nationalism had effectively socialized the cadres of rural communities. This was the decisive turning point in the transformation of what had been the political aspiration of a section of the political elite into a mass movement. Economic discontent springing from the extreme underdevelopment and rural poverty prevailing in Cyprus up to the Second World War, strengthened the appeal of nationalism which in this context took up the meaning of a protest against the neglect by the colonial government.[19] An additional stimulation came from the frustrated social aspirations of rising urban groups of professionals and intellectuals, recently returned from Athens where they had been trained at the National University and imbued with the ideals of Greek nationalism which up to 1922 was going through a particularly militant phase. Deprived from a voice in the affairs of the island by the exclusivist outlook of the British administration which disdained dealings with the "natives", they turned to militant nationalism.[20] Thus as all these new social groups were drawn into politics, their needs and aspirations for increased political participation were translated into pressures for more effective representation tied to incessant nationalist manifestations in favour of union with Greece.

In their nationalist clamouring, politically conscious Cypriots felt psychologically heartened by the principle of nationalities that was stirring European politics in the years before and after the Great War. In this connection one should emphasize the importance of the entire complex of psychological and moral appeals that contributed greatly to the momentum of the *enosis* movement — a dimension of the problem that Anglo-Saxon scholars have very often misjudged and failed to appreciate. It is true that nationalism in Cyprus as elsewhere emerged as a byproduct of social and political change, external influences and domestic political struggles as will be suggested in a moment. Its appeal and spiritual force, however, was largely due to the sense of dignity it helped infuse in the Cypriots, the yearning for national redemption after so many bitter historical experiences, a feeling of identity with a cultural entity which possessed a meaning wider than the parochialism of the Ottoman periphery. In the context of all this an ancient Hellenic culture which had survived the vicissitudes of foreign conquests seemed to find its becoming meaning and the historical heritage of Cyprus was endowed with what was felt to be its proper symbolic significance.[21]

The political struggles developing within Cyprus strengthened the dynamic of nationalist claims. The escalation of nationalist agitation by diverting attention from socio-economic needs and cultivating an emotional climate of solidarity in pursuit of a collective national goal, was preempting pressures from below that social change now made possible. Such potential pressures coming from lower social strata could question the monopoly of political authority enjoyed by those leading the nationalist movement — the Church and the lay notables who controlled economic life, the professions and the press. The creation of a Communist Party (KKK) in this period (1926) was just an indication of what forms social and political pressures from below could take. Finally, despite their shared control over the affairs of the Greek Cypriots, short and longer term disagreements and antagonisms between the ecclesiastical hierarchy and lay politicians tended to intensify nationalist agitation as the contesting parties tried to neutralize each other by outbidding the opponent in nationalist zeal.[22] Such was the dynamic of the political situation on the eve of the uprising of 1931.[23] With this spontaneous uprising Greek Cypriot nationalism reached its major peak in the pre-War period. The revolt began in the cities but found widespread responsiveness in the countryside, thus showing the great strides of nationalism among the Greek population of Cyprus.[24] At the same time this was a symptom of the widening process of ethnic differentiation.

As nationalism grew among the Greek Cypriots and as demands of broader political participation rose against British colonial rule, the Turkish Cypriots, as well, became increasingly conscious of their ethnic identity and their rights of participation in controlling the affairs of the island. The formal expression of this developing political outlook has been the consistent opposition voiced by the leaders of the Turkish Cypriots to the Greek nationalist demands and their drive for union with Greece. The Turkish Cypriot leaders usually sided with the British in blocking Greek nationalist aspirations, although instances of interethnic co-operation especially over financial issues, were not entirely absent in this period. The dire poverty and the pressing economic needs of the population induced interethnic co-operation in the Legislative Council during the opening decades of British rule. In the 1880s and 1890s co-operation was general in the effort to promote solutions to the financial problems and basic socioeconomic needs of the island. This pattern of sustained co-operation broke down around the turn of the twentieth century, when the Greeks insisted on raising the issue of union with Greece in the Council. Until then the *enosis* aspiration was voiced outside the Council and this made interethnic co-operation possible. The important fact, in any case, is that the interethnic disagreement over the national status of the island remained academic, was confined to the elite level and was never strained enough to cross the threshold of violent ethnic conflict.[25] It can be suggested, therefore, that although the dynamic of ethnic differentiation was in the making throughout the period up to the Second World War, this was still a period characterized by the absence of ethnic conflict: significantly, the Greek rising in 1931 marking the height of enosis agitation did not provoke any interethnic incidents.

A dimension of social mobilization that contributed greatly to ethnic differentiation was the expansion of literacy. As literacy grew and cultural symbols became more significant, the awakening of primordial sentiments[26] drew the two Cypriot communities apart. The crucial factor here was the development of the educational systems on the model of those of Greece and Turkey respectively. As the educational values and curricula of the mainlands were transplanted to Cyprus, the symbolism of nationalist antagonism that grew out of the historical confrontation of the two nations was also transposed to Cyprus. The shared folk piety and values of premodern rural society subsided as the traditional religious and linguistic differences developed into the bases of a distinct Greek and a distinct Turkish national consciousness. In the context of the new symbolism the Cypriots found themselves divided into two communities that felt themselves to be parts of two nations which fought their wars of independence against each other. As young Cypriots went to study in the universities of Greece and Turkey, this attachment to their respective motherlands was intensified. The ethic of Greek patriotism was even more stressed by the mainland teachers sent to Cypriot schools, and the nationalist historicism and ethnographic research that spread from Greece to Cyprus provided the scientific bases for the nationalist belief system.[27] The Turkish Cypriots were always a few steps behind in these developments, but belatedly they have also tried to build up their scientific apparatus to sustain their ethnic claims.[28]

The importance of this cultural aspect of ethnic differentiation cannot be adequately emphasized. It provided the context within which the two Cypriot communities became conscious of their primordial attachments and the basis of their socialization into Greek and Turkish nationalism respectively.[29] As a result, a commonly shared system of social communication that could conceivably form the basis of an integrated Cypriot society was precluded from developing.[30]

To round up this analysis of the internal dynamics of ethnic conflict one has to look at the economic aspects of its development as well. What should be noted in this connection is that for reasons going back to the internal social evolution of the Ottoman Empire, the Greeks along with other Christian nationalities, started on the road of economic modernization earlier than the Muslims. Thus, although landed property remained in the hands of Turkish beys, the new wealth coming from commerce was concentrated in the hands of the new Christian middle classes.[31] These nineteenth century developments in the economic history of the Ottoman Empire affected the long-term prospects of ethnic conflict in Cyprus in that the pattern of differential economic modernization of the two communities added an important structural dimension to their future antagonism. It is characteristic to note that at the end of the British period the Turkish Cypriots owned a percentage of agricultural land holdings slightly higher than their share of the population, but in their overall share of the island's wealth they were estimated to be worse off than what their numerical proportion of the population would warrant.[32] This clearly reflects their inadequate participation in the more modernized sectors of the economy such as commerce and industry — a problem originating in their historically conditioned delay in economic modernization. Such was the economic aspect of ethnic relations in Cyprus when the ethnic conflict erupted in the 1950s. The further ethnic segregation that was consolidated in the 1960s only intensified these inequalities in levels of economic development.

Social and cultural change provided the internal dynamic of ethnic differentiation, but the effective context for the process was set by British colonial policy.[33] In contrast to the French, who used French language and culture as a medium of assimilating their colonial subjects, the British, partly because of their experiences in India at mid-nineteenth century, followed a policy of indirect rule and tried to limit interaction with the peoples of the colonies to the necessary minimum.[34] As a consequence, they relied on local power structures and the communal organization of society in managing the domestic affairs of the colonies and as a rule discouraged social or ethnic integration.

In Cyprus this meant that the traditional Ottoman system of social organization based on the religious millets would survive under the British. Thus a regime which according to British imperial ideology aspired to bring the blessings of modern liberal civilization to its colonial peoples, was essentially creating the conditions for the survival of traditional corporate forms of social organization. Furthermore the politicization of these traditional corporatist structures and the ideals that sustained them, under the impact of modern nationalism, undermined decisively the prospects of a liberal political culture — something that British influence could conceivably have nurtured. This contradiction has provided still another condition making for ethnic conflict: the absence of a political culture that would view individuals in their own right regardless of their ethnic origin.

It is obvious that all this sustained very effectively the ethnic differentiation developing in societies with diverse religious, linguistic or racial groups—like Cyprus. The consequence was that the system of horizontal interethnic bonds forged in traditional society was gradually undermined and eventually broken. Thus British administrative practices not only contributed to the gradual destruction of the potential bases of an integrated society in Cyprus but by preserving and politicizing traditional power structures, most notably the Orthodox Church and its civil functions, it led the leadership to potential ethnic conflict.

The immediate benefits of this policy consisted in the manoeuvrability it allowed the colonial administration in playing one group against another and thus keeping ultimate control for itself — a policy implemented largely through the Legislative Councils of the colonies, an institution which Cyprus experienced between 1881 and 1931. A classic technique of colonial administrations (usually realized by pitting a minority community against the aspirations of the majority), in the longer run this policy meant that the infrastructure and mechanisms of confrontation would be present once ethnic differentiation had worked itself out in consolidating fully fledged and self-conscious communities and the approach of independence would trigger contests over prospective spoils.[35]

It is probably important to conclude this analysis of the dynamics and processes of ethnic differentiation by noting certain important instances in which traditional coexistence could be transformed into modern forms of organized interethnic co-operation in the face of the continuing consolidation of two distinct national communities. The identification of such cases in Cypriot historical experience essentially provides the empirical basis of a conception of alternative courses of development that could have led to the emergence of an integrated society in Cyprus, despite the existence of two different cultures.

The most important case in point has been the development since the interwar years of an organized working-class movement which, in promoting shared social claims, provided the context for the systematic co-operation of Greek and Turkish Cypriot workers. It is significant that this movement was led by the Left which because of the content of its ideology could stress the community of social rights and aspirations and thus de-emphasize the ethnic strains nurtured by the nationalism of the Right. Separate Turkish Cypriot trade unions did not appear until 1943 when the first symptoms of organized separatist tendencies emerge among the Turkish Cypriot political elite. Turkish Cypriot workers, however, continued to participate massively in the unified left-wing syndicates until the late 1950s. A Turkish Cypriot trade unionist who persisted in this attitude was murdered in 1965 by the extremists of his community because he opposed ethnic separation and stressed the need and possibility of coexistence.[36] Three years earlier, in 1962, two Turkish Cypriot journalists who were taking similar stands in their newspaper, had met with the same tragic fate. Well before these sinister trends could appear in ethnic relations, interethnic co-operation was making significant strides in municipal politics in the face of nationalist agitation in the 1940s, indicating still another case in which shared problems and interests could counteract and essentially arrest developing ethnic cleavages.[37] Finally in the countryside the forms of traditional agricultural co-operation (sharecropping, disposal through intermediaries of the other ethnic group) could naturally develop into common participation of Greek and Turkish Cypriot peasants in the Cooperative Movement which since the early part of the twentieth century provided credit and marketing opportunities for agricultural products.[38] In all these instances of organized coexistence one can detect the seeds of potential social integration. Subsequent developments in ethnic relations which have led certain foreign observers to stress the impossibility of coexistence in Cyprus because of a presumed incompatibility of culture, should be re-evaluated in the light of the evidence presented in this and the previous section.

IV.

The culmination of the process of ethnic differentiation in the consolidation of structurally and culturally distinct and often antagonistic communities, deeply conscious of their primordial attachments, sets, of course, the preconditions of ethnic conflict. In this context, the drift to ethnic violence can easily begin once antagonism and suspicion are created in view of certain events, policies and choices. This was essentially the pattern developing in Cyprus in the aftermath of the Second World War. Since this is not a history of ethnic relations in Cyprus, I will not attempt to detail the sequence of events stretching from the mid-1940s to the mid-1950s which built up to the point of ethnic explosion.[39]

The heightened hopes of self-determination raised by promises during the Second World War, the intransigence of the Cypriot nationalists bred by the repressive British policies following the abortive uprising in 1931 and the intensified political struggle in Cyprus between Left and Right found expression in the formulation of an uncompromising policy of self-determination, demanding nothing less than union with Greece in the shortest possible time.[40] The refusal of the British to even discuss any change in the status of Cyprus, a vital base for their Middle Eastern strategy, the example of anticolonial armed struggles elsewhere and the strong support for the cause of Cyprus's freedom voiced in Greece, nurtured the idea of an armed revolt to be carried out by a secret organization of Cypriot freedom fighters. The fighting broke out on 1 April 1955. Although the fighting raged between British troops and Greek Cypriot fighters, the prevailing tension and sense of urgency fostered a climate of ethnic suspicion.

The evolving political outlook of the Turkish Cypriot political elite meanwhile was showing the first symptoms of separatism. In 1943 a Cyprus Turkish Minority's Association was established, replaced in 1945 by the Cyprus Turkish National Party. Two years later this party took the stand that in case the British left Cyprus, the island should "go back to Turkey". The decisive turn, however, is indicated by the change of the party name to "Cyprus is Turkish Party" in 1955. From then on with British encouragement initially and systematic direction from mainland Turkey throughout, a group of organized extremists (known as Volkan and later TMT) managed to bring the entire Turkish Cypriot community in its firm grip and to impose a monolithic singleness of purpose in promoting the objective of ethnic separation and eventual partition.[41] This triumph and entrenchment of extremism among the Turkish Cypriots — something that the extremist fringes of EOKA, despite repeated attempts, failed to achieve on the Greek Cypriot side — has functioned as one of the most exacerbating elements in the ethnic conflict in the twenty years from the mid-1950s to the mid-1970s by providing one of the major domestic conduits of outside intervention and distortion of ethnic relations.

The mechanisms of the precipitation of ethnic violence were created soon after the outbreak of the liberation struggle in 1955, as a body of auxiliary Turkish Cypriot policemen was set up by the colonial administration to help in hunting down the Greek Cypriot fighters and as secret armed organizations of Turkish Cypriots were formed to promote Turkish plans for the future of Cyprus. The fatal example was already set with the anti-Greek riots instigated by the Turkish government in Istanbul and Izmir in September 1955. It took the killing of a few auxiliary policemen to trigger the eruption of ethnic conflict in its ugliest forms, with street rioting, killing and arson from 1956 onward. Ethnic antagonism was fortified by the support of Greece and Turkey for their ethnic communities in Cyprus. All available evidence points to the fact that the Turkish government consistently incited ethnic rioting which was initially tolerated by the British administration in order to force the Greeks to compromise.[42] The long process of ethnic differentiation had finally been exacerbated enough by external factors and influences that it plunged Cyprus into ethnic conflict.

With independence in sight, i.e., when the British finally indicated their willingness to discuss the future status of Cyprus, the two communities did not close ranks. As considerable comparative evidence suggests, the period just prior to independence is considered by feuding ethnic groups as providing the last possible chance for the achievement of their maximalist objectives. Inevitably conflicts over the spoils tend to erupt.[43] In Cyprus discord developed over both the form and the method of independence. The Greek Cypriots, pointing at their overwhelming majority in the population and at their historical claims on the island's past, clamoured for union with Greece through the exercise of the right of self-determination. The Turkish Cypriots, abandoning their initial wish for the continuation of British rule, asked for a partition of Cyprus between Greece and Turkey, if not a wholesale annexation of the island by Turkey, to be decided through international agreements by the interested outside powers, Britain, Greece and Turkey. Both positions encountered considerable difficulties. The aspiration of union with Greece faced almost insurmountable international opposition from every conceivable direction. The argument for partition was domestically an impossibility except at enormous human and material costs in view of the absence of any ethnically homogeneous regions on the island. At any rate, such a solution, although repeatedly suggested or threatened by Britain and actively promoted by Turkey, was bound to encounter all-out resistance on the part of the Greek Cypriots. The international ramifications of all this created what came to be known in the 1950s as the Cyprus Question.[44]

When considerable international pressure led to a compromise settlement in 1959 and after protracted negotiations Cyprus emerged as an independent Republic on 16 August 1960, the ethnic conflict remained unresolved and simmering beneath the surface of events.[45] Indeed, the ominous signs of future strife could be gleaned from the repeated disagreements that strained the work of the committees drafting the constitution of Cyprus in 1959–1960. Many of the points of contention that appeared then were to re-emerge as the major issues in the conflict that subverted the Republic of Cyprus in 1963–1964.[46]

The constitutional framework of the Republic of Cyprus was designed to accommodate, but not to resolve, the ethnic conflict. Through an apparatus of intricate formulas and cumbersome structures, all premised on ethnic dualism, it froze and sanctioned ethnic division. Instead of encouraging co-operation, it institutionalized separatist tendencies in its provisions for ethnic voting and split municipalities. As a consequence, the public life of Cyprus was oriented by the very spirit of its constitution in the direction of ethnic antagonism instead of turning towards the democratic development of socially based party politics. The nature of the fundamental law of the Republic of Cyprus was aptly described by a distinguished legal expert who observed that in this case "constitutionalism has run riot in harness with communalism."[47]

The tragic misconception of the Cyprus Constitution lay in the effort to overcome ethnic conflict by freezing ethnic divisions and distinctions and by stressing the bicommunal character of the state. The only way, however, to make the new state viable and capture the allegiance of the ethnically divided population for a political system which did not embody their symbolic aspirations, was by creating the machinery and services that would effectively meet the practical needs of the entire population. Effective performance of such services in the context of a development-oriented secular welfare state could have provided a basis of loyalty which national symbols and primordial sentiments could not furnish. Subsequent experience with economic development and prosperity during the fourteen years of the island's independent statehood made it possible for this instrumental loyalty to the Republic to emerge in an incipient and uncertain form in the political culture of Cyprus.[48] On such a basis a set of policies could be initiated in the direction of what Clifford Geertz has called an "integrative revolution."[49] What this would be aiming at might be described as the development not of any form of communal assimilation, which was undesirable to both sides, but a common stake in peaceful coexistence based on the shared benefits of socio-economic development and democratic politics.

Whatever potential there might have been for such a development, it was effectively blocked by the institutionalization of ethnic dualism in the 1960 Constitution and as the turn of events was to show, by outside interference. The hopelessness of the situation was to become evident in the divisive dynamics and the psychological uneasiness of postindependence politics in Cyprus, ridden (as it soon appeared to be) with disagreements and discord. The Greek Cypriots resented what they felt to be an unfair share of the bargain: although they had set aside their cherished aspiration of *enosis*, the final settlement gave them less than what their proportion in the population and their contribution to the economy would warrant. The disappointment of Greek nationalism encouraged a sense of deprivation among the Greek Cypriots and serious apprehensions concerning the eventual objectives of the Turkish Cypriots. The latter's uncompromising attitude over the immediate implementation of all the separatist provision of the Constitution, was felt by the Greeks to be motivated by a desire to promote partition.

Indeed, the Turkish Cypriots were overzealous in pressing for full enjoyment of the prerogatives awarded them by the 1960 Constitution, arguing that this was the only way to cope with the overwhelming numbers of the Greeks. Therefore, the Turkish Cypriots remained extremely suspicious of any suggestions of change in the constitutional *status quo*. The outcome of all this was tension and escalating antagonism culminating in the constitutional impasse of 1963 and the breakdown of the 1960 settlement amidst renewed ethnic violence.[50]

The eruption of a new wave of violence on Christmas 1963 and the communal fighting that punctuated the tragic year 1964, reaching a climax with the bombings of northwestern Cyprus by the Turkish air force, represent just a new and more intense phase of the ethnic conflict of the 1950s which had remained unresolved. A wave of rioting and street fighting erupted at the end of December 1963 following the submission of the thirteen amendments to the Cyprus Constitution proposed by President Makarios in November of that year. The new ethnic explosion was used by Turkey and later in 1964 by the United States as a pretext in order to impose partition upon Cyprus (Acheson Plan). Although this was averted in the face of active Cypriot resistance and international, especially Soviet, opposition, this new phase of ethnic conflict was marked by effective segregation of the two Cypriot communities from 1964 onwards. The ethnic confrontation was crystallized as the Turkish Cypriots consolidated their control over a number of territorial enclaves which became "no-go" areas for the Greek Cypriots and where a great part of the Turkish Cypriot community was insulated.

Territorially the enclaves were based mainly on the Turkish quarters of the major cities or on clusters of Turkish villages in the countryside and were formed by forced population movements into these areas. Initially, these population movements appeared, and indeed were presented to be, for safety and refuge during the charged atmosphere of ethnic confrontation in 1964. Gradually, separate administrative structures were developed to govern these areas which, however, remained economically unviable and utterly dependent on Turkey for their survival. The fact that many people were kept as idle refugees in the enclaves and were prevented from going back to their villages even after the relaxation of tensions in the late 1960s, suggests that the whole movement was designed to modify the ethnic demography of Cyprus and to create a partial geographical basis for some form of ethnic separation.[51] All evidence that has been made available later tends to corroborate this view of the intentions of Turkish policy.[52]

After the 1963–1964 breakdown, the consolidation of the enclaves and the consequent crystallization of ethnic confrontation, relations between the two Cypriot communities exemplify certain structural dimensions which can form the analytical basis for comparisons between the ethnic conflict in

Cyprus and similar phenomena in other ethnically diverse societies. The set of five dimensions of ethnic conflict suggested below is not, of course, intended to constitute a model or even a "middle-range" conceptualization for the analysis of ethnic conflicts, but it is presented here simply for heuristic purposes and as a departure for comparative observations.

A heuristic paradigm:

A. Quantitatively the conflict has been relatively simple: a single numerically dominant group (80 percent of the population) is confronted by a single strong and stubborn minority.[53]

B. Spatially the conflict does not fit into any conceivable pattern of geographic distribution of ethnic groups. There has been no pattern of regional concentration, no ethnic segregation on an urban-rural dichotomy. Ethnic mixture geographically has persisted even after the consolidation of the Turkish Cypriot enclaves. It has been violently subverted only after the Turkish occupation of Northern Cyprus and the refugee wave that has uprooted the Greeks from the north, temporarily one hopes.

C. Sociologically ethnic division in Cyprus has not involved a system in which ethnicity and stratification coincide. Communal division has not been identical with class or status, but ethnic differentiation is horizontal, not vertical, encompassing two parallel social structures, each with its own stratification.[54]

D. Politically neither the majority nor the minority has been predominant over the other or exercised a monopoly of power. Further, there has been no division of control over different sectors of social activity (e.g., economy vs. government).

E. Internationally linkages with external entities have been quite pronounced. Both groups in Cyprus feel strong attachments to wider ethnic unities outside the island, and these ties tend to intensify the conflict domestically and to telescope it internationally.

The preceding structural analysis should throw into relief the reasons for the intensity of conflict on Cyprus. Quantitatively the conditions of ethnic balance are absent; geographically the loci of potential friction have been many. The strong external linkages make domestic politics very vulnerable to foreign influences and international instability. The presence of fully fledged and autonomous social structures in each group may have been responsible for the crystallization of ethnic polarization.

In turn, as conflict tends to intensify and the groups pull further apart, the dynamic of confrontation acquires powerful social psychological momentum. So long as the groups keep apart direct communication is obstructed by the structural dimensions of conflict, reality is distorted by prejudice, insecurity and a lack of information. Misperceptions thrive on stereotypes and misunderstandings of the other side's objectives and interests, thus perpetuating suspicion and hostility. Consequently, conflict acquires an important subjective component, dependent on sets of values and perceptions of the motivations of the other side.[55] In the Cyprus situation, after the communal segregation of the 1960s, the failure of the Turkish Cypriots to believe that the Greek Cypriots sought independence and not union with Greece, despite occasional official allusions to the latter, froze the relationship of conflict.

A moment of reflection and self-criticism on the part of the Greek Cypriots over this issue will probably reveal that their own ideological ambivalence did not help much in inspiring confidence in their Turkish Cypriot compatriots. Furthermore it might be relevant to point out that more could and should have been done by way of practical measures and social policies to help build up such confidence among the grassroots of the Turkish Cypriot community, especially those who remained outside the enclaves. It is certainly true that all governmental gestures in the direction of normalization were systematically obstructed and blocked by the advocates of separatism and terror who dom-inated the ranks of the Turkish Cypriot leadership — but one cannot escape the thought that more persistence and more imaginative policies might have been more effective. The problem has been that the social and ideological framework within which the question of the Turkish Cypriots was faced by most of the Greek Cypriots, fell short of those conceptions and initiatives that might have led towards ethnic reconciliation and reintegration by bring-ing about the necessary social changes. If these were the failings of the Greek Cypriots, the persistence of the Turkish Cypriots in a separatist behaviour and their repeated reception of reconciliation gestures with evident bad faith, did nothing to allay the suspicions and fears of the Greeks concerning partition.[56] As a consequence, ethnic relations remained in a situation of stalemated conflict for most of the period 1964–1974.

V.

This analysis of the dynamics of ethnic conflict in Cyprus has yet to be rounded up by a brief discussion of the impact of outside influences and intervention, admittedly the most catastrophic and exacerbating source of conflict. But before turning to this topic, one still has to raise a critical question concerning the nature of ethnic conflict. It has been shown in this chapter that conflict tends to appear as an ethnically diverse society advances towards modernity. All comparative evidence tends to support this view, and recent theoretical arguments, starting from a consideration of this evidence, have very convincingly questioned the older social science ortho-doxy concerning the homogenizing and integrative effects of modernization.[57] Therefore, one is confronted with the question whether, and up to what point, ethnic conflicts with all their enormous human and other costs are inexorable and tied to some kind of determinism.

I think that a consideration of the experience of Cyprus can suggest the elements of an answer to this question, and I would like to conclude this chapter by looking at this problem. It has been suggested in a comparative study of the possibilities and strategies of conflict regulation in six divided societies that the crucial element in successful conflict management is the motivation of political leadership to gradually reduce the level of conflict and bring it under effective control.[58] *Prima facie* it would seem that the conflict in Cyprus reached the levels of intensity it did, especially in the 1956–1958 and 1963–1964 phases, because such a motivation to control it was absent and the political leaders concerned preferred to press for the full achievement of their objectives rather than accept compromise. This suggestion is put forward here as a point of discussion to be resolved by further research, but the evidence I have been able to examine so far seems to support this view.

However, a change in orientation is obvious, at least as far as the Greek Cypriot leaders who controlled the Government of Cyprus were concerned, after the 1963–1964 crisis. Their motivation to pursue a policy of conflict regulation is evident in the receptivity they showed to the mediating and peacekeeping activities of the United Nations in Cyprus. A very constructive gesture in this direction was the acceptance by the Government of Cyprus of the UN Mediator's Report on Cyprus, a document of enlightened statesmanship suggesting general principles, political guidelines and specific institutional arrangements designed to meet the basic requirements of all involved in the Cyprus conflict and to create the preconditions of peaceful coexistence of the two communities.[59] Although the Turkish Cypriots did not show the same receptivity and rejected the report and its recommendations, their acceptance of the presence of the United Nations Peacekeeping Force on Cyprus (UNFICYP) made it possible for the force to accomplish its remarkable record of reducing friction and practically eliminating violent clashes on the island in the years 1968–1974, thus setting the preconditions of security and safety that were necessary for any moves in the direction of conflict resolution.[60]

Indeed, with United Nations encouragement things seemed to be developing in that direction with the initiation of intercommunal talks in June 1968. Thus, a channel of direct communication between the two communities was established with the purpose to negotiate a commonly acceptable solution. In an atmosphere of relaxation of ethnic tensions the talks proceeded in several phases, and allegedly, disagreement was narrowed down to the problem of the extent and form of local government.[61] If all the other problems concerning the constitutional structure of the state had indeed been resolved, this can only mean that the Greek and Turkish Cypriot leaders had finally realized that a settlement was possible and they were trying to work it out. If this was so, their behaviour and motivation were in step with political and economic developments on the island which were pointing toward the direction of conflict resolution.

The growth of political realism and moderation in the late 1960s made it possible for a policy of independent statehood to be adopted as the safest course for Cyprus. This became official policy when in 1965 the recommendations of the UN Mediator were accepted by the government of Cyprus and were popularly endorsed in two democratic elections in 1968 and 1970. Thus, the fundamental objection of the Turkish Cypriots to *enosis* was satisfied and this should have opened the way for accommodation. In the postindependence political climate the all-encompassing nationalist alignment that inherited the political legacy of the liberation struggle, broke up and new political parties emerged representing the interests and aspirations of social classes.[62] This new socially based politics might have conceivably cut into the ethnic cleavage and contributed towards interethnic political co-operation over social issues. Earlier instances of Greek-Turkish co-operation in trade unions or over the cause of intercommunal coexistence, although suppressed when the ethnic conflict flared up, indicated that such development was possible.[63] Economically, the great strides of development and industrial expansion[64] were opening job opportunities for the Turkish Cypriot workers who were kept secluded and idle in the enclaves. An expanding economy could have easily allowed the resumption of increased economic contacts in all commercial and industrial sectors once the separatist policy "from Turk to Turk", pressed on the Turkish Cypriots by their leaders, had been abandoned. Thus, some form of economic reintegration of Cypriot society could have been attained which would have also provided a way of redressing the inequalities in the levels of economic development between the two communities.[65]

Against the arguments for the reintegrative potential of economic development, one might point out that in a Greek-dominated economy, the Turkish Cypriot workers could have been reduced to the condition of an exploited proletariat. This, however, need not necessarily be the case, since legislative measures and syndicalist organization can provide effective safeguards against such a turn of events. Furthermore syndicalist organization against possible exploitation by the employers in a capitalist economy could promote — as it had done in the past — interethnic co-operation.

As Cyprus was entering her second decade of independent life, the hopeful signs of development, prosperity and conflict resolution inspired a sense of optimism and confidence in her people. The continuing interethnic coexistence and co-operation in several mixed communities of rural Cyprus, historically a feature of the Cypriot countryside, was a living indication that despite the bitter experience of conflict, peace was a possibility within the prospects of the island.

We may now return to the question of the inexorability of ethnic conflict. It seems that modernization and social change may bring ethnic differentiation, rising ethnic consciousness and eventually conflict, but it is also reasonable to suggest that once the relative costs and benefits of conflict and coexistence are realized and the appropriate political motivations mature, change and development can, in fact, be seen to possess great potentialities which can contribute constructively to conflict resolution. The problem of ethnic conflict, therefore, becomes one of direction, at least after a certain point in the process of modernization. The critical issue, then, is motivation in the management of the effects of change.

The only effective way to achieve this, it would appear, is by means of imaginative social planning designed to redress inequalities, heal psychological traumas and insecurities, efface the antagonism of cultural symbols. All this might mean fundamental changes in the structure of society which would certainly have required courage, imagination and generosity to accomplish, especially on the part of the stronger, majority community. Perpetuation of conflict and the concomitant opportunities to foreign manipulation that this means, is essentially the result of a failure to conceive the problem in this way and of an unwillingness to proceed with the needed changes. It is by looking at the problem in this way that a sound method of social criticism can develop — a critical method that might also be suggestive in planning future courses of action.

A caveat should be immediately added, however. In making a claim about the manageability of conflict, I am fully aware of the great difficulties with the evidence. Whatever indications can be gleaned from the experience of Cyprus make a rather weak case, and many other important cases point in the opposite direction. Therefore, although cases of conflict resolution and successful integration can be found, one has to be very cautious in one's claims. In the particular case that concerns us here I would like to make it clear that by conflict resolution I certainly do not mean to suggest any form of ethnic assimilation and the creation of a new integral nationality — this I think has been empirically impossible in Cyprus, given the existence of two fully fledged and articulate communities, both very zealous about their identities. Further, I am not even sure whether a turn of events in the direction of assimilation was desirable. But other forms of integration, especially in the economy and other spheres of practical activity, certainly were both possible and desirable in an age of consolidation of wide economic units. Therefore, the hopeful trends and possibilities of conflict resolution which I indicated a moment ago, could be conceived as elements in a potential modus vivendi, in an accommodation of basic ethnic needs in a binational secular society — an accommodation that might appear even more attractive in view of the costs of the alternatives.

After the identification of these positive elements and incipient trends in the direction of conflict resolution, it is relevant to ask why they never came to fruition. It is at this point that the examination of outside influence and interference becomes the most important element in understanding the evolution of the ethnic conflict in Cyprus. This analysis has, therefore, to conclude by looking at the disastrous effects of the exogenous sources of conflict.

Enough has been written on this subject so that only a few reminders are needed here. The first source of outside instigation of ethnic conflict in Cyprus has been Turkey with its policy of partition. The idea of partition was suggested by the British in the 1950s and has been espoused by Turkey since then. Despite various ostensible modifications of this policy, Turkey has pursued this objective ruthlessly in the last two decades. Partition in the form of the geographical separation of the two ethnic communities and the concentration of the Turkish Cypriots in one region was proposed by

Turkey as the official Turkish position to the UN Mediator in 1965.[66] The ethnic conflict in Cyprus has been fostered by Turkey in order to undermine the independence of Cyprus in the pursuit of partition, and the intercommunal negotiations were repeatedly blocked from Ankara when they seemed to reach a point of agreement. This policy was justified by general security considerations and concern for the safety and welfare of the Turkish Cypriots. It seems, however, that the benefits in foreign policy bargaining and from the domestic manipulation of the Cyprus issue carried a heavier weight in the motivations of the decision makers in Ankara.[67]

Greece also embarked on a reckless policy designed to undermine the independence of Cyprus, once the military dictatorship was established.[68] Enough evidence is now available concerning the repeated attempts at violent overthrow of the government of Cyprus in order to achieve the union of Cyprus with Greece with considerable territorial concessions to Turkey, thus achieving partition disguised as union. To promote these policies the Greek dictatorship encouraged right-wing terrorism and subversion in Cyprus on a considerable scale. Since this campaign was conducted in the name of union with Greece, it scared the Turkish Cypriots and had generally adverse effects on the efforts to reach a resolution of the ethnic conflict through the intercommunal talks. The subversive activities culminated in the bloody coup of 15 July 1974 which succeeded in overthrowing temporarily the legitimate government of Cyprus, but also in precipitating the Turkish invasion and in bringing about the eventual disintegration of military rule in Greece.[69] As a consequence of the two Turkish offensives on 20–22 July and 14–15 August 1974, Cyprus has been partitioned with the northern part of the island under Turkish occupation. This disaster has been an enormous human tragedy for the island. Thousands have been killed and wounded and thousands more are missing; one third of the population have become refugees. Such have been the human costs — to say nothing of enormous material damages and economic losses — of what the Turkish government has described a "peace-keeping" operation purporting to resolve domestic conflicts and to restore order in Cyprus. The only relevant comment that one can make is to note a macabre statistical comparison: the human cost of the ten years of ethnic confrontation has been less than one thousand lives; in the few weeks of Turkey's "peace operation" more than six thousand people were killed.[70] As it has been persuasively argued elsewhere, the policy of partition despite its incredible human, political and material costs which have become tangibly apparent after the 1974 tragedy, has been supported and actively promoted first as a collective NATO policy and later as the United States "ideal solution" for the Cyprus problem — ideal for what were considered Western strategic interests in the Eastern Mediterranean. A policy premised on Cold War assumptions and based on glaring misinformation, this has remained the approach of the US to the Cyprus problem since the 1950s.[71] Although during the crises of 1963–1964 and 1967 the United States tried to cool the situation through mediation, the policy of partition was urged as a permanent solution in 1964 by the Acheson Plan and was permitted to be violently implemented by Turkey in 1974. In the wake of this tragedy evidence is becoming available concerning covert American intervention and destabilization activities in Cyprus, especially in the form of direct or indirect — via the Greek CIA — encouragement of terrorist subversion against President Makarios.[72] Thus, both ethnic antagonism and intra-Greek dissension provided opportunities which facilitated American intervention in Cyprus.

The connections of these empirical facts about external intervention in Cyprus with the workings of ethnic conflict, will be better realized if the whole syndrome is considered in a broader framework. The combined effects of nationalist influences from Greece and Turkey and British administrative practices initiated and gradually consolidated ethnic differentiation in Cyprus. What this in fact meant was that two systems of closely woven linkages would tie the Cypriot majority and minority communities respectively with each of the two neighbouring countries which they considered as their motherlands. These intimate national, social and emotional attachments furnished the most effective channels through which domestic social and political processes in Cyprus could be influenced and directed from outside. The dependent foreign relations and the entrenched external influences in the politics of the two mother countries, provided an additional system of linkages through which international power politics and the pursuits of post-War imperialism in the Eastern Mediterranean could directly be felt in the domestic affairs of Cyprus. By means of these two levels of external linkages internal conflict in Cyprus has been effectively internationalized and its development and forms of resolution became dependent on factors external to the realities and needs of the people of the island.[73] Thus foreign strategic interests dictated by the Cold War and power politics in the Middle East have been decisive factors in the development of ethnic conflict within Cyprus.

In the context of all this, domestic conflict and the failures of local political leadership only facilitated the promotion of foreign interests at the expense of internal peace. On balance however, despite the political failures that have been noted earlier, the evidence presented in this essay is clear in suggesting a fundamental success of the government of Cyprus. In ten years of continuing crisis marked by ethnic confrontation and relentless foreign pressures, it managed to secure the survival of Cyprus as an independent and unified Republic, thus setting a basic precondition of conflict resolution on the island. It seems that precisely for this reason this government and its policies had to be destroyed before foreign designs on Cyprus could be put to work. Therefore ethnic conflict was exacerbated by external encouragement of extremism on both sides. The external linkages of Cypriot domestic politics were effectively used to this end. Ethnic extremism and systematic destabilization directed and financed from outside, set the stage for the violent attack and invasion which was designed to remove the nuisance offered to Western interests by a democratic and neutralist Cyprus in the Eastern Mediterranean. As a consequence of the Turkish invasion and the presence of the occupation forces, ethnic relations have been further distorted by the violent destruction of ethnic settlement patterns, by the colonization of occupied Cyprus by settlers from Asia Minor (who belong to ethnic groups different from the Turkish Cypriots) and by the geographical separation of the two Cypriot communities, which makes the continuation of co-operation in many spheres almost impossible. It becomes therefore once again evident that the decisive factors in the escalation of conflict and the consequent distortion of ethnic relations, have been external, not domestic. This conclusion is probably the most significant contribution of the analysis of the Cyprus case to the comparative study of ethnic conflicts.

It is against these overpowering external odds that the weak and precarious trends of conflict resolution had to take root in the life of Cyprus. We have now come full circle back to Braudel's argument after showing the uses that the events of history have been making of the threatened life of a Mediterranean island. Braudel is correct in stressing the critical importance of the unchanging geographical environment in determining the course of history. The bitter fate that her strategic location has brought upon Cyprus has borne this out once again in the long history of the ancient sea. One may thus conclude with Braudel by noting the imprisonment of man "within a destiny in which he himself has little hand, fixed in a landscape in a which the infinite perspectives of the long run stretch into the distance both behind and before". But since by following Braudel's historical method one is led to the "very sources of life in its most concrete, indestructible and anonymously human expression",[74] the real conclusion of this analysis of the ethnic conflict in Cyprus should be a human protest over the lost opportunities and the injustices that the good-hearted people of Cyprus have had to endure for no wrong doing of their own.

Figure 9.1 "Black summer 1974". Woodcut by Telemachos Kanthos (1997).

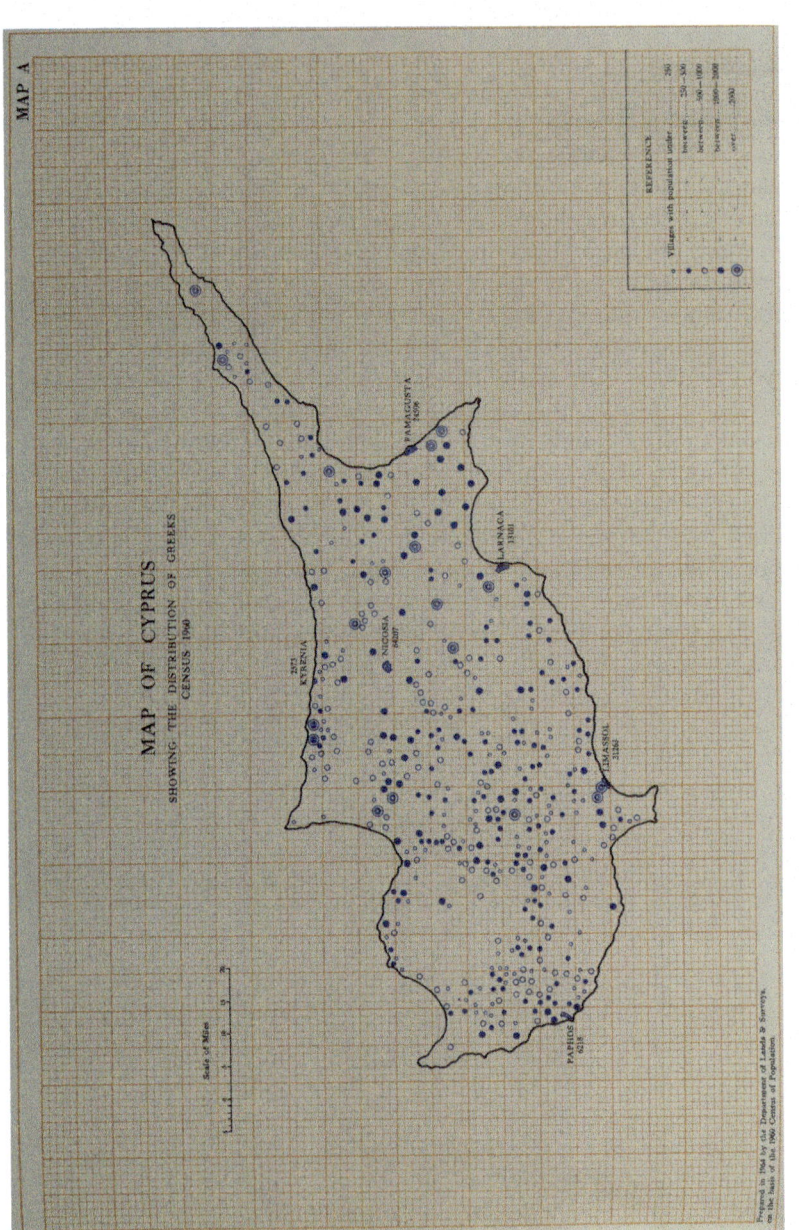

Figure 9.2 Map of Greek Cypriot villages, Cyprus (1960).

Source: Republic of Cyprus, *Statistical Data by Ethnic Group*, Nicosia, Cyprus: Dept. of Statistics and Research/Ministry of Finance, March 1964 Map A (Based on Census 1960)

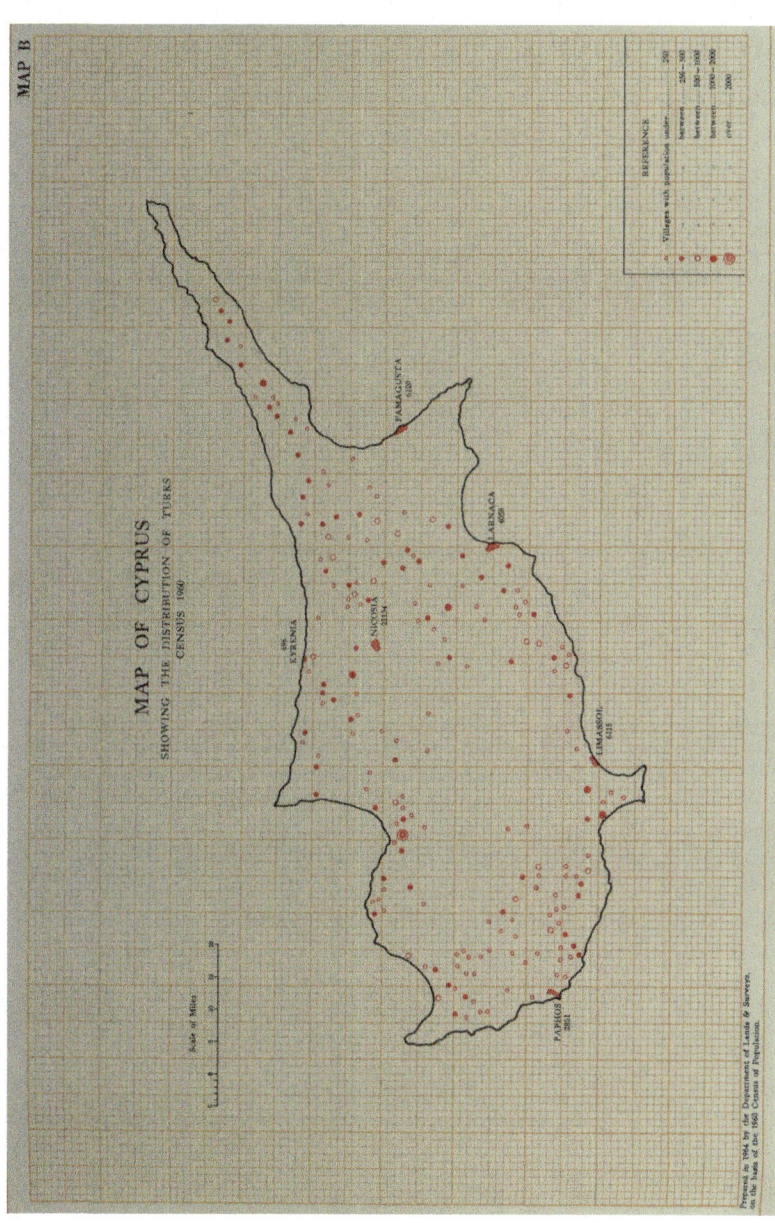

Figure 9.3 Map of Turkish Cypriot villages, Cyprus (1960).

Source: Republic of Cyprus, *Statisitcal Data by Ethnic Group*, Nicosia, Cyprus: Dept. of Statistics and Research/Ministry of Finance, March 1964 Map **B** (Based on Census 1960)

Appendix

A Statistical Profile of Ethnic Relations in Cyprus

Table 9.1 Population by religion at census years

Religion	1881	1891	1901	1911	1921	1931	1946	1960
Greek Orthodox	73.9	75.8	77.1	78.2	78.8	79.5	80.2	77.0
Muslim	24.4	22.9	21.6	20.6	19.8	18.5	17.9	18.3
Armenian Gregorian	0.1	0.1	0.2	0.2	0.4	1.0	0.8	0.6
Roman Catholic	1.1	0.4	0.4	0.3	0.3	0.7	0.2	0.8
Maronite	0.6	0.5	0.4	0.4	0.7	0.5	0.5	
Other	0.5	0.2	0.2	0.3	0.3	0.3	0.4	2.8

Table 9.2 Select characteristics of population by ethnic group: 1960 (%)

	Greek	Turkish
Urban[1]	68.7	20.4
Rural	81.8	17.0
University educated (Total: 100 per cent)	80.5	19.5

Table 9.3 Ethnic shares in select consumer goods and services: 1963 (%)

	Greek	Turkish
Motor Vehicles	85.2	14.8
Radio—TV	80.8	19.2
Telephones	90.4	9.6

Table 9.4 Ethnic shares in the economy (%)

	Greeks	*Turks*	*Armenians*	*Others*
Income Tax (1958)	29.7	1.8	1.0	67.52[2]
Land Holdings (1960)	78.3	20.43[3]		1.3
Crop Production (1963)	87.4	12.64[4]		
Vine Products (1962)	87	13		
Livestock Income (1963)	86	14		
Persons in Manufacturing (1962)	89.9	9.1		1.0
Mining Output (1962)	24.1	1.2		74.7
Imports 1(963)	78.7	3.2	5.3[5]	12.8
Exports (1963)	57.5	0.3	6.4	35.8

Sources: Table I, Statistics and Research Dept., Republic of Cyprus Statistical Abstract, 1970, No. 16 (Nicosia, 1970), p. 24. Tables II-IV, Dept of Statistics and Research, Republic of Cyprus, Statistical Data by Ethnic Group (Nicosia, March, 1964).

Comments:

1. Of all settlements (urban and rural) 50.3 per cent are purely Greek, 6.8 per cent are purely Turkish and 42.9 per cent, including all urban centres, are mixed in their population composition.
2. This sum was paid mostly by foreign mining companies, showing how inordinately big a share of Cyprus's national wealth was under foreign exploitation.
3. This statistic should be read in light of a parallel figure concerning the percentage of Turkish Cypriot landholders: although the overall communal share of landholdings is 20.4 per cent (above the Turkish share of 18.3 per cent in the population) only 15.1 per cent of the island's landholders are reported to be Turkish Cypriots. This discrepancy brings out graphically the higher concentration of land ownership among the Turks, which is a clear vestige of the quasi-feudal social structure of the community. This in its turn is not unrelated to the backwardness of the community in such modern sectors of the economy like manufacture and commerce.
4. In the production of the typical crops of traditional agriculture, wheat and barley, the Turkish shares were 20 per cent and 19 per cent respectively.The Armenian record in the import-export trade indicates that a minority could engage in modern sector economic activities without constraints—other than those of its own historical experience, which delayed Turkish development in this direction.

Notes

1 Fernand Braudel, *The Mediterranean and the Mediterranean World in the Age of Philip II*, translated by Sian Reynolds, New York: Harper and Row, 1972, Vol. I, p. 154.
2 For the ethnological evolution of the population of Cyprus in the Ottoman period see Th. Papadopoullos, *Social and Historical Data on Population,*

1570–1881, Nicosia: Cyprus Research Centre, 1965. On the origins of the Turkish Cypriots see C.F. Beckingham, "The Turks of Cyprus", *The Journal of the Royal Anthropological Institute* 87, Part II (1957), pp. 165–174. On the ethnic geography of Cyprus see Alexander Melamid, "The Geographical Distribution of Communities in Cyprus", *The Geographical Review* XLIV (July 1956), pp. 355–374 and the maps in illustrations 9.2 and 9.3 accompanying this chapter.

3 Purely Turkish villages with names of Christian Saints have been the following: in Paphos, Saint John, Saint Nicholas, Saint George; in Limassol, Saint Thomas; in Nicosia, Saint Epiphanios (Solea); in Famagusta, Saint Chariton; in Karpass, Saint Iakovos, Saint Andronikos, Saint Eustathios, Saint Symeon. Turkish Cypriots were also living in many mixed communities bearing names of Christian Saints.

4 The pertinent material is deposited in the folklore archive of the Cyprus Research Centre.

5 On the Cryptochristian group of the Cypriot *Linobambakoi* in the context of the religious syncretism of Ottoman society, see R.M. Dawkins, "The Cryptochristians of Turkey", *Byzantion* VIII (1933), pp. 247–275. See also K. Chantzioannou, *Τὰ ἐν διασπορᾷ*, Nicosia, 1969, pp. 240–241 which cites additional bibliography.

6 Cf. A.C. Aimilianides, "Ἡ ἐξέλιξις τοῦ δικαίου τῶν μικτῶν γάμων ἐν Κύπρῳ", *Κυπριακαὶ Σπουδαὶ* II (1938), pp. 207–212. This holds mostly in Islamic sacred law regarding women marrying Muslim men. Although Orthodox Canon Law excludes the possibility of marriages between Muslims and Christians, this doctrinal requirement did not inhibit the practice of intermarriage.

7 Speros Vryonis, Jr., *The Decline of Medieval Hellenism in Asia Minor and the Process of Islamization from the Eleventh to the Fifteenth Centuries*, Berkeley and London: University of California Press, 1971, pp. 444–497.

8 The meaning of the Ottoman conquest for the peasant masses of Cyprus is best conveyed I think, by the eighteenth-century historian Archimandrite Kyprianos who remarked that the peasants joined the Turkish armies believing that they might liberate them from the plague of the nobility. See his *Ἱστορία Χρονολογικὴ τῆς Νήσου Κύπρου*, Venice, 1788, pp. ix, 294, 331.

9 On the meaning of the *millet* system see Bernard Lewis, *The Emergence of Modern Turkey*, London: Oxford University Press, 1968, p. 335.

10 See briefly but authoritatively, Sir George Hill, *A History of Cyprus* IV: *The Ottoman Province, the British Colony*, ed. by Sir Harry Luke, Cambridge, Cambridge University Press, 1952, pp. 70–73, 74–75, 80–92, 92–99, 104–109.

11 Th. Papadopoullos, "Πρόσφατοι ἐξισλαμισμοὶ ἀγροτικοῦ πληθυσμοῦ ἐν Κύπρῳ" [Recent Islamizations of Rural Population in Cyprus], *Κυπριακαὶ Σπουδαὶ* XXIX (1965), pp. 27–48.

12 My recent researches at the Archivio di Stato in Venice have strengthened and broadened my views as to the nature of traditional coexistence in Cyprus. During these researches I have examined two series of archival materials on eighteenth century Cyprus (A.S.V./Ccnsolato di Cipro, especially vol. 20, 1703–1797 and A.S.V./Cinque Savii alia Mercanzia/Lettere dei Consoli/Cipro, vols. 647–653, 1721–1792). Besides many interesting details on interethnic relations at the grassroots, the clear evidence of the use of Greek, as the lingua franca of the island etc., this material suggests that in the context of incipient capitalist relations that tend to emerge in Cyprus as a consequence of the activity of foreign consuls, Christians and Muslims participate indistinguishably in the same economic networks. Cf. also C. P. Kyrris, "Symbiotic Elements in the History of the two Communities of Cyprus", *Proceedings of the International Symposium on Political Geography*, Nicosia, 1976, pp. 127–166 citing considerable

historical evidence on various forms of traditional ethnic coexistence in Ottoman Cyprus.

13 Harry Luke, *Cyprus under the Turks*, London: Oxford University Press, 1921, pp. 209–210. Cf. Hill, *A History of Cyprus*, IV, p. 231.

14 On this first manifestation of the *enosis* movement see E. Protopsaltis, Ἡ Κύπρος εἰς τὸν Ἀγῶνα τοῦ 1821, Athens, 1971, pp. 91–108.

15 A British consular report in 1866 notes that the townspeople had been inculcated with the Hellenic idea. Consular Correspondence, R.P.O., F.O. 329/1, 29 October 1866; cited in Hill, *A History of Cyprus*, IV, p. 496.

16 For accounts of the *enosis* movement under the British see Hill, *op. cit.*, pp. 488–568 which is detailed but obviously biased. It should be read in the light of Doros Alastos, *Cyprus in History*, London: Zeno, 1955, pp. 330ff. and Michael Dendias, *The Cypriot Question*, Athens: Pyrsos, 1937.

17 On the connection between the process of social change (generally defined as modernization) and the politicization of group consciousness see Samuel P. Huntington, *Political Order in Changing Societies*, New Haven and London: Yale University Press, 1968, pp. 32–39. The concept of social mobilization and its political consequences is used in this chapter as defined by Karl W. Deutsch, "Social Mobilization and Political Development", *The American Political Science Review* LV, no 3 (September 1969), pp. 493–514. Social and economic changes in Cyprus can be systematically document from the censuses collected by the British authorities every ten years since 1881.

18 According to a Colonial Office report at the beginning of the twentieth century the peasants were still unaffected by political agitation, but the spread of education was expected to stir them up too, P.R.O., Doc. No. C.O. 883/6, 30 August 1902. For the ways in which patronage networks and economic dependence helped in the penetration of nationalism in the rural areas see Michael Attalides, "Forms of Peasant Incorporation in Cyprus during the last Century", *Patrons and Clients in Mediterranean Societies*, ed. by Ernest Gellner and J. Waterbury, London: Duckworth, 1977, pp. 137–155.

19 François Crouzet, *Le Conflit de Cypre*, Brussels: Bruylant, 1973, pp. 61–93.

20 C. W. J. Orr, *Cyprus under British Rule*, London, 1918, pp. 165–169. Orr's view on the social dynamic of the *enosis* movement has been criticized by Dendias, *The Cypriote Question*, pp. 179–183. A Colonial Office report several years before Orr wrote, noted that people who studied law and medicine in Athens returned imbued with "Hellenic propaganda", bred on the precedent of the cession of the Ionian Islands to Greece, P.R.O., Doc. no C.O. 883/6, 28 November 1901.

21 Dendias, *The Cypriote Question*, retains its pertinence for an understanding of the moral and emotional significance of Greek Cypriot nationalism.

22 For the sociological dynamics of the development of nationalism in Cyprus, see Kyriacos C. Markides, "Social Change and the Rise and Decline of Social Movements: The Case of Cyprus", *American Ethnologist* I, no. 2 (May 1974), pp. 309–330.

23 For the details see Hill, *A History of Cyprus*, IV, pp. 543–548.

24 The best account of the 1931 rebellion is still that by Arnold Toynbee, *Survey of International Affairs 1931*, London: Oxford University Press, 1932, pp. 354–394. For additional evidence concerning the rural responses to the nationalist uprising see the documentary material edited by Paschalis M. Kitromilides in Κυπριακαὶ Σπουδαὶ XXXV (1971), pp. 191–209.

25 In the eighty years of British rule only one minor incident of Greek-Turkish political violence is reported over the Ottoman defeat in the Italo-Turkish war of 1911–1912. Hill, *History of Cyprus* IV, pp. 518–519.

26 For a definition of this concept and its political meaning see Clifford Geertz, "The Integrative Revolution: Primordial Sentiments and Civil Politics in New States", *Old Societies and New States*, ed. by Clifford Geertz, New York: Free Press, 1963, pp. 109–114.

27 For the development of Greek education in Cyprus under the Ottomans see Loizos Philippou, Τὰ Ἑλληνικὰ Γράμματα ἐν Κύπρῳ κατὰ τὴν περίοδον τῆς Τουρκοκρατίας I (1930), Nicosia. See especially pp. 175–176 and 189ff. for details on the spread of education in the rural areas. For a similar study of the following period of British rule see Kl. I. Myrianthopoulos, Ἡ Παιδεία ἐν Κύπρῳ ἐπὶ Ἀγγλοκρατίας 1878–1946, Limassol, 1946. The first serious attempt to provide a scholarly study of the Hellenic character of the civilization of Cyprus is that by A. Sakellarios who in 1855–1868 published in two volumes his Τὰ Κυπριακά in Athens. This was a study of the geography, history and language of Cyprus. A second enlarged edition enriched with folklore materials appeared in 1890–1891. This work essentially inaugurated the tradition of nationalist Greek scholarship on Cyprus. The first work by a Cypriot in this tradition was published in 1874 under the significant title, Φιλολογικαὶ Ἐπισκέψεις τῶν ἐν τῷ βίῳ τῶν νεωτέρων Κυπρίων μνημείων τῶν ἀρχαίων, by G. Louka, a student of Sakellarios, during the latter's stay in Cyprus as a teacher of Greek letters. The tradition of nationalist scholarship reached its culmination with the publication of scholarly journals like Κυπριακὰ Χρονικά, Larnaka, 1923–1937 and since 1937 Κυπριακαὶ Σπουδαί. For an interesting study of similar educational and cultural developments in another distant part of the Greek periphery in the nineteenth century, see Anthony Bryer, "The Pontic Revival and the New Greece", *Hellenism and the first Greek War of Liberation, 1821–1829: Continuity and Change*, J. A. Petropulos *et al.*, eds., Thessaloniki: Institute of Balkan Studies, 1976, pp. 171–190.

28 While the Greeks were actively engaged in the cultivation of nationalist scholarship and culture already in the nineteenth century, the Turkish Cypriot movement did not begin until the 1930s when a history of Cyprus in Turkish was published: Fikret Alasya, *Kibris Tarihi*, Nicosia, 1939. This was a clear symptom of the nationalist influences of Ataturkism emanating from Turkey to Cyprus. On the political significance of the upsurge of nationalist scholarship in Turkey in the 1930s under the impact of Ataturkism, see Bernard Lewis, "History writing and National Revival in Turkey", *Middle Eastern Affairs* IV (1953), pp. 218–227. Cf. *idem, The Emergence of Modern Turkey*, pp. 318–355, 431–436. For the ethnic differentiation of the Turkish Cypriots and the transformation of their Islamic identity into Turkish national consciousness see C. F. Buckingham, "Islam and Turkish Nationalism in Cyprus", *Die Welt des Islams*. N.S. V (1957), pp. 65–83. For educational development see Ali Suha, "Turkish Education in Cyprus", Πρακτικὰ τοῦ Α΄ Διεθνοῦς Κυπρολογικοῦ Συνεδρίου, Nicosia, 1973, Vol. III, Part 1, pp. 355–375.

29 On this point cf. the study as to how history teaching helped in the cultivation of the symbolism of nationalist antagonism: *Cyprus School History Textbooks: A Study in Education in International Misunderstanding* by the Education Advisor Committee of the Parliamentary Group for World Government, (London, n.d.).

30 For the theoretical foundation of this view cf. Karl W. Deutsch, *Nationalism and Social Communication*, Cambridge: M.I.T. Press, 1953.

31 Bernard Lewis, *The Emergence of Modern Turkey*, pp. 448–456.

32 Stahis Panagides, "Communal Conflict and Economic Considerations: The Case of Cyprus", *Journal of Peace Research* 5 (1968), pp. 133–145.

33 Cf. Adamantia Pollis, "Inter-Group Conflict and British Colonial Policy, The Case of Cyprus", *Comparative Politics* 5, no. 4 (July 1973), pp. 575–599.

34 Ronald Robinson and John Gallagher, *Africa and the Victorians*, New York: Doubleday, 1968, pp. 10–11.

35 Captain Orr, who sincerely believed in the blessings of liberal civilization brought by British rule to the peoples of the Empire, was probably the first to question the wisdom of an administration which relies "on the permanent hostility between two sections of the population to carry into effect the policy of the Government" by noting its potential detrimental consequences. See *Cyprus under British Rule*, p. 106.

36 For details on interethnic co-operation in the trade union movement see Χρονικὸ τῆς Σύγχρονης Κυπριακῆς Τραγωδίας published by the Central Committee of AKEL, Nicosia, 1975, pp. 189–196. The following statistics are suggestive concerning the politics of trade unionism in Cyprus: the first trade union was established in 1932 with 84 members under left-wing leadership; by 1960 the left wing trade union movement had 35544 members and by 1970 36000 members; the first Turkish Cypriot union was created in 1943 with 43 members; by 1960 the Turkish trade unions had 4381 members and by 1970, 3000 members; in 1944 a right wing trade union federation was set up with 758 members its membership rising to 5587 in 1960 and 21,000 in 1970. See Republic of Cyprus, *Annual Report of the Ministry of Labour and Social Insurance for the year 1970*, Nicosia 1971, p. 99.

37 For details see Pl. Servas, Ἡ Κυπριακὴ Τραγωδία, Athens, 1975, pp. 21–35.

38 There is a general study of the Cooperative Moment in Cyprus by K. Angastiniotis, Ὁ Συνεργατισμός, Γένεσις καὶ Ἀνάπτυξις του ἐν Κύπρῳ, Nicosia, 1965. For an English language text, see *idem*, "Co-operative Development", *Cyprus: A Handbook on the Island's Past and Present*, Nicosia: Greek Communal Chamber, 1964, pp. 223–234. The significance of the movement in the promotion of interethnic co-operation deserves a more systematic examination.

39 The history of the conflict between 1946–1959 is recorded in great detail in a recent synthesis of all available sources in François Crouzet, *Le Conflict de Chypre*, Brussels: Établissements Émile Bruylant, 1973, 2 volumes.

40 Ibid., Chapters V–VII, shows in detail that despite their sharp ideological antagonism left and right followed in this period a militant policy of self-determination that tended to mutually reinforce the demand for union with Greece.

41 For more details see Michael Attalides, "The Turkish Cypriots: Their Relations to the Greek Cypriots in Perspective", *Cyprus Reviewed*, ed. by M. Attalides, Nicosia, 1977, pp. 71–97.

42 C. Christides, Κυπριακὸ καὶ Ἑλληνοτουρκικὰ, Athens, 1967, pp. 309–318 (in Greek) and Stephen G. Xydis, *Cyprus: Reluctant Republic*, The Hague: Mouton, 1973, pp. 125–130.

43 Immanuel Wallerstein, "The One-Party States of West Africa", *Political Parties and Political Development*, J. La Palombara and M. Weiner, eds., Princeton: Princeton University Press, 1966, p. 205 and Cynthia H. Enloe, *Ethnic Conflict and Political Development*, Boston: Little, Brown, 1973, p. 22.

44 The two volumes by Stephen G. Xydis, *Cyprus: Conflict and Conciliation 1954–1958*, Columbus: The Ohio State University Press, 1967 and *Cyprus: Reluctant Republic*, as well as Crouzet, *Le Conflit de Chypre*, constitute the most important sources on the Cyprus Question in the 1950s. For a discussion of the relevant literature see N. P. Diamandouros and P. M. Kitromilides, "The Birth of The Republic of Cyprus", *Reviews in European History* II, No. 2 (June 1976), pp. 297–303.

45 For the 1959–1960 settlement see Crouzet, *Le Conflit de Chypre* II, pp. 1073–1154 and Xydis, *Cyprus: Reluctant Republic*, pp. 337–460. For an incisive critique of the "solution" of the Cyprus problem, see C. Chrestides, Κυπριακὸ καὶ Ἑλληνοτουρκικά, pp. 407–445.

46 Xydis, *Cyprus: Reluctant Republic*, pp. 477–514.

47 S. A. de Smith, *The New Commonwealth and its Constitutions*, London: Stevens, 1964, p. 285.

48 For a formulation of this changing outlook see T. Papadopoullos, "Η κρίσις τῆς Κυπριακῆς Συνειδήσεως", *Φιλολογική Κύπρος* (Nicosia, 1964), pp. 204–209.

49 Clifford Geertz, "The Integrative Revolution: Primordial Sentiments and Civil Politics in the New States", *The Interpretation of Cultures*, New York: Basic Books 1973, pp. 255–310.

50 The issues of the 1963 crisis are most adequately covered in Stanley Kyriakides, *Cyprus: Constitutionalism and Crisis Government*, Philadelphia: University of Pennsylvania Press, 1968. Note his analysis of the constitution (pp. 53–71), the constitutional tension areas (pp. 72–103) and the subsequent crisis and break-down (pp. 104–134). The events of the crisis are also chronicled in Charles Foley, rev. ed., *Legacy of Strife: Cyprus from Rebellion to Civil War*, New York: Praeger, 1966, pp. 168–191. For the legal aspects of the 1963–1964 crisis see Thomas Ehrlich, *Cyprus 1958–1967*, Oxford University Press, 1974, pp. 36–89.

51 Cf. Kemal Karpat, "Solution in Cyprus: Federation", *The Cyprus Dilemma: Options for Peace*, New York, 1967, pp. 35–54, which presents the Turkish case on precisely that argument.

52 This evidence comes mostly from United Nations documents. See for instance, Report of the Secretary General on the UN Operation in Cyprus, 12 December 1964, paras. 32 (19 *UN SCOR*, Supp. October-December 1964, pp. 230–231) and 10 March 1965, paras. 53–56 (20 *UN SCOR*, Supp. January-March 1967, pp. 118–119).

53 Cf. Geertz's typology in "Integrative Revolution", pp. 266–268.

54 Cf. D. Horowitz, "Three Dimensions of Ethnic Politics", *World Politics* 23, No. 2 (January 1971), pp. 232–244.

55 Cf. John W. Burton, *Conflict and Communication*, New York: Free Press, 1969 and Herbert C. Kelman, ed., *International Behavior*, New York: Holt Rinehart and Winston, 1965.

56 John W. Burton, *World Society*, London: Cambridge University Press, 1972, pp. 55–59, 68–69, 75–77.

57 Walker Connor, "Self-Determination: The New Phase", *World Politics* 20, no. 1 (October 1967), pp. 30–35 and *idem*, "Nation-building or Nation-destroying", *World Politics* 24, no. 3 (April 1972), pp. 319–355. For a recent empirical exam-ination of this problem see Milton M. da Silva, "Modernization and Ethnic Conflict: The Case of the Basques", *Comparative Politics* 7, no. 2 (January 1975), pp. 227–251.

58 Eric A. Nordlinger, *Conflict Regulation in Divided Societies*, Cambridge, MA: Center for International Affairs, Harvard University, 1972.

59 Galo Plaza, "Report of the United Nations mediator on Cyprus to the Secretary General", *United Nations Security Council Official Records, Supplement* (Jan-uary–June 1965). Doc s/6253 26 March 1965.

60 Details on the operations of UNFICYP can be found in the relevant reports of the Secretary General to the Security Council, published in Supplements of the *SCOR* twice a year (in June and December) since 1964. See also Michael Har-bottle, *The Impartial Soldier*, London: Oxford University Press, 1970.

61 Polyvios G. Polyviou, *Cyprus in Search of a Constitution: Constitutional Negoti-ations and Proposals, 1960–1970*, Nicosia, 1976, pp. 81–315 gives a detailed

account of the four phases of intercommunal talks (1968–1974) based for the most part on a systematic transcription of the repeated proposals of the two sides. A valuable addition to the bibliography on the Cyprus Question, it gives a sense of the evolution of the respective positions of Greek and Turkish Cypriots up to the eve of the coup and the invasion. Note in particular pp. 265–315 outlining the constitutional agreement allegedly reached in late 1973: this agreement provided essentially the constitutional basis for conflict resolution in Cyprus. Despite the progress on constitutional issues achieved in the talks and despite the constructive dynamic of conflict resolution through direct communication that this context provided, certain fundamental shortcomings pointed out by the critics of this method of negotiation as applied to Cyprus, have to be acknowledged: first the talks were held in secrecy — secrecy that kept the concerned citizens and political parties of Cyprus in the dark, as to what was discussed. Secrecy in addition made possible the exertion of external pressures which distorted the progress of the talks. Secrecy over the content of the discussions and the agreements announced from time to time, made it easy for the negotiations to be repeatedly obstructed by the Turkish side which on many occasions went back on earlier agreements. This was a tactic used by the extremists on the Turkish side to forestall any agreement that might bring normalization to the island.

62 A first attempt in the direction of an analysis of the political situation emerging in the early 1970s is made in Paschalis M. Kitromilides, *Patterns of Politics in Cyprus*, unpublished Honours thesis, Wesleyan University, 1972.

63 For some glimpses into incipient trends in reintegration cf. Attalides, "The Turkish Cypriots: Their Relations to Greek Cypriots in Perspective", *Cyprus Reviewed*, ed. by M. Attalides, Nicosia, 1977, pp. 71–97.

64 For the achievements of economic development in Cyprus in a broad comparative perspective see *The UNESCO Courier*, February 1970, pp. 22–23. For more details see the Second and Third Five-year Development Plans, prepared by the Planning Bureau of the Republic of Cyprus.

65 On the economic situation of the Turkish Cypriots cf. Attalides, 'The Turkish Cypriots: Their relations to Greek Cypriots in Perspective'.
    In this connection it is interesting to note the observation of Paul Swcezy, "antagonism between the Turkish minority and the Greek majority [...] could have been alleviated, or perhaps wholly overcome, in a healthy society such as would have been possible had Cyprus been able to dispose over the wealth of Mavrovouni," referring to the exploitation of Cyprus's mineral resources by an American corporation. See his "Foreign Investment", *Monthly Review*, June 1965.

66 Report of the U. N. Mediator, parags. 73–79, 97–98, 107–109. For the evolution of the Turkish views on partition since the 1950s, see Xydis, *Cyprus: Conflict and Conciliation*, pp. 78–79, 88–89, 92–93, 107–108, 166–167, 242–246, 334–345, 385–389, 511–512, 518–519.

67 For the manipulation of the Cyprus issue in Turkish domestic politics cf. Richard D. Robinson, *The First Turkish Republic*, Cambridge: Harvard University Press, 1965, p. 188 and Ferenc Vali, *Bridge across the Bosporus: The Foreign Policy of Turkey*, Baltimore: Johns Hopkins Press, 1971, pp. 78–114, 358–364.

68 On the policy of the Greek dictatorship toward Cyprus see Alexander G. Xydis, "The Military Regime's Foreign Policy", *Greece Under Military Rule*, Richard Clogg and George Yannopoulos, eds., New York: Basic Books, 1972, pp. 191–209. Some radical critics have argued that one of the major reasons for the advent of the dictatorship was the urgency of NATO and the USA to promote the partition of Cyprus, a policy opposed by both the government of President

Makarios in Cyprus and the Papandreou government in Greece. See for instance Andreas Papandreou, *Democracy at Gunpoint: The Greek Front*, New York: Double-day, 1970, pp. 124–141. Greek attempts to undermine, the independence of Cyprus by promoting a NATO-oriented solution began already under the governments that followed the Papandreou administration in 1965. See. Ch. Chresides, Κυπριακὸ καὶ Ἑλληνοτουρκικά, pp. ix–exxii and *idem, Ἄκρως Ἀπόρρη-τον: Τὸ Πρωτόκολλο τῆς 17 Δεκεμβρίου 1966*, Athens, 1973.

69 The fullest account of these recent developments yet available is Laurence Stem, "Bitter Lessons: How We Failed in Cyprus", *Foreign Policy*, no. 19 (Summer 1975), pp. 34–78. Another report on Greek-instigated subversion in Cyprus is J. Bowyer Bell, "Violence at a Distance: Greece and the Cyprus Crisis", *Orbis* XVIII, no. 3 (Fall 1974), pp. 791–808, which, however, remains completely silent on American involvement.

70 A number of Congressional publications contain valuable information on the 1974 crisis, the invasion and the drama of the refugees. House Foreign Affairs Committee, *Cyprus 1974*, Hearings, 93rd Congress, 2nd sess., 19 and 20 August 1974 (Washington, DC: Government Printing Office, 1974); Senate Committee on the Judiciary, Subcommittee on Refugees, *Humanitarian Problems on Cyprus*, Hearings, 93rd Congress, 2nd sess., 26 September 1974 (Washington, DC: Government Printing Office, 1974) and *Crisis on Cyprus: 1974*, Study Mission Report to the Subcommittee on Refugees, 14 October 1974. These documents incorporate many useful press reports on the problem. See also Stanley Karnow, "America's Mediterranean Bungle", *The Atlantic*, February 1975, pp. 6ff.

71 See Van Coufoudakis, "United States Foreign Policy and the Cyprus Question: A Case Study in Cold War Diplomacy", *U.S. Foreign Policy toward Greece and Cyprus. The Clash of Principle and Pragmatism*, ed. by Theodore A. Couloumbis and Sallie M. Hicks, Washington, DC: The Center for Mediterranean Studies, 1975, pp. 106–138.

72 Stern, "Bitter Lessons", gives some indications in this direction. This view of the situation tends to be corroborated by the evidence of two other serious journalists, Eric Rouleau, in *The Guardian Weekly*, 24 August 1974 and Christopher Hitchens, "How Cyprus was Betrayed", *The New Statesman*, 24 October 1975. See also Christopher Hitchens, "Détente and Destabilization: Report from Cyprus", *New Left Review*, No. 94 (November-December 1975) pp. 61–75 for the political context of these activities. The investigations of congressional committees in the USA (especially by the Pike Commission, autumn 1975), have also produced evidence implicating American secret services in subversive activities in Cyprus. It is hoped that the full transcripts of these hearings will be made public to facilitate judgement on these controversial issues.

73 This conceptualization draws on George Modelski, "The International Relations of Internal War" *International Aspects of Civil Strife*, ed. by James Rosenau, Princeton: Princeton University Press, 1964, pp. 14–44 and James Rosenau, *The Scientific Study of Foreign Policy*, New York: Pree Press, 1971, pp. 307–338.

74 Braudel, *The Mediterranean* II, p. 1244.

10 Ethnic conflict in a strategic area
The case of Cyprus

Introductory[1]

Social change has been viewed by successive generations of scholars and by diverse theoretical doctrines as a process of development and improvement with generally desirable consequences. The origins of this understanding which has conditioned many theories of modernization, can be traced back in the Enlightenment idea of progress and in nineteenth-century social optimism over the prospects of humanity—as well as in an unstated belief in the universal relevance of the Western liberal experience. Nevertheless the actual experience of the transition from traditional to modernizing society which at a heightened pace has been under way on a global scale since the Second World War, has clouded the long-cherished optimism by dramatizing the enormous costs at which change is achieved. Indeed one could say that this new awareness of the price of change is alerting the attention of social theorists to a problem that the achievements of Western society have tended to obscure: the heavy human and other costs which had to be paid in the long process towards the consolidation of modernity in Europe and North America.

In our recent experience the most telling indication of the costs of change has been the increase in the incidence and scale of violence within changing societies. The decade of the 1960s has been marked by a generalized rise in the occurrence of civil violence in both modernizing and highly advanced societies. Civil violence accompanies the movement of social change and tends to assume the form either of praetorianism in the absence of effective political institutions, social revolution against existing social and political structures or communal conflicts over the scope of a political system in encompassing diverse ethnic groups and national communities.[2]

Communal violence and ethnic conflicts have appeared with increasing frequency and intensity since the dissolution of the colonial empires in the 1950s and 1960s. The first instance of widespread ethnic violence has accompanied the attainment of Indian independence in 1947 and the partition of the Indian subcontinent. By the 1960s communal conflicts had erupted in many other recently independent states but in a variety of forms ethnic divisions were intensified to the point of violent explosions in advanced, postindustrial societies (notably the

United States) as well. In view of this generalized experience it has been persuasively suggested that modernization fosters ethnic conflict as social mobilization and the politicization of primordial attachments tend to disrupt the fragile structures of ethnically diverse societies. Modernization tends to intensify and politicize rather than stamp out ethnic diversity.[3] It would seem, nevertheless, that ethnic conflicts in developing and highly advanced societies coming as they do at different points in the continuum of social change, are not exactly identical phenomena and consequently explanatory theories of ethnic conflicts will have to consider this distinction and account for the differences.

Although older scholarly orthodoxy regarding the relation between modernization and ethnic integration has been incisively criticized, there is still a great deal to be learnt about ethnicity and ethnic conflicts for the existing lacunae and deficiencies in the theoretical literature to be remedied.[4] Before attempting generalizations and theory building it is best to proceed inductively by looking at the dynamics of particular conflicts. The following analysis of the ethnic conflict in Cyprus is attempted in this spirit. We hope that the empirical evidence from the study of the sources, conditions and various characteristics of the conflict between the two Cypriot ethnic communities offered here, will contribute towards the development of a more effective conceptualization for the comparative analysis of ethnic conflict.

Dimensions of the latest tragedy

Developments in Cyprus in the late 1960s and early 1970s were marked by a general relaxation of ethnic tensions, economic boom and a continuing intercommunal effort in search of a negotiated settlement of the ethnic conflict in accordance with the basic needs and requirements of both ethnic communities. The constructive involvement of the United Nations in containing friction and in reducing the level of confrontation by means of the policing and mediating activities of the UN Cyprus peacekeeping force (UNFICYP) in the military field, as well as in promoting a resumption of Greek-Turkish Cypriot contacts aimed at reaching a commonly acceptable constitutional arrangement in the political sphere, had set in motion several hopeful trends foreshadowing a successful resolution of the ethnic conflict in Cyprus.

Noting all this an observer might have concluded that Cyprus could potentially develop into a paradigmatic case of conflict resolution which in a comparative perspective could be of considerable value as a model to other ethnically troubled parts of the world. At the same time however, observing the growth of terrorist extremism on the right-wing fringes of the Greek Cypriot community, the procrastination and repeated delays in the intercommunal negotiations and the escalation of covert and overt foreign interference in the affairs of Cyprus, one was also becoming increasingly aware of the dangers of a new catastrophic explosion.

During the first half of the year 1974 a series of events which largely fell beyond the Cypriots' own control, led to the realization of the second of the two possible scenarios outlined above. The strained relations between the democratically elected government of Cyprus's President Archbishop Makarios with the military dictatorship then ruling Greece, culminated in the coup of 15 July 1974. The coup was planned in Athens and executed by the Greek officers of the Cyprus National Guard and the Greek military contingent stationed in Cyprus (in accordance with the 1960 Treaty of Alliance).

The coup met with considerable armed resistance and caused violence and bloodshed among the Greek Cypriots but it managed to set up a short-lived puppet regime. Archbishop Makarios was rescued out of Cyprus by the United Nations forces and the British Royal Air Force. Realizing the dangers involved in their adventure, the anti-Makarios putschists avoided systematically to attack or threaten the Turkish Cypriots and appealed to them to cooperate with the new regime for a continuation of the intercommunal discussions.

The overthrow of the legitimate constitutional order, however, afforded a perfect opportunity for Turkey to execute a policy adopted since the 1950s. This policy aimed at the partition of Cyprus. Seizing the pretext furnished by the coup and arguing that Cyprus's independence had been violated by Greece, while also invoking her rights and obligations under the 1960 Treaty of Guarantee to intervene and restore the upset status quo, Turkey mounted an invasion of Cyprus with air, sea and land forces in the early hours of Saturday, 20 July 1974. Britain, also a guarantor of Cyprus's independence, had earlier in the week rejected a Turkish proposal for a joint intervention.

In the battle of Cyprus that raged between the 20th and the 22nd of July 1974, the invading Turkish forces, despite superior numbers and equipment, suffered many losses and met with fierce resistance on the part of the poorly armed and badly organized Cyprus National Guard. When a ceasefire was arranged by the United Nations in the afternoon of the 22nd of July the Turkish forces had managed to establish themselves on a limited beachhead west of Kyrenia on the northern coast of Cyprus. After repeatedly violating several ceasefire agreements—including one signed at Geneva by the Foreign Ministers of Great Britain, Turkey and Greece on the 30th of July 1974—the invading Turkish forces proceeded on the 14–15 of August on a new offensive which culminated in the partition of Cyprus along a line running from Kokkina in the west through the Turkish quarter of Nicosia to Famagusta in the east. The occupied area includes the entire Kyrenia district, the western and northern regions of Nicosia district, almost all of Famagusta district with the Karpass peninsula and parts of Larnaca district—in all about 40 per cent of the territory of the Republic of Cyprus. The map that appears in Figure 10.1 shows the advances of the occupation forces in Cyprus.[5]

These events have left Cyprus in an immense human tragedy. The human toll of the violence has been five thousand dead and up to fifteen thousand wounded. In addition there are about three thousand missing persons, especially young men who vanished during the fighting in the summer of 1974. All this gave rise to a sense of grief which permeated all aspects of life in Cyprus in the several months following the invasion.

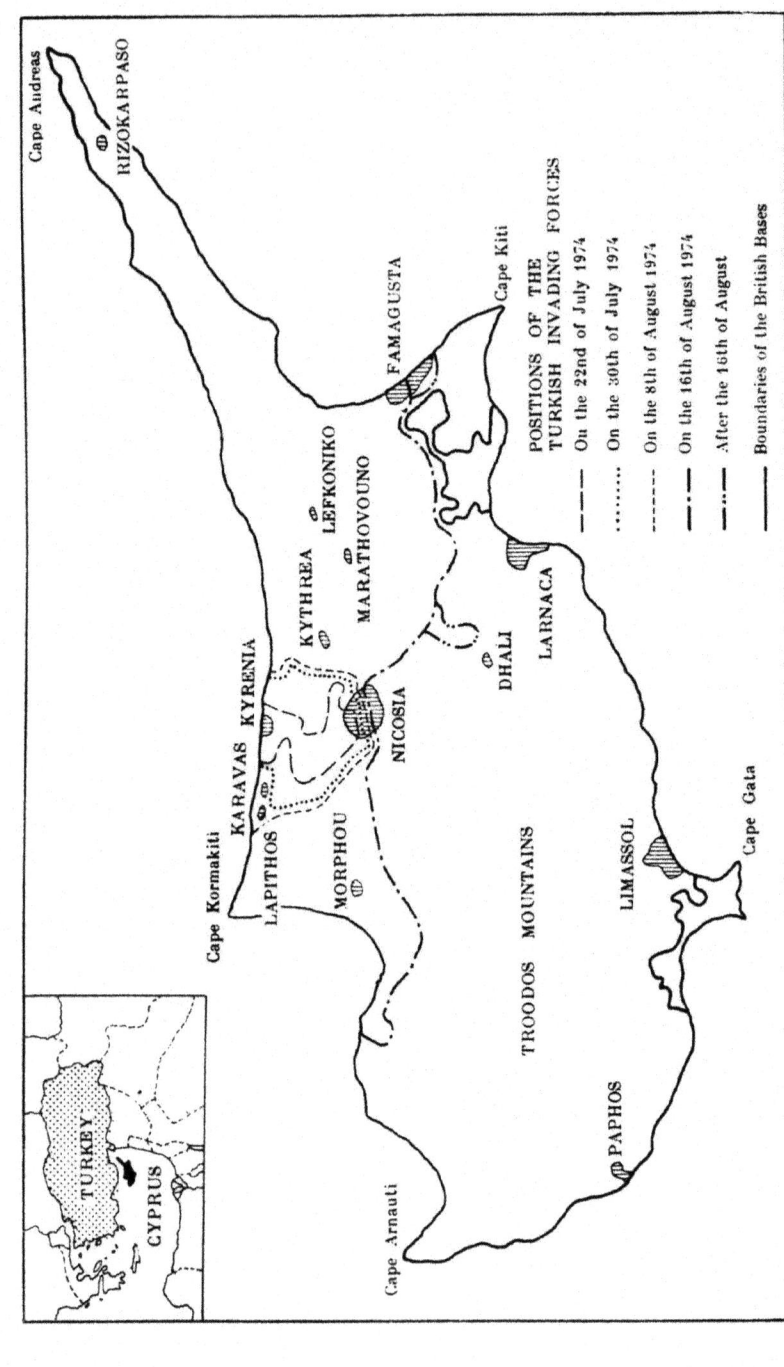

Figure 10.1 Advances of the Occupation Forces in Cyprus, July 22–August 16, 1974.

As a result of the invasion, the war and the occupation of Northern Cyprus, a refugee wave uprooted one third of the population of Cyprus from their homes. Out of a population of approximately 650 thousand an estimated 180,800 Greek Cypriots and about 17,000 Turkish Cypriots have become refugees. The predicament of these people is described in Table 10.1 which presents a detailed account of the various categories of persons who have been affected by the war and the occupation.[6]

As the winter of 1974–1975 set in, the most acute problem was that of shelter and accommodation since many refugee camps became uninhabitable with the coming of rainy and windy weather. Although most of the refugees have found shelter in all sorts of available structures from schools and monasteries to stables and warehouses or managed to squeeze in with friends and relatives, there are an estimated twenty thousand who still remain under inadequate shelter and thus are exposed to the vicissitudes of changing weather. As of this writing the Cypriot refugees are facing their second winter under tents. Relief pouring in from Greece, the Hellenic diaspora and international organizations (United Nations and International Red Cross) has been barely sufficient to cover the essentials of subsistence.

All this is just the material and tangible dimension of refugee life. The whole ordeal has affected deeply the Cypriots' outlook on life and the confident optimism bred by the prosperity of the recent past has been gradually replaced by a sense of desperation and anguish. Out of this grows a living consciousness and appreciation of the tribulations of other people who have been less fortunate than the Cypriots in their recent history.

The intense human suffering of the refugees has been, of course, the most serious of Cyprus's recent problems. However, there have been many other problems as well. The coup, the war and the occupation shattered the island's flourishing economy. The sheer physical destruction has been enormous: it began with the demolition of public buildings the day of the coup and culminated with the raids of the Turkish air force which set huge areas of Cyprus's best forests afire and bombed to ruins hospitals, schools, hotels, industrial buildings and tourist attractions. Then came the looting of the occupied areas and the destruction of a great part of the crops and livestock all over Northern Cyprus. Preliminary estimates of overall economic damage and material destruction as of September 1974, put the costs up to the equivalent of the expenditures of the last eleven years in Cyprus's general budget.[7]

As a consequence of the fact that the most important of Cyprus's natural resources and the most economically developed areas are in the occupied northern region, the economy suffered huge losses in production, exports and tourism. It has been estimated that about 4.5 million dollars in economic production were lost every day during the several months after the invasion. In addition, there are the losses resulting from the idleness forced on the refugees—roughly one third of the economically active population—and the costs of their maintenance estimated at 4.6 million dollars a month.

Table 10.1 Displaced Persons and Others in Need on Cyprus (as of November 1, 1974)

I. Refugees:	
1. Greek Cypriots in Government-controlled areas:	
Satisfactorily sheltered with friends/relatives or in second homes rented	57,600
Living in public buildings, schools, etc.	5,800
Housed in permanent structures, but over-crowded conditions & will have to move	89,700
Living in shacks, garages, unfinished structures	11,000
Living in tents	9,000
Living in the open, under trees, in makeshift open shelters	7,700
Total	180,800
2. Turkish Cypriots in Government-controlled areas:	
Living in tents on British Sovereign Base areas	8,500
In isolated villages, cut off, or in controlled villages/enclaves	22,000
Total	30,500
3. Greek Cypriots in Turkish-occupied areas:	
Living in cut off villages, or displaced	9,000
4. Turkish Cypriot refugees in Turkish-occupied areas:	
Moved from the south to the north, and includes some refugees from 1963-64	8,500
II. Prisoners of war and detainees, both sides:	
All have been released under UN auspices	6,000
Total	234,800

Source: *Crisis on Cyprus: 1974* (Study Mission Report of the Subcommittee on Refugees of the US Senate Committee on the Judiciary. October 24, 1979), p. 19.

The economic growth and prosperity of the past ten years have accumulated enough reserves to meet the emergencies of the first several months, but the extent of the devastation has been such that the outlook for the future appears very grim indeed unless normal economic activities are resumed immediately.[8]

The picture of human pain and material destruction that opens this chapter, conveys just a dim sense of the tragedy that has so suddenly replaced Cyprus's many achievements and hopes in her fourteen years of independent statehood. Still our distressing description has not so far accounted for the origins of the conflict and the historical sequences of events that led up to today's depressing situation. Although the humanitarian facet of the problem certainly looms larger than anything else in the wake of the latest crisis, there is a background in politics and conflict which must be examined if the whole issue is to be comprehended. Indeed, Cyprus's grievous experience underscores the urgency of the problems raised by ethnic conflicts and points out the pressing need to attain a better understanding of the issues involved—in the hope that out of our analytical efforts more appropriate and humane resolution strategies will develop.

In the following pages we will try to first present a general survey of the politics of ethnic conflict in Cyprus and then we will outline and evaluate a number of initiatives, attempted at a variety of levels, aiming at a resolution of the problem in one direction or another. Our purpose is to present in general the relevant material that has been made available by considerable scholarly research and the publication of pertinent primary sources. We hope that our survey of sources and research and our outline of events and problem areas will provide an adequate introduction to the general problem of ethnic conflict in Cyprus. Although our focus remains political, we appreciate the need of a comparative study of the deep historical roots and the structural and attitudinal dynamics of the conflict between the two Cypriot communities.[9] A few relevant hints offered in the following pages, are meant to suggest the direction that future research should follow.

The politics of ethnic conflict: from coexistence to segregation

The origins of the contemporary problem of Cyprus go back to the Ottoman conquest of the island from the Venetians in 1570–1571. The most momentous effect of the Turkish conquest was the creation of a Muslim minority in Cyprus. According to Ottoman practice, part of the invading forces settled in Cyprus as sipahis—or military landholders—taking over as their *timars* or *chifliks* the feudal estates of the former Frankish nobility. If these were the original forefathers of the Turkish minority, its numbers were soon swelled by the Islamization of Greek inhabitants who were induced to escape the lot of subject *rayas* by joining the religion and enjoying the privileges of the ruling *millet*.[10] These Islamizations can be systematically documented from tax registers which have survived from the period of Ottoman occupation. There is convincing evidence that there were conversions of Greek Cypriot villagers to Islam as late as 1825–1828. The best testimony however is afforded by the names of Christian saints borne by several Turkish villages in Cyprus—e.g., St John, St Nicholas, St George—and the fact that until recently many of the Turkish Cypriots, especially in the Paphos area, were in fact Greek speaking Muslims.[11]

These Muslims lived in peace with the Greek Cypriots who formed the overwhelming majority of the population throughout the centuries of the Ottoman occupation of Cyprus—thus extending to Cyprus the pattern of peaceful symbiosis of Orthodox Christian and Muslim peasants that prevailed in Anatolia, especially in such areas as Cappadocia and Pontos, until the Greeks were expelled from Asia Minor in 1922–1924. This peaceful coexistence manifested itself in a shared folk piety and a common lifestyle that survived intact in those areas of Asia Minor that remained away from the battlegrounds of the Greek-Turkish war that raged during 1919–1922 in Western Anatolia. The memories of this peaceful past are still invoked by the moving receptions of those Greeks who in recent years have been returning to visit their erstwhile villages. The same is largely true of those parts of rural Cyprus where Greeks and Turks lived in mixed or neighbouring villages. In this context an undeniable tradition of mutual help and cordiality in the personal sphere survived the vicissitudes of political history.[12]

This was the social legacy of intercommunal relations inherited by the British when they took over the administration of Cyprus in 1878 in the context of a rearrangement of power relations in the Near East sanctioned by the Treaty of Berlin.[13] In the span of eighty years of British rule between 1878 and the late 1950s, only one minor incident of intercommunal violence is reported.[14]

It is true that in the intricate politics of the Legislative Council which functioned from 1881 to 1931, the colonial rulers managed repeatedly to play the representatives of the two communities against each other.[15] Political representation in the Legislative Council reflected the traditional Ottoman system of social organization based on religious communities (millets) which was retained by the British and formed the fundamental principle of their handling of the politics of Cyprus. In the context of this policy the millet system was gradually politicized and provided the organizational foundation for the national differentiation of the Cypriots.[16] Despite this process, which was encouraged by British policy, the Turkish members of the Council sided occasionally with their Greek compatriots to promote the common interests of the island, especially regarding taxation and finance. Even over the issue of *enosis*, the demand for union with Greece for which the Greek Cypriots had been clamouring for generations, the two communities did not come to blows. True, the Turkish Cypriot leaders registered consistently their opposition to *enosis* but this disagreement was never strained so far as to be expressed in violence.

The *enosis* movement emerged in the nineteenth century and it essentially represented an extension to Cyprus of the wider historical phenomenon of European nationalism. In its social character and political aspirations, the *enosis* movement was similar to the Italian Risorgimento, the movement for German unification and the irredentist movements of the Balkan nations. Similar *enosis* movements aspiring at unification with the Kingdom of Greece had developed in Crete, Macedonia and the Seven Ionian islands in the nineteenth century. Timid under the Ottomans in the nineteenth century, the *enosis* movement was intensified under the British and reached a peak in the nationalist rebellion of October 1931.[17] Meanwhile, in 1925 Cyprus became a British Crown colony after Turkey had renounced all rights of sovereignty over the island by the Treaty of Lausanne of 1923.[18]

The 1931 uprising, aspiring to *enosis* with Greece, was forcefully put down by the British and the civil liberties of the Cypriots were suppressed. The repression of all political life and national expression that followed this uprising, was largely responsible for the intransigence that the Enotist leaders manifested in dealing with the constitutional proposals of the British government after the Second World War.

In the wake of the Second World War the national demands of the Cypriots were formulated as a claim of self-determination in the context of the movement of decolonization.[19] A plebiscite organized by the Ethnarchy of Cyprus in 1950 — after the British rulers refused to conduct one — showed an overwhelming majority of the Greek Cypriots favouring union with Greece.[20] The British refused to discuss the future of Cyprus even in the face of increasing political agitation in the island.[21] The subsequent intransigence growing on all sides in the years 1950–1955, culminated in an anticolonial guerrilla rebellion lasting between 1955 and 1959 and spearheaded by EOKA, the underground National Organization of Cypriot Fighters.[22]

Until then the conflict had been primarily between the Greek Cypriots and the British while the Turkish Cypriots remained relatively uninvolved. It was not until 1957–1958 that the tensions prevailing in Cyprus generated intercommunal violence on a considerable scale for the first time. The eruption of ethnic violence in the late 1950s came as the result of a process of increasing differentiation between the two Cypriot communities which had until then coexisted in a traditional society. Socio-economic modernization, slow but steady under the British, and the spread of literacy transformed the traditional religious and linguistic differences into the bases of the development of a distinct Greek and a distinct Turkish national consciousness. In the political sphere, as nationalism grew among Greek Cypriots and as demands for broader political participation rose against British colonial rule, the Turkish Cypriots as well became increasingly conscious of their ethnic identity and their rights of participation in Cypriot affairs. Further, as the educational systems of the two communities were modelled on those of Greece and Turkey respectively, the symbolism of nationalist antagonism that grew out of the long historical confrontation of the two nations, was transposed to Cyprus. As a result of all this a commonly shared system of social communication that could conceivably form the basis of an integrated society, was precluded from developing.[23]

Against this background there emerged the contention over the spoils of independence which was felt to be imminent once the British indicated their willingness to hand over the government of the island to the Cypriots themselves.[24] Fortified in their antagonism by the support of their respective motherlands and by British colonial policy which as a rule discouraged ethnic integration in the territories of the Empire,[25] the two Cypriot ethnic communities found it increasingly difficult to compromise. Discord developed over both the form and the method of independence. The Greek Cypriots fought for union with Greece through the exercise of the right of self-determination. The Turkish Cypriots expressed interest in continuing British rule or securing a partition of Cyprus between Greece and Turkey to be decided by these outside powers and Britain. The irreconcilability of these positions led to heightened tensions which exploded in violence. Thus the workings of social mobilization and the political choices of the years 1945–1955 resulted in the translation of the traditional religious and linguistic differences into ethnic conflict.

Accommodation or drastic surgical solutions were extremely difficult in view of the communal demography and ethnic geography of Cyprus. As Table II of Chapter 9 indicates, the Turkish Cypriot community never exceeded 25 per cent of the population. Indeed, since the 1920s its numbers had dropped below 20 per cent. Being thus an overwhelming majority of the population, the Greek Cypriots remained intransigent in their claim of self-determination by majority rule. Conversely, the extreme dispersion of Turkish Cypriot settlements all over the island, shown in Figure II shown in Figure 9.3 of Chapter 9, made it impossible to find a geographic basis for partition—a solution suggested first by the British and espoused by Turkey since the mid-1950s.[26]

The continuing anti-British guerrilla struggle of the Greek Cypriots, the consequent endemic diplomatic confrontation between Britain, Greece and Turkey and mounting pressures from NATO and the world community, built up to such a point of tension that the parties to the conflict finally settled for a compromise: on 16 August 1960, following the Zurich and London agreements of the previous year and protracted negotiations in Cyprus thereafter, Cyprus emerged as an independent state.[27]

The Zurich and London agreements, concluded in February 1959, reflected the ethnic duality of Cyprus as well as the power balance of the contracting parties. The British acquiesced to the loss of a colony, but secured rights to sizable sovereign bases on Cyprus. Further, in the confrontation between Greek and Turkish Cypriots, it appears that the mainland Greeks felt so pressed to reach a settlement that they gave up more than their fair share of bargaining chips to the Turkish side. The United States, being intimately involved with both Greece and Turkey, applied continuous pressure on both junior allies as well as on the Cypriots to settle amicably and to heal the "festering sore" in the southeastern flank of NATO.[28]

The Zurich and London agreements, and the Constitution which was based on them, set up the Republic of Cyprus, which was given the status of sovereignty and independence and soon attained UN membership. However, on independence day Cyprus was bound by three treaties. The Treaty of Guarantee between Cyprus, Britain, Greece and Turkey (the three guarantors) was designed to safeguard the territorial integrity and independence of Cyprus, simultaneously permitting the "guarantors" in concert or independently, to intervene in Cyprus to uphold the state of affairs created by the 1960 treaties and to prevent either *enosis*, the Greek maximalist position, or *Taksim* (partition of the island between Greece and Turkey), the Turkish answer to *enosis*, The Treaty of Alliance committed Greece and Turkey to come to the aid of Cyprus in case of external aggression and allowed them to station one military contingent each on Cyprus on a 60/40 ratio. By the Treaty of Establishment Great Britain secured two sovereign base areas at Dhekelia and Akrotiri-Episkopi in southern Cyprus.[29]

The basic principles of the constitutional organization of the Republic of Cyprus were agreed upon at Zurich between the Prime Ministers of Greece and Turkey. During the subsequent London conference they were presented to the Cypriots to guide the work of the commission which was to draft the Constitution of Cyprus. The Constitution took more than a year to draft and its major provisions were as follows: Cyprus would have a presidential regime with a Greek Cypriot President and a Turkish Cypriot Vice President, each elected by his respective community and each possessing final veto power on matters dealing with foreign affairs, defence and internal security. The Council of Ministers should include three Turkish Cypriots out of its ten members. At least one of three important ministries (Defence, Foreign Affairs or Finance) should go to a Turkish Cypriot citizen. The Turkish Cypriots also secured quotas of 40 per cent in the Army and the Security Forces and 30 per cent in the Civil Service—well in excess of their 18 per cent share in the population. The fifty-member legislature was to be composed of Greek and Turkish Cypriot deputies on a 70/30 ratio. Each ethnic community was to elect its deputies separately. Separate majorities in each ethnic caucus were required to pass legislation on such matters as taxation, electoral procedures and the municipalities. Exclusively communal affairs were to be administered by the Greek and Turkish Communal Chambers. Further there were provisions for separate Turkish and Greek municipalities, separate taxation and separate administration of justice. The Treaties of Guarantee and Alliance were annexed to the Constitution. Article 182 of the Constitution declared the provisions of final veto, separate majorities and fixed ethnic ratios as well as the two incorporated treaties as basic and unalterable.[30]

It is obvious that this constitutional framework of the Republic of Cyprus was designed to contain and accommodate the ethnic conflict by satisfying some of the most basic requirements of the two Cypriot communities—e.g. by ruling out both union and partition. Beyond this however the Cyprus constitution, premised on ethnic dualism, did not contribute anything towards a substantive resolution of the past and potential intercommunal conflict. Its intricate formulas and cumbersome structures were precisely designed to freeze and perpetuate the ethnic division. Instead of encouraging cooperation it institutionalized separatist tendencies in its provisions for ethnic voting in parliament and split municipalities, thus the public life of Cyprus was oriented by the very spirit of the constitution in the direction of ethnic antagonism instead of turning towards the democratic development of socially based party politics.

Constitutional experts everywhere concurred that the Cyprus constitution, despite its "ingenuity", was practically unworkable.[31] In real life efficient government proved impossible and controversies quickly arose. The danger points centred on the question of the Army's composition (i.e. at what level should the units be ethnically integrated), the passage of tax legislation, the establishment of separate municipalities and the implementation of the 70/30 ratio in the composition of the civil service.[32]

Predictably the psychological dynamics of the postindependence situation in Cyprus intensified these disagreements. The Greek Cypriots resented what they felt to be an unfair share of the bargain: although they had set aside their cherished aspiration for enosis the final settlement gave them less than what the hard facts of their proportion in the population and their contribution to the economy would warrant. On the other hand the Turkish Cypriots were quite zealous in pressing for full enjoyment of their prerogatives under the Constitution, arguing that this was the only way to cope with the overwhelming numbers of the Greeks. Therefore the Turkish Cypriots remained extremely suspicious of any suggestions of change in the status quo.

The outcome of all this was tension and escalating discord—to the point that by 1963 the Government could not collect taxes because the Turkish members of the House would not vote for the income tax bill—not out of any reservations regarding its fairness to their community, but as a tactical move to force the establishment of separate municipalities and the immediate implementation of the ethnic ratios provided by the Civil Service clauses of the Constitution.[33]

In November 1963, with this stalemate in the background, President Makarios offered for consideration thirteen amendments designed to make the 1960 Constitution workable.[34] These amendments sought primarily to abolish the requirement for separate ethnic majorities in the legislature, to merge the separate judicial systems for the two communities and to eliminate the veto powers of the President and the Vice President. While the Turkish-Cypriot community was studying these proposals, Turkey immediately and flatly rejected them and admonished the President to respect the provisions of the externally guaranteed Cyprus Constitution.

In the ensuing climate of heightened tensions a small incident escalated into all-out violence between the two fired-up communities during the last week of December 1963. Turkey threatened to intervene militarily as the new year was dawning. Active American pressure on all sides averted the escalation of the conflict into a Greek-Turkish war.[35]

The communal violence that erupted in 1963 and punctuated the following year, was a later and more intense phase of the ethnic conflict which had emerged in the late 1950s. It not only underlined the fact that ethnic conflicts tend to be of long duration and to persist over time despite intervals of (usually) uneasy peace, but it also showed that the bicommunal experiment conceived at Zurich and London primarily to meet NATO objectives, was ill founded and failed to contribute towards conflict resolution because it ignored the real issues and further distorted the relations of the two Cypriot communities by institutionalizing external interference in the politics of Cyprus.

Following the crisis of Christmas 1963 the British intervened using troops stationed at their bases to re-establish order, separate the combatants and achieve a cessation of hostilities. It was at that time that the "Green Line" was drawn along a narrow street in the old city of Nicosia by the British military authorities. This line has since separated the Turkish quarter of Nicosia from the remainder of the city and has remained a symbol of ethnic division.

In the critical days following the British intervention the initiative shifted to the old British metropolis. London, with strong US backing, attempted to set up a multinational NATO emergency force whose task would be to police the tenuously established truce lines. Greece and Turkey reluctantly agreed with this proposal, but Archbishop Makarios — fearing partition— staunchly opposed a NATO-generated "solution" on Cyprus. After a conference in London between the three guarantor powers and representatives of the two Cypriot communities failed in February 1964, the Government of Cyprus brought the problem to the UN Security Council.

With its resolution of 4 March 1964, the Security Council called on all member states to refrain from actions that might endanger the territorial integrity and independence of Cyprus, urged restraint on all parties and recommended the establishment of an international peace keeping force to be dispatched to Cyprus.[36]

The UN Cyprus Peace Keeping Force (UNFICYP) had as its primary purpose to interpose itself between the combatants after the ceasefire and to act as an objective observer and facilitator of peaceful bargaining. The size of UNFICYP has fluctuated from 6,400 at its peak to about 2,400 at the time of this writing.

UNFICYP was staffed primarily with contingents from Britain, Finland, Canada, Denmark, Ireland and Sweden. It has been divided into brigades, companies, squadrons and other units which are commanded by their national commanders, who, in turn, take their orders from UNFICYP's commanding officer. The force was dispersed throughout the island, patrolling city streets and countryside, in order to discourage the accidental outbreak of local incidents. The UN Secretary General has been represented by a special envoy in Cyprus.

UNFICYP has been responsible to the UN Security Council, which authorizes and renews the Force's life twice a year. However, most day-to-day authority over this Force has been delegated to the Secretary General. Its activities have included the following:

UNFICYP has been acting both as a buffer and a link between the two ethnic communities. UNFICYP's mandate, however, has clearly excluded the "forceful imposition of peace" in Cyprus. So, whenever armed hostilities break out, the role of UNFICYP becomes more political-diplomatic and less military.

In the ten years of its operation between 1964–1974 UNFICYP has performed quite admirably and has been welcome to all sides. The only criticism voiced occasionally argued that UNFICYP unwittingly contributed to the freezing of the status quo (i.e. the de facto separation of the communities), and that its presence has become addictive for all the islanders who have grown psychologically dependent on this externally administered "pain killing" operation. In short, it could be said that UNFICYP managed to control but not to eliminate ethnic conflict, especially when the latter was exacerbated by externally planned interventions in the political affairs of Cyprus.[37]

Since 1963–1964 a stalemate developed between the two communities involving a de facto separation of Greek from Turkish Cypriots. The Turkish Cypriot community was insulated in enclaves scattered throughout the island. These enclaves have been primarily based on the Turkish quarters of the six major cities and on a number of clusters of Turkish villages in the countryside. In the climate of tension and fear prevailing during the ethnic confrontation in 1964, a number of small and isolated Turkish villages and the Turkish quarters of some mixed Greek and Turkish villages were abandoned by their population which moved to the areas that later were consolidated into the enclaves.

Originally this movement appeared as the result of a quest for safety and refuge during the charged up atmosphere of hostilities. As time went by however and life was returning to its normal pace, especially after 1968, it became evident that the creation and sealing off of the enclaves was a measure designed to modify the ethnic demography of Cyprus and create at least a partial geographical basis for a political federation of the island, to replace the unitary state of the Republic of Cyprus.[38] Documentary evidence that has been made available subsequently tends to corroborate this view.[39] The Turkish Cypriot enclaves remained inaccessible to the government of Cyprus and have been virtual no-go areas for Greek Cypriots. The Turks gradually developed separate administrative structures (military, police, taxation and justice) within the enclaves and withdrew from participation in the Cypriot government which remained as the only internationally recognized authority in the island.[40]

It will be realized that the intensification of ethnic differentiation precipitated by the growth of Greek and Turkish nationalism in Cyprus, and the ethnic violence of the 1950s prevented, once Cyprus attained independence, an "integrative revolution" from taking off on the island.[41] In the case of Cyprus the preconditions of some form of social, though probably not ethnic, integration were present in the sociological substratum of traditional coexistence still surviving in the countryside. The institutionalization of ethnic dualism however in the Cyprus constitution and the consequent political climate of communal divisiveness effectively blocked any policy initiatives which might have exploited the potentialities of social change in the direction of some form of integrative evolution rather than foster conflict.

In addition a number of powerful exogenous factors also arrested the possible pattern of coexistence from developing. At the origins of the ethnically based political disintegration of the Republic of Cyprus lay the legacy of British colonial policy, which, as noted earlier, tended to solidify ethnic divisions by means of separate organization of communal groups in the colonial territories.

An even more powerful factor has been the close linkages between the two Cypriot communities with Greece and Turkey respectively.

Since independence, and especially since the constitutional breakdown of 1963–1964 the interethnic intransigence of both Cypriot communities had been considerably fortified by the policies of Greece and Turkey. Both countries, Turkey more effectively than Greece, have been dealing with their respective ethnic communities on Cyprus with scant regard to Cypriot sovereignty. Clearly support and directives emanating from Ankara to the

Turkish Cypriot leadership, have been a major factor in the creation of the enclaves and the promotion of the separation of the two Cypriot communities throughout the 1960s.[42]

Support from Ankara also made possible the neutralization of all moderate elements in the leadership of the Turkish Cypriots and the solidification of the separatist course advocated by the extremists. The escalation of extremism among Turkish Cypriot political elites in turn enabled Turkey to exercise total control and to maintain a firm grip over the enclaves which remained dependent on economic aid and military protection from the mainland.[43]

Conversely, the vitality of the Cypriot economy and the effective political leadership of President Makarios combined to allow a considerable degree of independent initiative in the effort of the Cyprus government to secure the continuing independence of the island. The military dictatorship that came to power in Greece after the coup of 21 April 1967, however, had attempted systematically to quell the independent line of Archbishop Makarios by undermining his authority. The intraethnic conflict that developed among the Greek Cypriots as a consequence, complicated further all attempts at ethnic conflict management in Cyprus, to which we should now turn.

From legal arguments to attempts at conflict resolution: 1964–1974

During the ten years of ethnic crisis (1964–1974), both communities have advanced sets of well-developed legal arguments designed to bolster their respective positions while working substantively on the political level in order to crystalize a status quo consonant with their interests.[44] Archbishop Makarios, the unchallenged spokesman of the Greek Cypriot point of view, has followed the road of seeking a solution through direct negotiations between the communities, while making maximum use of the good offices of the UN General Assembly and minimizing, to the extent possible, influences from Greece, Turkey, Britain, the United States and NATO in general. President Makarios has consistently argued that the 1960 Constitution and the treaties had been forced upon the Cypriot people and that these treaties have been blatantly inequitable.[45] He feels that the provisions of the Treaty Guarantee permitting the intervention of third states (the guarantor powers) as well as the fact that amendment of the Constitution, on which the Cypriot people never had the opportunity to vote, is excluded in eternity, are clearly incompatible with internationally recognized principles of sovereignty and independence.[46]

On the political side the Greek case rests heavily on General Assembly Resolution 2077 (XX) of 18 December 1965 which takes "cognizance of the fact that the Republic of Cyprus, as an equal member of the United Nations is, in accordance with the Charter of the United Nations, entitled to enjoy and should enjoy, full sovereignty and complete independence without any foreign intervention or interference". The Assembly has further called upon all nations, "in conformity with their obligations under the

Charter, and in particular Article 2, paragraphs 1 and 4, to respect the sovereignty, unity, independence and territorial integrity of the Republic of Cyprus and to refrain from any intervention directed against it".[47]

Resting therefore its case on the international recognition of Cyprus's sovereignty and evoking the generally acknowledged principle of majority rule and minority rights, the Cypriot government has offered consistently the following concessions in an attempt to reach compromise over this most thorny interethnic issue:

1. The adoption of a code of fundamental rights to protect the minority;
2. The requirement that the Turkish Cypriot participation in Parliament should be on the basis of proportional representation to the population of the Cypriot Turks;
3. The authorization for the minority to direct the "education, culture, religion and personal status of its members";
4. The acceptance of a UN Commission which would oversee the protection of minority rights for a specified period of time.[48]

The Turkish Cypriot position has also adopted a mixture of legal and political arguments in order to protect its interests. The Turkish Cypriots have accused President Makarios of failing to implement faithfully and equitably the 1960 Constitution from the very beginning. His Thirteen Amendments (November 1963) fly to the very face of Article 182 of the Cyprus Constitution which prohibits amendments. Beyond that, it is an accepted principle of international law that treaties are not subject to unilateral abrogation (*pacta sunt servanda*).[49]

The Turkish view continues by denouncing the Greek Cypriot majority's policies of "exclusion and oppression" which have allegedly been designed to drive the Turkish minority from the island. Thus, the Turkish Cypriots purported to justify their stern resistance and the support they are securing from mainland Turkey on the foundation of Article 4 of the Treaty of Guarantee (1960) which states:

> In the event of a breach of the provisions of the present treaty, Greece, Turkey, and the United Kingdom undertake to consult together with respect to the representations or measures necessary to ensure observance of those provisions.
>
> In so far as common or concerted action may not prove possible, each of the three guaranteeing powers reserves the right to take action with the sole aim of re-establishing the state of affairs created by the present Treaty.[50]

In short the Turkish view initially was that the Zurich and London treaties and the 1960 Constitution remained valid and, as a minimum for a settlement, the parties involved should return to the status quo ante (1963). These remained the positions of the two communities during the period 1964–1974.

While the conflict has been simmering during the past ten years, reaching on occasion (twice in 1964 and once in 1967) peak levels threatening a simultaneous Turkish and Greek intervention in Cyprus which could escalate into a full-scale war between the two countries,[51] efforts have been made to solve the Cyprus problem on at least four levels: a) international; b) regional; c) subregional; and d) local. Basically these four levels could be more simply divided in two: a) solutions imposed on the Cypriots by outside powers versus b) solutions arrived at by intercommunal negotiations between those directly involved by virtue of being the inhabitants of Cyprus.

On the international level of conflict management and resolution efforts the major focus should be on the activities and initiatives of the United Nations in the Cyprus question. During the 1950s, while the struggle for decolonization was going on in Cyprus, Greece and the Greek Cypriots chose the UN as an instrument of policy. Although excluded from the process that brought about the Zurich and London agreements, the UN has proved a useful echo chamber and world public opinion forum generating some serious pressures upon the British to relinquish colonial control over the island. The role of the UN in the 1960s, the postindependence period for Cyprus, has been considerably more active and decisive than in the 1950s largely because the government of Cyprus placed more trust in the mediating efforts of the international organization, insisting that the Cyprus problem was not a Greek-Turkish dispute to be resolved by NATO.[52] We have already spoken about UNFICYP.

Further, the UN Secretary Generals, through their official mediators Sakari S. Tuomioja of Finland and Dr Galo Plaza of Ecuador tried to promote a policy of peaceful coexistence and engagement between the two communities while recognizing the unitary nature of the Cypriot state and recommending as the most likely path to a permanent solution direct negotiations between the Greek and Turkish Cypriots, with the encouragement (but not intervention) of all outside interested parties. In this question particular mention should be made of the Report on the mediating activities submitted by Dr Galo Plaza to the Secretary General in March 1965.[53] This is a document of highly enlightened statesmanship which with its suggestions of political formulas and structural arrangements and its pervading concern for human welfare, could be an invaluable basis of all resolution efforts. The Report, counselling against persistence in the pursuit of union or partition and recommending ample safeguards of the rights of the Turkish Cypriots in a unitary state, was accepted by the government of Cyprus but rejected by the government of Turkey and consequently by the leadership of the Turkish Cypriot community.

So, to summarize, the approach of the international factor has been to leave the solution of the problem to the Cypriots alone and to provide good offices and other mediating and facilitating services from the outside while discouraging great power (US, USSR) and middle power (Great Britain, Greece and Turkey) intervention in the internal affairs of the island.

On the regional level, efforts to solve the Cyprus problem have tended to follow the very direction that the government of Cyprus had constantly tried to avoid. The predominant element on this level has been the efforts of Britain and the United States through NATO to eliminate the last remaining *casus belli* in the affairs of Greece and Turkey, regardless of what this might mean for the fate of Cyprus.[54] As we indicated above, between December 1963 and February 1964 Britain attempted to organize a NATO regional force to supervise the truce in Cyprus.[55] This would have involved a three-month renewable NATO-recruited and British-commanded multi-national force of 10,000 men which would have been placed under the political guidance of a committee of NATO ambassadors. Negotiations would have been enhanced through the efforts of an appointed mediator from a NATO country, other than Greece, Turkey, Great Britain and the United States. Turkey and Greece assented to this plan with some important qualifications. President Makarios, however, objected and asked instead for a force which would have been responsible to the UN rather than NATO. This, of course, was in keeping with the Cypriot policy of strategic nonalignment and active participation in the Third World movement.

The NATO level activities assumed a far more aggressive and interventionist nature under the initiative of the United States. In July of 1964 President Lyndon B. Johnson appointed the veteran diplomat Dean Acheson as a special mediator for Cyprus. Acheson's view was that the problem should be solved by direct agreement of Greece and Turkey within the spirit of the NATO alliance. This meant that the Cypriots, above all Archbishop Makarios, need not and should not necessarily be consulted. In the last analysis, a solution would have to be imposed upon the two warring Cypriot communities. Specifically, the plan woven by the aging diplomat would have taken the outward form of enosis of Cyprus with Greece, and by extension, assured entry of Cyprus into the NATO complex. The Turkish side, however, would have been pacified with territorial concessions in the form of a sizable sovereign or leased base, extensive guarantees for the Turkish minority and the development of Turkish cantons in the Greek- controlled portion of Cyprus.[56]

The Greek and Turkish governments initially accepted, in principle and quite cautiously, the Acheson proposals. President Makarios, however, denounced the plan as a barely disguised form of partition of Cyprus which was totally unacceptable to the interests of the Greek Cypriot population. Despite difficult odds and unbearable pressures upon the Archbishop, his views somehow managed to withstand the regional/strategic pressures orchestrated by the United States in the framework of the NATO alliance.

Perhaps the most important dimension added by the US to the Cyprus imbroglio has been in the US's restraining influence over Greece and Turkey to avoid an outbreak of war between them. For example, the US through a series of emissaries and mediators, has continuously counselled prudence and urged a negotiated settlement to be reached between Greece and Turkey. George Ball's trip to Cyprus in February 1964, Lyndon Johnson's telegram to Premier

Inonu in July 1964 strongly counselling against Turkish intervention in Cyprus, Dean Ache – son's mediating efforts in July 1964, and Cyrus Vance's frenzied activity in November of 1967, all illustrate this type of activity. A major departure from this style has been Secretary Henry Kissinger's orchestrated apathy vis-a-vis the bloody events of July–August 1974 in Cyprus.

The subregional level focuses on the efforts of Greece and Turkey to safeguard their national interests in Cyprus. Whether one speaks of the pre- or postindependence period of Cyprus (i.e. before and after 1960), it would be a safe assumption to make that both Greece and Turkey have placed their own general security requirements, and by extension their NATO obligations, as well as their domestic political exigencies on a higher priority than any concern they might have had with the welfare of their ethnic brothers in Cyprus.

As we have already pointed out, both Greece and Turkey have attempted to penetrate and control their respective ethnic counterparts in Cyprus, perceiving the two Cypriot communities as clients or, more euphemistically, junior partners. Naturally, Turkey has found it much easier to control the utterly dependent and economically depressed Turkish enclaves. On the contrary, President Makarios and the Cypriot government have proven a harder nut to crack, to the point that, particularly in the post-1967 period, one could say that the controlling influence of the Athens government was considerably weakened in Nicosia. This was made abundantly clear in February 1972, when President Makarios ignored a public ultimatum from Athens to drastically restructure his government or resign. He did neither and survived.[57]

It was thus becoming increasingly clear that in view of the Cypriots' resistance — which was eloquently expressed in the overwhelming popular support enjoyed by President Makarios — as well as because of the objections voiced by the Soviet Union, NATO could not impose an Acheson type solution, short of using drastic military means. This created the political preconditions of a negotiated settlement to be reached through intercommunal talks, presumably premised primarily not on foreign strategic interests but on considerations over the welfare and interests of the Cypriots themselves.

This leads us to the local level of settlement efforts through direct negotiations of the two Cypriot communities. Thus we come full circle since the objectives and methods of conflict resolution encouraged on the international level have been essentially the same as the strategy of the intercommunal talks. Negotiations were initiated in June 1968 and continued in several phases until mid-1974 between Messrs Clerides and Denktash representing the two ethnic communities. At a later stage two constitutional experts from Greece and Turkey were included to assist the two principal negotiators. The special representative of the UN General Secretary in Cyprus, attended as well.

The discussions covered many of the constitutional problems raised by the ethnic conflict and although the content of the negotiations remained secret, informed sources repeatedly intimated that significant progress was being made. At the later stages of the talks, substantive disagreement was narrowed down over the issue of local government—the Greek side conceding that considerable decentralization was desirable but also insisting that the jurisdiction and functions of local government should not be such as to create essentially the infrastructure of a communal Turkish state within the unitary state of Cyprus.[58]

We believe that the intercommunal negotiations were the appropriate method of conflict resolution because they provided a channel of direct communication between spokesmen of the two ethnic Cypriot communities. In such a context misperceptions and misconceptions could be discussed and cleared up, common interests realized and the bases of agreement identified, if only good will would prevail.[59] The preconditions of a successful strategy of conflict resolution were indeed present in Cyprus and should have been apparent to any perceptive observer of the situation on the island during the past several years, despite the muted confrontation of the two communities.

To begin with there was the sociological basis of interethnic coexistence and co-operation which had not just been historically the feature of life in Cypriot traditional society but had survived largely intact in the ethnically mixed communities of rural Cyprus. The constructive record of the UNFICYP in conflict containment, added another useful precondition of conflict resolution. The UNFICYP could be used as an impartial police force to provide the necessary protection and security to all Cypriots once all other armed forces were removed from the scene. If the Greek and Turkish contingents and military personnel were removed from Cyprus and the National Guard and the Turkish Cypriot fighting units were disbanded, not only the probability of recurrent collisions and explosions would be effectively checked, but also considerable funds would be economized to finance the stationing of a neutral and periodically rotating international force on a semipermanent basis in Cyprus to act as an arbitrator and observer of the would-be settlement.[60] We think that such a situation would guarantee effectively the security of the Turkish Cypriots so that they could feel free and safe to come out of the self-imposed seclusion of the enclaves and participate in the life of Cyprus. By guaranteeing peace and security therefore a permanent Cyprus UN police force could help create both the practical mechanisms and the psychological climate of ethnic reintegration.

But most important of all the new directions emerging in the political life of Cyprus and the dynamics of economic development seemed to be working in favour of an accommodation of the conflict. Politically the growth of moderation and realism had led to the conclusion that the pursuit of independent statehood was the safest course for Cyprus. This became official policy when in 1965 the government of Cyprus formally accepted the recommendations of UN Mediator Dr Galo Plaza who explicitly counselled against persisting in the pursuit of enosis. In repeated democratic elections the Greek Cypriot community had confirmed this policy by casting overwhelmingly their votes in support of Archbishop Makarios and his supporters and the "feasible" solution (i.e. independence) they advocated. This meant that the most fundamental and uncompromising demand of the Turkish Cypriots was met and consequently the way for an accommodation should have been open. Another hopeful indication in this direction was the emergence of socially based political parties which could conceivably cut into the ethnic cleavage as earlier instances of interethnic co-operation in trade unions or in the cause of Cypriot independence might suggest.[61]

Economically the fast rate of growth and industrial expansion[62] had broadened the labour market and thus Turkish Cypriot workers who were kept secluded and idle in the enclaves could join the labour force and thus be economically reintegrated into Cypriot society as they had been in the past. Normal contacts could be resumed in all commercial and industrial areas once the separatist policy "from Turk to Turk" pressed on the Turkish Cypriots by their leaders, was modified or dropped. The economic reintegration of Cypriot society might also provide the means of redressing the inequalities in the levels of economic development of the two communities, thus removing one of the underlying structural sources of conflict.[63] Indeed by the early 1970s increasing numbers of Turkish Cypriot workers were employed in projects of public works and general economic exchanges tended to be resumed between the two communities. Normal economic relations had never of course been severed in the agrarian economy of mixed rural communities.

With these trends in mind it is plausible to argue that the social and political context was ripe for a commonly acceptable Constitutional formula satisfying the basic needs and long-standing objections of both sides and setting up the institutional framework of effective conflict resolution and social reintegration. To meet these requirements a viable model for Cyprus would have to be based on independence by ruling out all forms of union and partition. The institutional set-up should be premised on decentralization to allow ethnic autonomy and sharing in the central institutions of power to secure the integrated character of the state. The constitutional infrastructure of reintegration could be established if a number of divisive provisions of the 1960 Constitution were amended. For instance the Greek President and the Turkish Vice President would have to be elected by the entire population of the island. The representation of the Turkish side in Parliament, the bureaucracy and the security forces would have to be analogous to the percentage of Turkish population (18 per cent) rather than ranging up to 30 or 40 per cent. On the other hand considerable autonomy and self-management would have to be recognized to the Turkish communities of the island in conducting their local and broadly cultural affairs (religion, education, etc.) to reassure them in their desire to preserve their highly valued ethnic identity.[64] International guarantees could have been adopted to oversee and secure the effective operation of this autonomy. The Parliament however would have to be divided into Greek and Turkish caucuses voting separately only on residual matters dealing exclusively with intracommunity affairs. The experience of 1960–1963 had amply demonstrated that the entire Parliament would have to vote as a cohesive unit, abolishing the requirement of securing separate majorities of each ethnic caucus on all important legislation.

This was not an inconceivable way in which events could have developed and Cyprus might have become a model case of a fair resolution of ethnic conflict. Unfortunately the positive trends outlined above, were not allowed to come to fruition. Ethnic dualism has not been the only or even the primary cause of conflict in Cyprus. The dynamics of conflict resolution were effectively blocked by outside interference. Thus every time the intercommunal talks seemed to reach a point of substantial agreement on fundamental issues, the trend was reversed by the behind the scenes manipulation of the Turkish Cypriot negotiator by the Turkish government in Ankara.[65] Writing with events since July 1974 in mind, we can assert with considerable certainty that despite its grudging endorsement of the interethnic negotiations, Turkish policy never abandoned the pursuit of partition which was first suggested by Britain in the 1950s and was later presented as the official Turkish view on Cyprus to the UN Mediator in 1965.[66] In the background of this posture was the fact that manipulation of the Cyprus issue in Turkish internal politics had proved a convenient diversion of attention from pressing domestic problems.[67]

In the pursuit of this aim Turkey was fortified by US policy which has favoured some form of partition of Cyprus between Greece and Turkey—thus achieving both the eradication of a cause of conflict threatening the solidity of the southeastern flank of NATO and the incorporation of Cyprus, a territory with some strategic value,[68] within the boundaries of two members of the Western alliance. The disappearance of Cyprus as a sovereign Republic would also terminate the independent and neutralist outlook in the foreign policy of President Makarios — a policy resented by the Cold Warriors in Washington. This is adequately indicated, we think, by US insistence on a settlement of Cyprus within NATO in the 1950s, by the Acheson plans promoted during the crisis of the mid-1960s and finally by American acquiescence in if not support for the Turkish invasion and violent partition of Cyprus in the summer of 1974. Probably the most eloquent indication of American attitudes on the problem of Cyprus is offered by the vote the USA cast against the innocuous resolution affirming the independence and sovereignty of Cyprus, passed by the UN General Assembly in December 1965.[69]

Greece was also converted to the line of some form of NATO-oriented partition, once the military dictatorship rose to power in 1967.[70] The Athens colonels felt that some territorial concessions to Turkey would be desirable in order to satisfy the atavistic aspirations of Greek irredentist nationalism. Apparently such a foreign manoeuvre was expected to generate some popular sympathy for the repressive military regime. Hence the encouragement and direction of the several moves to unseat President Makarios.

The pattern of intraethnic discoid that the Greek military regime encouraged in the ranks of the Greek Cypriot community escalated in the formation of extremist underground armed groups like the National Front (1969–1970) and EOKA-B (1971–1974) which preached a revival of the enosis movement.[71] These developments in turn exacerbated the fears of the Turkish Cypriots and undermined further the efforts at an accommodation of ethnic differences. Deprived of popular sympathy the campaigns of extreme right-wing subversion and terrorism failed to unseat President Makarios who won re-election for a third term in 1973. Several documents captured during police operations against EOKA-B terrorism, clearly implicated the Greek junta and Greek officers serving in Cyprus. In a now famous letter to the figurehead President of dictatorial Greece, Archbishop Makarios expressed his abhorrence for military regimes and demanded the termination of the disastrous activities of the junta in Cyprus. As political oppression and bankruptcy were reaching their climax in Greece, the junta responded by engineering the coup of 15 July 1974. This coup and the subsequent Turkish invasion have left Cyprus in the tragic condition which we described at the beginning of this chapter.[72]

From the point of view of the future of the ethnic conflict the most momentous effect of the Turkish invasion, is the forceful demographic change imposed on the occupied areas of Northern Cyprus. This consists of a policy of moving Turkish settlers (either infiltrators from the south or colonists from Asia Minor) into Greek villages and towns to occupy the properties of refugee Greek Cypriots.[73] The process of forceful demographic transformation is placed in its proper symbolic context by turkicizing place names, by destroying monuments of Greek culture, by turning Orthodox churches into mosques and by erecting statues of Kemal Ataturk in the occupied areas. We cannot forecast what the precise outcome of all this is going to be but there can be no doubt that it will have a powerful impact on the future pattern of interethnic relations in Cyprus and elsewhere.

Epilogue

Whenever Cyprus captured the attention of students of politics it did so as an international problem, an element in strategy and power relations in the Eastern Mediterranean. What has come to be known as the Cyprus Question, essentially a leftover of the Eastern Question of old, has fundamentally involved the issue of control over a strategically located island on the threshold of the Near East. In this chapter we have tried to shift focus from the international to the domestic aspect of conflict over Cyprus by considering the emergence and unfolding of the ethnic dispute which has dominated the politics of the island for many years. (For the benefit of those readers who are interested in the international aspects of the problem of Cyprus, we have included all the relevant literature in the references.)

From a theoretical point of view we have tried to point at the relation between the workings of social change and the evolution of the ethnic conflict. The most significant finding in this connection seems to have been the fact that despite the effort to concentrate on domestic social and political processes, it is ultimately impossible to consider the nature of ethnic conflict in Cyprus without discussing international politics — especially at all those points when instability and strife escalate on the island. This points at the

close linkages between the politics of inter- and intraethnic conflict in Cyprus
with international power politics in the area. Instability in Cyprus tends to be
telescoped and engulf the politics and foreign relations of Greece and Turkey,
and through the 1950s and early 1960s British imperial policy in the Middle
East as well. All this in turn affects the international equilibrium in
a sensitive and fragile geopolitical region. Conversely, conflict and instability
in Cyprus are influenced, and domestic developments are often distorted by
the attempts of outside powers to shape the political situation in the Eastern
Mediterranean in their own interest. Thus through a variety of social and political processes internal conflict in Cyprus is internationalized and therefore
its outcome becomes dependent upon external factors.[74]

Throughout this chapter it ought to have been clear that external sources
contributed greatly to the stimulation and exacerbation of conflict within
Cyprus. At the initial stages British colonial policy and the nationalist influences emanating from Greece and Turkey provided the context and the
momentum needed for the escalation of ethnic strife. Later on, Cold War
American policies advanced through NATO nurtured the conflict indirectly
first and more directly in the recent past (early 1970s)[75] in order to achieve
the partition and NATOization of Cyprus. In this phase both Greece and
Turkey became — willingly and consciously — the channels through which
systemic NATO pressures were exercised on Cyprus, a nonmember of the
alliance. The close historical, national and social ties of the island with
these two countries ultimately provided the most effective conduits to those
who knew how to manipulate these intimate ethnic bonds in order to undermine and subvert the Republic of Cyprus. The contribution that the experience of Cyprus has therefore to make to the comparative study of ethnic
conflict concerns primarily the importance of exogenous sources in the creation and intensification of communal antagonism.

Still the force of this claim rests significantly on the evidence that one can
adduce in support of an argument that in the absence of outside pressures
ethnic conflict could have been regulated in the context of democratic coexistence and elimination of violent confrontation. In this chapter we have
pointed out a number of indications, possibilities and trends which could be
interpreted in this light. Indeed the history of Cyprus is as much one of
ethnic diversity and conflict as it is a history of ethnic coexistence.
A reading of this history clearly suggests that ethnic conflict may have been
equally the result of certain political choices and political misjudgements
within Cyprus as it was the outcome of outside policies. But it is equally
clear from the historical record that after the bitter experience of violent
conflict both a maturity of political wills and the direction of social developments were pointing confidently toward conflict resolution.

There is nothing inexorable about ethnic conflict: complete ethnic assimilation and the creation of new unified nationalities is probably unrealistic to
expect — and certainly we should not be understood to mean this when we
talked of the possibilities of conflict resolution and political reintegration.

But this is beside the point: ethnic coexistence based on mutual accommodation of fundamental needs and aspirations has proved possible wherever appropriate motivations could be put to work.[76] What outside interference did in Cyprus was precisely to stifle the motivation for conflict regulation whenever it appeared. As a consequence Cyprus was never given even the chance to resolve its ethnic and political problems on its own. On the contrary both ethnic conflict and intraethnic dissension were always effectively manipulated by outside powers to promote their own objectives and designs on Cyprus. In this sense conflict within Cypriot society provided the needed opportunities to foreign intervention.

Therefore the claim that communal separation is the only workable solution to ethnic conflicts and, in the case of Cyprus, partition is the only alternative to continuing violence, appears very much like a self-fulfilling prophecy and conceptually is perhaps not unrelated to the failure of theories of ethnic conflict and political integration to take into account the disruptive effects of foreign interference. Characteristically the argument for partition is advanced in the case of Cyprus but not in connection with many other ethnically diverse societies ridden with communal problems. Indeed in Cyprus partition could be achieved only at the price of a bloody invasion, a vicious war and a policy of genocide designed to destroy the basis of ethnic coexistence before any other alternative strategies of conflict resolution could be tested: the development of class-based democratic politics to supplant ethnic cleavages, the new loyalties that a development-oriented welfare state could have nurtured, the shared stakes in a developing economy, a cultural dialogue to replace the antagonism of traditional nationalist symbols and stereotypes with the discovery of common experiences and values. All of these carried real possibilities of peace and co-operation and it is for this reason that the fate of Cyprus is all the more tragic.

Postscript

This profile of ethnic conflict in Cyprus was originally written in an attempt to increase awareness over the basic issues of the problem, after the dramatic explosion of the summer of 1974. The chronicle of ethnic politics on the island and pertinent international developments draws on relatively well-established facts of history. Caught as we are in a continuing and fast-moving crisis, however, we must update in this postscript our references to more recent events. When this chapter was written, an economic collapse of the badly shaken Republic of Cyprus, seemed within the sphere of probability. Fortunately, this has not happened. Instead a miracle of economic survival seems to have been achieved, with outside assistance of course but drawing largely on the mobilization of the island's own human and material resources. This achievement points once again at the soundness of public policy and the viability of a Cypriot polity. Survival, nevertheless, does not mean recovery; and full recovery cannot be realistically contemplated before the root cause of the disaster is removed: that is foreign occupation of a large part of the island must first be terminated before reconstruction can be attempted on safe foundations. The fact of survival only points at the will and ability of the Cypriots to come to grips with their predicament.

This note of optimism is not meant to suggest that the odds of the problem are decreasing. If anything the possibility of a settlement is made more remote by the intensification of certain trends which we noted in closing our account of ethnic relations in the main body of the chapter. The colonization of occupied nothern Cyprus, by settlers from Asia Minor was stepped up in the fall of 1975. Anatolian peasants, out of the ethnological mosaic of Asia Minor, continued to be transported to Cyprus to change the ethnic balance in the population. The colonization has provoked not only the outcry of the Greek Cypriots, especially the refugees at whose expense the colonists are settled in occupied villages and towns, but also it has met with the discontent of the Turkish Cypriots who resent the presence of the intruders and in general the ruthless comportment of the occupation forces.

One of the most unfortunate developments in ethnic relations in the second half of 1975 has been the forced emigration to the north of the Turkish Cypriots of southern Cyprus. These people were forced, at the insistence of their leadership, to abandon their villages and urban quarters in Paphos, Limassol and Larnaca and become involuntary migrants to the north. This was the product of a deal during intercommunal talks in Vienna in July 1975. The movement of the Turkish Cypriots from the south was secured in exchange of the toleration of the continuing presence of the Greek Cypriot population in occupied Karpass and the improvement of their treatment by the occupation forces. However a few months later, pressures on this unfortunate rural population are escalated to force them away from their ancestral hearths.

Thus the pattern of ethnic coexistence as it was set by a long-shared history, is in the process of radical transformation. All this of course is brought about in order to create the conditions of a settlement that will finally meet the traditional Turkish objective of expansion in Cyprus, which at the moment is presented in the legal nomenclature of bizonal federation (after assuming in the past successively the names of partition, functional federation, cantonization, etc.). There can be no doubt that any such arrangement will not solve the problem, but it will only perpetuate the confrontation in all its intensity. Bizonal federation in the form, demanded by Turkey will bring not only effective partition but also the establishment of a Turkish protectorate over the whole of Cyprus. The endemic instability that will certainly result will provide Turkey with new pretexts to complete the annexation of Cyprus in its entirety.

In any case the invasion and consequent dismemberment of Cyprus has radically altered the nature of the problem. It is not anymore a question of finding a constitutional modus vivendi between two ethnic communities. This of course remains one of the central issues but the most immediate and urgent problem at this moment is the fact of foreign invasion and occupation of a large part of the territory of a sovereign Republic. The problem is now more than ever before truly international and it is up to the international community to exercise pressures and impose sanctions upon its delinquent member to abide by the rules of world society and the law of nations. Only after the rectification of this grave violation of international law, can the problem of ethnic relations and the efforts for an accommodation return to the centre of the stage where they deserve to be. Once again we fall back on the international dimension of the problem and the distortion of ethnic politics by outside factors. And by way of conclusion we may note that Congressional investigations under way in Washington at the moment of this writing, are producing evidence vindicating our allegations about direct American involvement in the latest crisis. After all it seems that either frenzied shuttle diplomacy or orchestrated apathy have always been designed to promote the same objectives. Once the full details of this activity are made public, it will be up to a critical social science, studying the nature of contemporary imperialism, to establish the precise reasons for this involvement.

Figure 10.2 "Flight". Woodcut by Telemachos Kanthos (1977).

Notes

1 In preparing this chapter we benefited from the comments of Simon Simeonides of the Harvard Law School and Daniel P. Tompkins of Swarthmore College.

2 See Samuel P. Huntington, "Civil Violence and the Process of Development", *Adelphi Papers*, no. 83 (December 1971), pp. 1–15. Civil violence is used here to denote violence within states in contradistinction to international violence.

3 See Walker Connor, "Self Determination: The New Phase", *World Politics* 20, no. 1 (October 1967), pp. 30–53 and *idem*, "Nation Building or Nation Destroying?", *World Politics* 24, no. 3 (April 1972), pp. 319–355. For a recent analysis of the relation between social change and ethnic conflict see Daniel Bell, "Ethnicity and Social Change" in *Ethnicity: Theory and Experience*, ed. by Nathan Glazer and Daniel P. Moynihan, Cambridge, MA: Harvard University Press, 1975, pp. 141–174.

4 The recent volume edited by Glazer and Moynihan, *Ethnicity, op. cit.*, is a significant contribution but does not cover the experience of all ethnically diverse societies.

5 As of this writing sources on the 1974 crisis include mainly press reports and primary documents. For good political accounts by an experienced journalist see the series of articles by Stanley Karnow in the *New Republic*, 7 September to 5 October 1975 and *idem*, "America's Mediterranean Bungle", *The Atlantic*, February 1975 (vol. 235, no. 2), p. 6 ff. Useful reports on the crisis have appeared in all major news publications. Note for instance *The New York Times*, 9 September 1974, p. 8 and *Le Monde Diplomatique*, August 1974, no. 245, pp. 1, 4–6. The following Congressional documents contain valuable information on the crisis and the role of the United States: House Foreign Affairs Committee, Subcommittee on Europe, *Cyprus 1974*, Hearings, 93rd Congress, Second Session, 19 and 20 August 1974, Washington, DC, 1974; Senate Committee on the Judiciary, Subcommittee on Refugees, *Humanitarian Problems on Cyprus*, Hearings, 93rd Congress, Second Session, 26 September 1974, Washington, DC, 1974 and Senate Committee on the Judiciary, Subcommittee on Refugees, *Crisis on Cyprus: 1974*, Study Mission Report, 93rd Congress, Second Session, 14 October 1974, Washington, DC, 1974.

6 Detailed documentation on the problem of the refugees is available in the Study Mission Report, *Crisis on Cyprus 1974*, cited above, pp. 18–43 and in Senate Committee of the Judiciary, Subcommittee on Refugees, *World Hunger, Health and Refugee Problems, Part V: Human Disasters in Cyprus, Bangladesh, Africa*, Hearings, 93rd Congress, Second Session, 20 August 1974, Washington, DC 1974, pp. 1–23, 163–196. For the human aspect of the regugee problem see the two articles by Brigadier Michael Harbottle in *The Times* (London), 17 and 21 October 1974.

7 According to a Memorandum made available to the authors by the Government of Cyprus, some quantitative indicators of destruction are the following: (a) Overall economic damage: 350 million Cyprus pounds; (b) Damage to household properties: 100 million Cyprus pounds; (c) Forest destroyed: 100 square miles (20% of the total forested area in Cyprus); (d) Losses from tourism: 30 million Cyprus pounds.

8 See the reports in *The New York Times*, 27 January 1975, p. 12 and ibid., 29 January 1975, p. 6 and *Christian Science Monitor*, 8 January 1975, p. 3A. The Planning Bureau of the Republic of Cyprus has compiled a useful factual report: *Economic Consequences of Turkish Invasion*, Nicosia, Public Information Office, October, 1974.

9 For an analysis of these aspects of the problem see the interpretative essay by Paschalis M. Kitromilides, "Cyprus: The Nature of Ethnic Conflict", in *US Foreign Policy toward Greece and Cyprus*, eds by Th. A. Couloumbis and S. M. Hicks, Washington, DC: The Center for Mediterranean Studies, 1975, pp. 83–97, an expanded version of which appears as chapter IX in this collection.

10 For the meaning of *millet* and the *millet* system see Bernard Lewis, *The Emergence of Modern Turkey*, London: Oxford University Press, 1968, p. 335.

11 For the history of Cyprus as an Ottoman province see Sir George Hill, *A History of Cyprus* IV, Cambridge: Cambridge University Press, 1952, Part I, pp. 1–400; Sir Harry C. Luke, *Cyprus under the Turks 1571–1878*, London: Oxford University Press, 1921; Doros Alastos, *Cyprus in History*, London: Zeno Publishers, 1955, pp. 234–301. For the ethnological evolution of the population of Cyprus in this period see Theodore Papadopoullos, *Social and Historical Data on Population, 1570–1881*, Nicosia: Cyprus Research Centre, 1965. For the problem of conversions to Islam see the evidence presented in *idem*, "Πρόσφατοι Ἐξισλαμισμοὶ Ἀγροτικοῦ Πληθυσμοῦ ἐν Κύπρῳ", *Κυπριακαὶ Σπουδαὶ* 29 (1965), pp. 27–48. Cf. C. F. Beckingham, "The Turks of Cyprus", *The Journal of the Royal Anthropological Institute* 87, Part II (July–December 1957), pp. 165–174.

12 For the historical character of the phenomenon of Greek-Turkish symbiosis see the monumental work by Speros Vryonis, Jr., *The Decline of Medieval Hellenism in Asia Minor and the Process of Islamization from the Eleventh to the Fifteenth Century*, Los Angeles: University of California Press, 1971, especially pp. 444–497. Cf. Paschalis M. Kitromilides, "Ὁ εξισλαμισμός της Μικρας Ασίας και οι ιστορικές καταβολές των ἑλληνοτουρκικῶν σχέσεων', *Μικρασιατικὰ Χρονικὰ* XVI (1975), pp. 318–337.

13 For a detailed account see D. E. Lee, *Great Britain and the Cyprus Convention Policy of 1878, Harvard Historical Studies*, no. 38, Cambridge, MA, 1934.

14 Hill, *A History of Cyprus*, pp. 518–519.

15 For politics under the British *ibid.*, Part II and Alastos, *Cyprus in History,* pp. 302–381. For the earlier period of British rule the most detailed account is that by Philios Zannetos, *Ἱστορία τῆς Νήσου Κύπρου ἀπὸ τῆς Ἀγγλικῆς κατοχῆς μέχρι σήμερον* II, Larnaca, 1911.

16 For an analysis of this process see Adamantia Pollis, "Systemic Factors and the Failure of Political Integration in Cyprus", paper presented at the International Studies Association Convention, Washington, DC, February 1975, pp. 14–21.

17 The account of the *enosis* movement in Hill, *op. cit.,* pp. 488–568 is very detailed but obviously biased and lacks any wider perspective. It should be read in the light of Alastos, *op. cit.,* p. 330 ff. and Michel Dendias, *La Question Chypriote au point de vue historique et de droit international*, Paris: Sirey, 1934 which is still the most adequate treatment of the enosis movement. The best account of the 1931 uprising is still perhaps that by Arnold Toynbee, *Survey of International Affairs, 1931*, London: Oxford University Press, 1932, pp. 354–394.

18 Cf. *Treaty of Peace with Turkey,* Signed at Lausanne on 24 July 1923, Cmd 1929, London, H.M. Stationary Office, 1923. Note Article 16 (p. 21) by which Turkey renounces all rights of sovereignty on territories outside her frontiers as specified in the treaty; and Article 20 (p. 23) by which Turkey recognizes the annexation of Cyprus by Britain.

19 Developments in Cyprus between 1946–1959 are covered in detail in the recent two volume work of François Crouzet, *Le Conflit de Chypre, 1946–1959*, Brussels: Bruylant, 1973.

20 *Ibid.*, Vol. I, pp. 266–277. For the reactions of the Turkish Cypriots, pp. 303–307.

21 *Survey of International Affairs 1954*, by Coral Bell, London: Oxford University Press, 1957, pp. 173–184. The British attitude was expressed in the refusal of Prime Minister Eden to discuss the future of Cyprus with Greek Prime Minister Papagos and in the statement by the Minister of State at the Colonial Office Henry Hopkinson in the House of Commons that change of sovereignty over Cyprus could never be contemplated. All this could and was interpreted

by the Greek government and the Greek Cypriots to mean that a settlement through direct Anglo-Greek diplomacy was not possible. For relevant documents see *Documents on International Affairs 1954*, ed. by D. Folliot, London: Oxford University Press, 1957, pp. 227–242. See also Stephen G. Xydis, "Toward Toil and Moil in Cyprus", *The Middle East Journal* 20, no. 1 (Winter 1966), pp. 1–19, for events leading up to the outbreak of the anticolonial struggle in Cyprus.

22 On the EOKA struggle see Doros Alastos, *Cyprus Guerilla: Grivas, Makarios and the British*, London: Heinemann, 1960 and Charles Foley, *Island in Revolt*, London: Longmans, 1962. Crouzet, *Le Conflit de Chypre* II, pp. 481–649 provides the most recent and synthetic account drawing on voluminous documentation.

23 For the theoretical foundation of these views cf. Karl W. Deutsch, *Nationalism and Sosial Communication*, Cambridge, MA: M.I.T. Press, 1953. For a conceptualization of the political implications of socio-economic change, on which the previous discussion is based, see *idem*, "Social Mobilization and Political Development", *The American Political Science Review* LV, no. 3 (September 1961), pp. 493–514.

24 On the precipitation of ethnic conflict by the approach of independence cf. Cynthia H. Enloe, *Ethnic Conflict and Political Development*, Boston: Little, Brown, 1973, p. 22: "... as soon as independence or foreign economic pressures make interdependence and pooling of scarce resources imperative, institutional expressions of cultural separateness become threats to stability, instead of the assurances of social harmony they once were".

25 See Adamantia Pollis, "Intergroup Conflict and British Colonial Policy, The Case of Cyprus", *Comparative Politics* 5, no. 4 (July 1973), pp. 575–599. For the historical origins of this policy cf. Ronald Robinson and John Gallagher, *Africa and the Victorians*, Garden City: Doubleday, 1968, pp. 10–11.

26 The escalation of conflict in the 1950s has stimulated voluminous writing on the Cyprus Question, including many accounts by journalists, official papers and many pamphlets explaining the respective viewpoints of those involved. The bibliography of primary sources in Crouzet, *Le Conflit de Chypre* II, pp. 1155–1166, though incomplete is very useful. Robert Stephens, *Cyprus. A Place of Arms*, London: Pall Mall, 1966 is a useful account by a distinguished journalist with great experience in the politics of the Eastern Mediterranean. Important scholarly studies of this phase of the problem of Cyprus are, in addition to Crouzet, Stephen G. Xydis, *Cyprus: Conflict and Conciliation, 1954–1958*, Colombus: Ohio State University Press, 1967; Leontios Ierodiakonou, *The Cyprus Question*, Stockholm, Almquist and Wiksell, 1971, and Pantazis Terlexis, *Διπλωματία και Πολιτική του Κυπριακού: Ανατομία ενός λάθους*, Athens: Rappas, 1971. The most serious statement of the Turkish point of view is that by Suat Bilge, *Le Conflit de Chypre et les Chypriotes Turcs*, Ankara: Publications de la Faculté des Sciences Politiques de l'Université d'Ankara, 1961. Finally a valuable source of information, criticism and insights is Ch. Chrestides, *Κυπριακό κα Ελληνοτουρκικά: Πορεία μιας εθνικής χρεωκοπίας*, Athens, 1967.

27 The pertinent documents appear in Royal Institute of International Affairs, *Documents on International Affairs 1958, 1959*, ed. by G. King, *1960* (ed. by R. Gott), London Oxford University Press, 1962, 1963, 1964, pp. 376–395, 541–552, 422–427, respectively. The complex diplomacy of the years 1958–1960 leading up to the independence of Cyprus, is studied in great detail in Stephen G. Xydis, *Cyprus: Reluctant Republic*, The Hague: Mouton, 1973.

28 For the impact of the Cyprus problem on the politics of Greece see Theodore A. Couloumbis, *Greek Political Reaction to American and NATO Influences*,

New Haven: Yale University Press, 1966, p. 93 ff. For Turkey, Frank Tachau, "The Face of Turkish Nationalism as reflected in the Cyprus Dispute", *The Middle East Journal* XIII, no. 3 (Summer 1959), pp. 262–272. For the British decision to relinquish sovereignty over Cyprus see Naomi Rosenbaum, "Success in Foreign Policy: The British in Cyprus, 1878–1960", *Canadian Journal of Political Science* III, no. 4 (December 1970), pp. 605–627.

29 For the text of the Treaties of Guarantee and Establishment see *United Nations Treaty Series* 382, 1960, pp. 3–16. Several pages of Annexes to the Treaty of Establishment follow. The Treaty of Alliance appears *ibid.* 397, 1961, pp. 287–295.

30 The Cyprus Constitution is analyzed in Stanley Kyriakides, *Cyprus: Constitutionalism and Crisis Government*, Philadelphia: University of Pennsylvania Press, 1968, pp. 53–71.

31 Cf. the analysis and evaluation in S. A. de Smith, *The New Commonwealth and Its Constitutions*, London: Stevens, 1964, pp. 282–296. Note the characteristic remark on p. 285: "Constitutionalism has run riot in harness with communalism".

32 Kyriakides, *op. cit.*, pp. 72–103.

33 *Ibid.*, pp. 85–86 for revealing views of Turkish Cypriot deputies.

34 The text of President Makarios's thirteen proposed amendments appears in *International Relations* (Athens) II, no. 5, April 1964, pp. 8–24. Cf. Dimitri Bitsios, Κρίσιμες Ώρες, Athens 1973, pp. 134–137 [English translation: *Cyprus, Vulnerable Republic*, Thessaloniki 1975], on the encouragement given to the Archbishop in this initiative by the then British High Commissioner in Cyprus.

35 For accounts of the 1963–1964 crisis see Charles Foley, *Legacy of Strife: Cyprus Form Rebellion to Civil War*, Baltimore: Penguin, 1964; Stephens, *Cyprus: A Place of Arms*, pp. 168–191; Kyriakides, *Cyprus: Constitutionalism*, pp. 104–134, which is based on detailed primary source documentation; George S. Harris, *Troubled Alliance: Turkish-American Problems in Historical Perspective, 1945–1971*, Stanford: Hoover Institution Press, 1972, p. 105 ff, which brings the story up to the 1967 crisis. On US involvement in that crisis see Edward Weintal and Charles Bartlett, *Facing the Brink*, New York: Scribner, 1967, pp. 16–36. For relevant documents see *American Foreign Policy Current Documents 1964*, Department of State Publication 8253, Released August 1967, pp. 555–603.

36 Text of the resolution in *19 United Nations Security Council Official Record, Supplement*, January-March 1964, pp. 102–103, UN Doc. S/5575 (1964). For the appeal and the debates see *19 UN SCOR*, Meetings 1094 to 1103 (17 February to 13 March 1964).

37 Detailed accounts on the activities of the UNFICYP are provided in the reports submitted by the UN Secretary General to the Security Council every six months since 1964 and published in the Supplements of the SCOR (usually in the June and December issues). An important contribution to the subject is that by Michael Harbottle, *The Impartial Soldier*, London, Oxford University Press, 1970. Cf. also James Stegenga, "UN Peacekeeping: The Cyprus Venture", *Journal of Peace Research* 7, no. 1 (1970), pp. 1–15.

38 Cf. Kemal H. Karpat, "Solution in Cyprus: Federation", *The Cyprus Dilemma: Options for Peace*, New York: Institute for Mediterranean Affairs, 1967, pp. 35–54. This essay expressing the Turkish view on Cyprus, states that the concentration of the Turkish Cypriot community in certain areas of the island following the 1963–1964 breakdown, created the geographical basis for a cantonal federation. The author suggests that four Turkish Cypriot and six-seven Greek Cypriot cantons could be formed and united in a federal structure which, he

suggests, due to the special needs of Cyprus, ought to be tighter than that of Switzerland.

39 Cf. "Report of the Secretary General on the UN Operation in Cyprus", Doc. S/ 6102, 12 December 1964, paragraph 32, *19 UN SCOR*, Supp. October-December 1964, p. 230–231; "Report of the Secretary General on the UN Operation in Cyprus", Doc. S/6228, 10 March 1965, paragraphs 53–56, *20 UN SCOR*, Supp. January-March 1905, pp. 118–119. For the role of Turkey in all this cf. "Report of the Secretary General on the UN Operation in Cuprus", Doc. S/5764, 15 June 1964, paragraph 119, *19 UN SCOR*, Supp. April-June 1964, pp. 239–240.

40 The foreign diplomatic missions to Cyprus and UN officials continued to consult with the Turkish Cypriot leadership. Dr Kuchuk and after February 1973 Mr. Denktash were considered as the Vice President of the Republic.

41 Cf. Clifford Geertz, "The Integrative Revolution: Primordial Sentiments and Civil Politics in the New States", *Old Societies and New States*, ed. by Clifford Geertz, New York: Free Press, 1963, pp. 105–157.

42 The Turkish insistence on the partition of Cyprus in the guise of geographical separation of the two communities, was formally reiterated to the UN Mediator. See "Report of the United Nations Mediator on Cyprus to the Secretary General", Doc. S/6253, 26 March 1965, par. 73–75, 97–98, 107–109, *20 UN SCOR*, Supp. January-March 1965, pp. 199–253.

43 For details see A. Pollis, "Systemic Factors and the Failure of Political Integration in Cyprus", pp. 31–34.

44 A very good recent study of the legal aspects of the disputes over Cyprus in their political context is Thomas Ehrlich, *Cyprus 1958–1960*, London: Oxford University Press, 1974.

45 Cf. Xydis, *Cyprus: Reluctant Republic*, Chapter XI, p. 420 ff for the reservations of Archbishop Makarios concerning the agreements and the pressures exerted on him by the Greek government.

46 For the full arguments of the Government of Cyprus concerning the Treaty of Guarantee cf. *19 UN SCOR*, 109th Meeting (27 February 1964), pp. 15–21. Cf. also the Charter of the United Nations, Articles 2 (1), 2(4) and 103, all of which can be invoked against the validity of the Treaty of Guarantee. This treaty also contravenes Article 53 of the 1969 Vienna Convention on the Law of Treaties, which, remarkably, has been voted for by Turkey.

47 *20 UN General Assembly Official Records*, 1402nd Plenary Meeting, 18 December 1965, pp. 2–11. The vote on this resolution was 47 for, 5 against, 54 abstaining. Text of Resolution 2077 in *20 UN GAOR, Annexes* III, p. 13.

48 Cf. Greek Cypriot official views as outlined in the "Report by the UN Mediator on Cyprus to the Secretary General", paragraphs 92–93.

49 For a fuller statement of Turkish arguments see *19 UN SCOR*, 1045th Meeting (18 February 1964), pp. 34–40.

50 *UN Treaty Series* 382, p. 6

51 The unfolding of the conflict in the 1960s has not yet formed the object of scholarly studies comparable to those that analyze events in the 1950s. For general surveys see Ierodiakonou, *The Cyprus Question*, pp. 249–300; Kyriakides, *Cyprus: Constitutionalism*, pp. 135–170; Linda B. Miller, *Cyprus, The Law and Politics of Civil Strife*, Occasional Papers in International Affairs, Center for International Affairs, Harvard University, Cambridge, MA, 1968.

52 The involvement of the United Nations in the Cyprus problem and the discussion of the issue in the Security Council and General Assembly repeatedly since 1964 is covered regularly in successive volumes of the *UN Monthly Chronicle*.

53 For full citation see note 41 above. For the substantive proposals of the Mediator note in particular paragraphs 132–148 on the issues of independence, self-determination and international peace; 149–157 on the structure of the state and 158–165 on the protection of the individual and minority rights.

54 The involvement of NATO in the 1963–1964 crisis is assessed in Philip Windsor, "NATO and the Cyprus Crisis", *Adelphi Papers*, no. 14, London: Institute of Strategic Studies, 1964.

55 *For the relevant documents cf. American Foreign Policy Current Documents 1964*, pp. 556–557.

56 For an official US assessment of the Cyprus problem see George Ball, "The Responsibilities of a Global Power", *Department of State Bulletin* 51 (1964), pp. 476–477. For Acheson's own account of his activities see Dean Acheson, "Cyprus: The Anatomy of the Problem", *Chicago Bar Record* XLVI, no. 8 (May 1965), pp. 349–356. For details about the provisions of the Acheson plan see *Tò Βήμα*, Athens, 1 September 1964, p. 1.

57 For an excellent analysis of the relations between the governments of Greece and Cyprus in the period 1960–1972 see the essay by Alexander G. Xydis, "Τό Ψυχολογικό Πλέγμα" (The Psychological Complex), in *Ὁ Μακάριος καὶ οἱ Σύμμαχοι του*, eds by A. G. Xydis, Sp. Linardatos, K. Chadjiargyris, Athens: Gutenberg, 1972, pp. 11–40.

58 Cf. C. A. Theodoulou, "Quelques aspects de la crise chypriote actuelle", *Politique Etrangère* 37, no. 2 (1972), pp. 221–233. Agreement was repeatedly reported as being very close at hand, but in all those occasions the following pattern would recur in the behavior of the Turkish side: the Turkish Cypriot negotiator would fly to Ankara to brief the Turkish government on the progress of the talks. Upon his return to Cyprus, however, the Turkish views would be invariably announced as hardened and the previous points of agreement discarded. This systematic subversion of all agreements reached in intra-Cypriot negotiations by Ankara, was last manifested in the rejection of an agreement over the operation of Nicosia International Airport, after the abortive resumption of talks in January 1975. See *The New York Times*, 24 January 1975, p. 3 and ibid., 1 February 1975, p. 2.

59 For the social psychological dynamics of such situations and the importance of direct communication for the resolution of conflict see John W. Burton, *Conflict and Communications: The Use of Controlled Communication in International Relations*, London: Macmillan. 1969. Cf. Herbert C. Kelman's evaluation of this work, "The Problem-Solving Workshop in Conflict Resolution", in *Communication in International Politics*, ed. by Richard L. Merritt, University of Illinois Press, 1972, pp. 168–204. For an argument that by the late 1960s the Cyprus conflict was becoming a problem of misperception cf. John W. Burton, *World Society*, Cambridge: Cambridge University Press, 1972, pp. 55–59, 68–69, 75–77.

60 It should be added here that the government of Cyprus had repeatedly argued for demilitarization of the island in the context of a settlement. See for instance the "Report of the UN Mediator", paragraph 92.

61 The emergence of political parties and electoral politics in their social context are examined in Paschalis M. Kitromilides, *Patterns of Politics in Cyprus*, unpublished thesis, Wesleyan University, 1972. Cf. Peter Loizos, *The Greek Gift: Politics in a Cypriot Village*, Oxford: Blackwell, 1975, pp. 235–288.

62 The best sources on economic planning and development in Cyprus are *The Second Five Year Plan, 1967–1971* and *The Third Five Year Plan, 1972–1976*, both prepared by the Planning Bureau of the Republic of Cyprus and containing all the relevant statistical information on achievements, targets

and problems in the economic development of Cyprus. The performance of Cyprus can be best appreciated in a comparative perspective as presented in the special report on economic development published in *The UNESCO Courier*, February 1970 (23rd year), pp. 22–23: in a survey of 69 developing countries Cyprus is classified in the category of those with both the highest growth rate and per capita income in the decade of the 1960s.

63 Cf. Stathis Panagides, "Communal Conflict and Economic Considerations: The Case of Cyprus", *Journal of Peace Research* 5 (1968), pp. 133–145.

64 According to the 1960 Constitution such matters were to be administered by the Communal Chambers. See Constitution of Cyprus, Part V, Articles 86–111, in A. J. Peaslee, ed., *Constitutions of Nations,* The Hague, Nijhoff, 1968, Vol. III: *Europe,* pp. 170–178. In his 13 ammendments in 1963 President Makarios proposed the abolition of the Greek Communal Chamber and the delegation of its functions to a Ministry of Education for reasons of increased governmental efficiency. He stated however that the Turkish Cypriot community was free to retain its Communal Chamber.

65 See note 57.

66 Cf. note 41. For an informative survey of the views of the various political parties of Turkey on Cyprus see Ferenc Vali, *Bridge across the Bosporus: The Foreign Policy of Turkey,* Baltimore: Johns Hopkins Press, 1971, pp. 78–99.

67 Cf. Richard D. Robinson, *The First Turkish Republic*, Cambridge, MA: Harvard University Press, 1965, p. 188. For the manipulation of the public's sensitivity over Cyprus in Turkish domestic politics, cf. Vali, *Bridge across the Bosporus,* pp. 99–114, 358–364.

68 The following view is revealing as to how Cyprus is perceived in certain American quarters: "As a center of operations directed toward the Soviet bloc-presuming overflight rights with Turkey-Cyprus has great potential. Moscow is only 1500 air miles from Cyprus airstrips; Baku, the Soviet oil center on the Caspian Sea, lies only 1000 miles away; Rostov, a main industrial center on the Don River is 900 miles distant; Sverdlovsk, a center of Soviet heavy industry, is situated at a distance of 2000 miles, and the oil fields of Rumania are as near as 800 miles. In fact, Batum, the nearest point in the Soviet Union from Cyprus is only 830 miles away and the nearest city in the Soviet bloc, the Bulgarian city of Akhtopol, is a mere 550 air miles. Cyprus thus occupies a peculiarly strategic location as an air base". T. W. Adams, *AKEL: The Communist Party of Cyprus*, Stanford: Hoover Institution Press, 1971, p. 87.

69 The study of US policy toward Cyprus has been placed on an entirely new basis by the research of Van Coufoudakis who has presented convincing arguments and documentation supporting a view of a continuity of American policy since the 1950s in pursuit of the partition of Cyprus as the ideal solution from the vantage point of Americam interests. See Van Coufoudakis, "United States Foreign Policy and the Cyprus Question: A Case Study in Cold War Diplomacy", in *US Foreign Policy toward Greece and Cyprus*, eds. by Couloumbis and Hicks, pp. 106–138.

70 More correctly it can be said that Greece agreed to cooperate in undermining the independence of Cyprus already under the governments that came to power after the fall of the Papandreou government in 1965. For an incisive ctitique see Ch. Christidis, Κυπριακό και Ελληνοτουρκικά, pp. IX-CXXII and *idem.*, Ακρως Απόρρητον: Το Πρωτόκολλο της 17ης Δεκεμβρίου 1966, Athens, 1973. On the policy of the Greek military junta toward Cyprus see Alexander G. Xydis, "The Military Regime's Foreign Policy", *in Greece under Military Rule*, ed. by Richard Clogg and George Yannopoulos, New York: Basic Books, 1972, pp. 191–209. A strand of radical opinion tends to attribute the advent of the military

dictatorshio in Greece to the increasing urgency felt by NATO and the USA to quell the independent stands taken by the Papandreou government in opposing the partition of Cyprus. Cf. Andreas Papandreou, *Democracy at Gunpoint: The Greek Front,* Garden City, Doubleday, 1970, pp. 129–141, and Constantine Tsoucalas, *The Greek Tragedy,* London: Penguin, 1969, pp. 153–165, 189–191.

71 For the sociological character and social bases of this movement see Peter Loizos, "The progress of Greek nationalism in Cyprus, 1878–1970", in J. Davis, ed., *Choise and Change: essays in honour of Lucy Mair, LSE monographs on Social Anthropology,* no. 50 (1974), pp. 114–133 and Kyriacos Markides, "Social Change and the Rise and Decline of Social Movements: The Case of Cyprus", *American Ethnologist* I, no. 2 (May 1974), pp. 304–330.

72 The fullest account of these developments yet available is that by Laurence Stern, "Bitter Lessons: How We Failed in Cyprus", *Foreign Policy,* no. 19 (Summer 1975), pp. 34–78. On the domestic processes leading up to the crisis see K. C. Markides, "Internal Weakness and External Intervention: The Collapse of the Cyprus Republic", Paper presented at the Midwest Political Science Association, Chicago, May 1975. An incisive forecast of the tragedy is Ch. Chrestides, Ἡ Αυτο-καταστροφή των Ἑλληνοκυπρίων, Athens 1973; *Idem, Ἀπό τον Ἰούλιο 1974 εκλεισε χρόνος,* Athens 1975 and Ploutis Servas, Ἡ Κυπριακή Τραγωδία, Athens 1975 offer critical analyses of the problem and its handling by the governments of Greece and Cyprus.

73 *The New York Times,* 2 November 1974, pp. 1, 7; ibid., 17 January 1975, p. 8; ibid., 10 February 1975, p. 10 and ibid., 3 July 1975, p. 2. On the pressures on the Greek Cypriots to leave the occupied area see *The Manchester Guardian Weekly,* 1 March 1975.

74 This and the following paragraph draw on the conceptualizations advanced in James M. Rosenau, ed., *International Aspects of Civil Strife,* Princeton: Princeton University Press, 1964, pp. 1–44 and *idem, The Scientific Study of Foreign Policy,* New York: Free Press, 1971, pp. 307–338.

75 Increasing indications of covert American involvement, destabilizing activities and encouragement of local subversion in Cyprus, are becoming available. Cf. Stern, "Bitter Lessons", for some hints in this direction.

76 See Eric Nordlinger, "Conflict Regulation in Divided Societies", *Occasional Papers in International Affairs,* no. 29 (January 1972), Center for International Affairs, Harvard University.

11 An unexplored case of political change

This brief chapter is no more than a research note aiming to offer some hints on the electoral history of Cyprus and of the nature of sources of pertinent data that might be of interest to students of political change and political behaviour. Considered in a comparative framework this entirely unexplored material appears quite promising as a source for the study of political mobilization and political cleavages in the context of a changing society.

In the perspective of Cypriot history, these phenomena are characterized by particular complexity given the multidimensional nature of political conflict in an ethnically segmented society, highly vulnerable to external influences because of its geographic location and historical ties. Accordingly political change as registered in electoral politics, has been the product of conflict on four distinct but interconnected levels: intracommunal social and political conflict; intercommunal antagonism escalating in violent ethnic conflict; native resistance to the foreign colonial regime whose establishment, however, inaugurated the process of modernization; and finally international conflict among external powers with interests in the strategically sensitive geopolitical space of the island. It is amidst all these interlocking pressures and tensions that the contest of democratic government through electoral participation had to be fought. The systematic study of the relevant evidence, therefore, could derive fruitful insights in connection with some central empirical, but also evaluative, concerns of political analysis.

Electoral politics before Independence, 1878–1960

The experience of Cyprus with electoral politics did not begin with the island's advent to independent statehood. Different forms of institutionalized popular participation in public affairs has been known since the beginning of British rule. The island's transfer from Ottoman to British administration in 1878 marked the establishment of formal ties that connected integrally traditional Cypriot society with modern Western practices. Among the latter was the introduction of popular suffrage by the new British rulers through the institution of a Legislative Council. A typical institution of British administrative practice in the colonial territories,[1] the Legislative Council was in essence meant to be an agency for the legitimation of foreign rule through the semblance of consultation of the native population. It was composed of both elected native members and appointed members among the British officials of the colonial administration.[2]

The mechanisms of operation of the Council were such that the elected members could never block the passage of official legislation because their majority vote could be overridden by decrees issued by the British High Commissioner or Governor. The Council, as established in 1882, was composed of six appointed official British members, nine elected Greek members and three elected Muslim members. The twelve non-official members were elected on separate electoral lists for Greeks and Turks and this was one of the crucial policy measures that tended since the beginning of British rule to institutionalize ethnic distinctions on the island. The balance in the Council was such that the Muslim members could — and they usually did —block the promotion of legislation proposed by the elected majority by siding with the official members. However even when interethnic cooperation in the Council could assure a majority vote for legislation favoured by a majority of the elected members, such legislation could — and was— annulled by executive orders-in-council.[3]

For electoral purposes Cyprus was divided into three constituencies, each one comprising two of the six normal administrative districts instituted by the British on the island. The suffrage was enjoyed by the great majority of the island's male population over the age of 21, specifically by all payers of some form of property or income tax. In 1925, under the constitutional changes introduced upon the declaration of Cyprus as a Crown Colony, the number of official members of the Legislative Council was increased from six to nine to counterbalance an increase in the number of Greek elected members from nine to twelve.[4] Although this increase in the number of Greek members corresponded more faithfully to the numerical proportion of Greeks in the overall population of Cyprus (four-fifths), the constitutional changes left the former balance of forces in the Council unaffected.

Despite the virtual annulment of the essence of representative government in the operation of the Legislative Council, its presence among the political institutions of Cyprus exposed the population for the first time to the experience of modern balloting.[5]

Elections to the Council were held in 1883, 1886, 1888, 1889, 1890, 1891, 1896, 1901, 1904, 1905, 1906, 1911, 1916, 1925 and 1927.[6] The relevant statistical data which have remained in the archives of the colonial administration of Cyprus and have never been examined by scholarship concerned either with the political history of Cyprus or with electoral studies of any sort, constitute the most important source for a historical study of the forms and constraints of political mobilization in a rural and impoverished society.[7] These initial forms of political participation were suppressed with the abolition of the Legislative Council by the British administration following the nationalist uprising in October 1931.[8]

British rule also brought to Cyprus the institutions of local government with the popular election of municipal and communal councils.[9] These elections too provided outlets to the contest among local political forces. Municipal and communal elections over the years registered the increasing disaffection with British rule as reflected in the growth of the nationalist movement in favour of union with Greece. Despite the growth of Greek Cypriot nationalism, however, the practice of local self-government which remained freer from the obstruction of official intervention, also provided opportunities for interethnic cooperation between Greek and Turkish Cypriots. This constitutes another significant aspect of the politics of Cyprus under British rule that deserves closer scrutiny.

In connection with the process of political mobilization in the history of Cyprus, the municipal elections provide perhaps the most important indicators in that they not only registered the strides of nationalism in the 1920s as observed so perceptively by Arnold Toynbee,[10] but, following the repressive measures of the 1930s, they recorded the expansion of the left-wing movement in the 1940s as well.[11] In this regard the municipal elections of 1943, 1946 and 1949 are of particular interest for the study of political change.

The experience of modern electoral politics introduced in Cyprus by the institutions of colonial government was not the only form of the popular exercise of the suffrage in the history of the island. Another form of electoral experience more integrally connected with the traditional culture of the island has been the popular participation in episcopal elections in the Greek Orthodox Church of Cyprus. An old tradition of the Christian Church, participation of the laity in the election of the ecclesiastical hierarchy, has survived to this date in the Church of Cyprus alone among all Orthodox Churches. The practice has been incorporated in the constitutional charter of the Church of Cyprus that was approved by the Holy Synod in 1914. The procedure involves indirect lay participation in episcopal elections in two stages: the male members of age 21 and over in each parish of the Church elect the so called "special representatives" who in turn elect the "general representatives" of each diocese who along with the higher clergy compose the electoral assembly that elects the bishops by majority vote.[12] This practice has been observed in every episcopal and archiepiscopal election in twentieth-century Cyprus and constitutes one of the factors of the intimate involvement of the Church in the political life of the island. In certain occasions the ecclesiastical elections were intensely politicized as it happened during the so called "Archiepiscopal Question" of 1900–1910 and again with the archiepiscopal elections of 1946–47 which reflected the intense polarization of the politics of Cyprus between Left and Right.[13]

Electoral politics in the Republic of Cyprus

After a four-year anticolonial revolt in 1955–1959, Cyprus emerged as an independent republic within the British Commonwealth and the United Nations. The independence of the island and its constitutional status were settled by the Zurich Agreements concluded in February 1959 by the Prime Ministers of Greece and Turkey and were formalized later on that month in the London Agreements between Great Britain, Greece, Turkey and the official representatives of the Greek and Turkish Cypriot communities.[14] No plebiscite was held in Cyprus to consult popular opinion on the Agreements. This issue was contested in the first presidential elections held in December 1959 which produced a two third majority vote for Archbishop Makarios who stood in favour of the Agreements. The 1960 Cyprus Constitution[15] provided for a presidential regime with a President elected directly by universal suffrage by all Greek Cypriots over 21 years of age and a Vice President elected separately in the same manner by all Turkish Cypriots. Legislative authority was vested in a fifty member House of Representatives comprising thirty-five Greek Cypriot and fifteen Turkish Cypriot deputies elected in six electoral constituencies coinciding with the six administrative districts of Cyprus with separate electoral lists for each ethnic community. The electoral system provided for universal suffrage of all citizens over 21 years of age, multimember constituencies and election based on simple majority or plurality of the popular vote polled by each candidate regardless of party affiliation. All elective offices in the executive and legislative branches are for five-year tenure. The distinctive characteristic of electoral politics in the Republic was the institutionalization from the outset of the ethnic cleavage in the society.[16] It thus precluded any form of political integration from developing in the context of democratic politics.

The operation of electoral politics in the republic was seriously obstructed by the constitutional crisis of 1963 and the ensuing ethnic violence and communal segregation.[17] One important political consequence was the withdrawal of Turkish Cypriot officials from the government of the republic and from the legislature. Another technical consequence were the serious delays caused in holding elections in Cyprus. This explains the irregular intervals between electoral contests in the 1960s. Contested presidential elections were held in 1959 and 1968 with Archbishop Makarios winning both of them. In 1973 and 1978 the incumbent president was returned unopposed.[18] General elections to the House of Representatives were held in 1960, 1970 and 1976. The 1960 election was settled by an electoral pact between the two major political formations, the nationalist Patriotic Front composed of followers of Archbishop Makarios and the leftist AKEL. It was contested at the polls by a few right-wing supporters of union with Greece who, however, received a completely negligible share of the vote. The 1970 and 1976 electoral contests reflected the differentiations undergone meanwhile by the political sociology of independent Cyprus, and were contested by five political parties in each case. The one-year delay in holding the 1976 parliamentary elections was due to a new major upheaval in the history of contemporary Cyprus, the Turkish invasion of 1974.[19] Local government elections to the village communal councils were held in 1962 for the first time since 1931 but their results were soon annulled amidst the constitutional crisis of 1963.[20]

Despite these pressures, all electoral contests in Cyprus have been remarkably free and orderly. Electoral statistics pertaining to these elections have been officially published by the Public Information Office of the Republic and were reproduced in the local press. The statistics for the 1970 and 1976 elections, published in several volumes, are particularly detailed. The data are available on precinct and district level with specific counts for each candidate as well as for party lists. For parliamentary candidates both a personal and a party count of the vote are available, and this allows very interesting comparisons which can yield important insights into the political sociology and the character of political mobilization in Cyprus.

Cypriot electoral data could be subjected to quantitative analysis in conjunction with the rich census statistics collected annually by the Statistics and Research Department of the Republic (demographic, economic, social, educational and other indicators). Despite the interesting evidence that electoral studies of this sort could produce for the comparative study of political change, practically nothing has been done in this direction by political scientists. The only exception is a detailed study of the 1970 parliamentary election, which attempted to examine the workings of democratic politics in the context of a society dominated by networks of personal ties and obligations.[21] A similar study of the 1976 parliamentary election is highly desirable for comparative purposes in that it could examine the question of the impact of the trauma of the 1974 invasion on the character of political behaviour. One partial explanation of the paucity of electoral studies dealing with Cypriot politics is the fact that the domestic political life of the island, though fascinating in its complexity, has been overshadowed by the international aspects of the Cyprus Question which has received considerable attention by political historians and students of international politics.

It is hoped, nevertheless, that this brief note on Cypriot electoral politics will alert students of comparative politics to the research possibilities of an unexplored and quite promising case which can adduce new evidence to the study of politics and social change in a Mediterranean perspective.

Notes

1 See Martin Wight, *The Development of the Legislative Council*, London: Faber and Faber, 1946, pp. 66–99.
2 See G. S. Georghallides, *A Political and Administrative History of Cyprus 1918–1926 with a Survey of the Foundation of British Rule*, Nicosia: Cyprus Research Centre, 1979, pp. 41–47.

3 On the long-term consequences of this policy for ethnic relations, see Paschalis M. Kitromilides, "From Coexistence to Confrontation: The Dynamics of Ethnic Conflict in Cyprus", in this collection.

4 See Georghallides, *op. cit.*, pp. 335–337.

5 For an interesting view by a contemporary observer see G. Louka, "Ἡ ἐν Κύπρῳ μέχρι τῆς 4ης/17ης Ἰουνίου 1908 τριακονταετὴς ἀγγλικὴ κατοχὴ", ed. by Theophano Kypri, *Κυπριακαὶ Σπουδαί* 40 (1976), pp. 115–59.

6 See Filios Zannetos. *Ἡ Κύπρος εἰς τὸν Ἀγῶνα τῆς Παλιγγενεσίας 1821–1930*, Athens, 1930, pp. 142–143. On particular elections, see Georghallides, *op. cit.*, pp. 235–236, 345–348.

7 On this point the testimony of Sir Ronald Storrs opens an important perspective. See *Orientations*, London: Nicholson and Watson, 1939, p. 491.

8 For the relevant background, see Arnold Toynbee, *Survey of International Affairs. 1931*, London: Oxford University Press, 1932, pp. 354–394.

9 Sec C. W. J. Orr, *Cyprus under British Rule*, London, 1918, reissued: London: Zero Publishers, 1972, pp. 74–75. See also Zannetos, *op. cit.*, pp. 143–144.

10 Toynbee, *op. cit.*, pp. 364–368.

11 A Communist Party of Cyprus (KKK) was founded in 1926. It was proscribed by the British in 1931 and remerged under the name of AKEL [Working People's Uplifting Party] in 1941. It has been since then the largest and best organized political party on the island controlling through its mass front organizations between one third and two fifths of the electorate. A study of the implantation of the communist movement in Cyprus on the model of Sidney Tarrow, *Peasant Communism in Southern Italy*, New Haven and London: Yale University Press, 1967, could be a very valuable contribution both theoretically and empirically.

12 See *Καταστατικόν τῆς Ἁγιωτάτης Ἐκκλησίας τῆς Κύπρου*, Nicosia, 1914, pp. 8–12, articles 20–31. Cf. John Hackett, *A History of the Orthodox Church of Cyprus*: London: Methuen, 1901, pp. 261–263, 282–303.

13 In connection with the political activities of the Church of Cyprus one should add the plebiscite organized by the Church in 1950 which produced a vote of over 95 per cent in favour of union with Greece.

14 On the relevant background see Stephen G. Xydis, *Cyprus: Conflict and Conciliation*, Columbus, OH: Ohio State University Press, 1967 and *idem, Cyprus Reluctant Republic*, The Hague and Paris: Mouton, 1973. François Crouzet, *Le conflit de Chypre*, Brussels: Bruylant, 1973, 2 vols offers a magisterial synthesis. On the anticolonial rising, the most recent and detailed though analytically naïve source is Nancy Crawshaw, *The Cyprus Revolt*, London: Allen and Unwin, 1978.

15 For the text, see A. J. Peaslee, ed., *Constitutions of Nations*, 3rd ed., The Hague: Nijhoft, 1968, Vol. III, pp. 138–216 and for a good analysis, see S. A. de Smith, *The New Commonwealth and Its Constitutions*, London: Stephens, 1964, pp. 282–296.

16 Another institutional expression of ethnic separation was the creation of separate Greek and Turkish Communal Chambers whose jurisdiction covered the affairs of each community in the fields of education, culture, religion, personal status etc.

17 See Stanley Kyriakides, *Cyprus: Constitutionalism and Crisis Government*, Philadelphia: University of Pennsylvania Press, 1968.

18 Archbishop Makarios, re-elected President in 1973 died in office on 3 August 1977 and was succeeded according to the Constitution by the Speaker of the House Mr. Spyros Kyprianou who was in turn elected President in February 1978.

19 The most informative source is Laurence Stern, *The Wrong Horse*, New York: Quadrangle Hooks, 1977. On the domestic background, see Kyriacos C. Markides, *The Rise and Fall of the Cyprus Republic*, New Haven and London: Yale University Press, 1977 which offers an account of the political sociology of the republic refer- ring also tangentially to the electoral contests of the period.

20 See Kyriacos C. Markides, Eleni S. Nikita, Elengo N. Rangou, *Social Change in a Cypriot Village*, Nicosia: Social Research Centre, 1978, pp. 61–66.

21 See Paschalis M. Kitromilides, *Patterns of Politics in Cyprus*, Honors Thesis, Wesleyan University, Middletown, CT, 1972, pp. xi + 263. Peter Loizos, *The Greek Gift. Politics in a Cypriot Village*, Oxford: Blackwell, 1974, pp. 235–288 discusses the impact of this election on the life of a rural community.

12 Political community in plural societies

The question I propose to address in this brief chapter concerns the political preconditions of the integration of ethnic minorities in a national community. I should like to suggest that this question constitutes one of the major challenges to contemporary political theory and political practice. The complications arising out of the problem of minorities for political practice are well-known and obvious to everyone who has paid even cursory and incidental attention to efforts to construct national states, cope with social change and regulate the smooth functioning of political institutions in plural societies: just consider the civil wars attendant upon the dissolution of colonial empires, racial strife in the USA, the nationalities problem in the USSR and more recently, the centrifugal tendencies of "peripheral" nationalism in the ancient nation-states of Europe. The challenges posed by the issue of minority integration to political thought are registered in the fact that none of the theories of the state prevalent in modern political philosophy can provide an adequate analytical framework for the examination of the problem. This is due to the fact that nationalism, with its parochial and morally outrageous values, has consistently remained outside the purview of political analysis, which is distinctly universalist in its normative premises and ethical claims.[1]

The preconditions of minority integration in the larger society are fundamentally identical with the range of problems posed by the phenomenon of nationalism. How can an ethnic minority be made to feel a part of a larger national society at the lowest possible human cost, is a question that raises all the empirical and normative problems about national identity and national sentiment. The broad range of issues associated with these forms of human expression have not received the attention they deserve in social theory—with some notable exceptions, of course. Classical political thought has largely ignored nationalism, as becomes obvious if an attempt is made to bring the perspectives of liberal and republican theories of the slate to bear on the pertinent problems. This is amply demonstrated if one considers the host of problems that remain unresolved and the critical questions which arise if the issue of minority integration is considered in the context of the "nightwatchman" minimal state of the liberal tradition or, alternatively, in connection with the participatory republic of civic virtue visualized by the radicals. The liberal state which leaves all individuals and groups to their own devices in the struggle for survival can hardly be considered a good place for socially disadvantaged minorities in need of affirmative action programs in order to cope with the structural constraints imposed upon them by an environment of social inequality. At the very least, the liberal state might be a tolerable place for religious and other intellectual minorities, since in principle it will leave them alone to cultivate their faiths as they see fit. The republican state, however, with its tendency to invade the privacy of the citizen with its participatory demands and the civil religion it requires in order to motivate participation and dedication to the common weal, could very well be a quite intolerable environment for a dissenting minority. A dominant national doctrine is bound to be the most usual content of the civil religion, and for the national community to work, those who might have doubts about official nationalism or are suspected of nurturing alternative loyalties might well "be forced to be free".

Thus classical political theory, with some rare exceptions which, however, approach the question of national minorities only to beg it, has generally overlooked the problem. More recent modes of political discourse, most notably some strands in twentieth-century Marxism and the empirical theories of modernization, have attempted to come to grips with the issues of nationality and "nation-building".[2] However, the specific problem of creating political community in societies where articulate ethnic minorities are present has not been adequately treated. Marxism, despite the important contributions of Eastern-European Marxist thinkers to the analysis of nationality,[3] has optimistically sidestepped the problem by delegating its solution to a future socialist society that will achieve the freedom of all its members, including members of national minorities, from the forms of oppression and alienation nurtured by capitalism. Modernization theory, on the other hand, although it has included political "integration" among its major concepts, has delegated the problem of minorities to a secondary place. With some notable exceptions, modernization theory has used the concept of integration to analyze the process of the extension of the power of state institutions and the regimentation of society through unifying policies. The cultivation of national identity and the emergence of nationalism are considered part of this process. This has generally been the analytical approach to the problem of national community in the most influential sources on modernization and political change.[4]

Despite the seminal contribution of one of the pioneers of the study of modernization, Rupert Emerson, who has laid out in all its complexity the problem of minority integration in the process of national self-assertion,[5] it has provoked only tangential interest in the mainstream of the empirical theory of political change. It is true that studies of "political development" in Africa and Asia in the 1950s and 1960s have not failed to notice the centrality of ethnic conflict in the process of state building. This emphasis, however, was confined to particular case studies and, with rare exceptions, did not provide the focus of theoretical reflection. Only belatedly has the problem of minorities, ethnic relations and civil conflict been given the attention it deserves in political analysis.[6] This can be considered a characteristic instance of the modification of theory and of change in analytical emphasis under the pressure of actual problems and political experience. Overall, however, the issue of minorities has tended to be left to sociologists and social psychologists who have focused on ethnic stratification, race relations and prejudice,[7] or to scholars of international law and relations who have treated minorities as one more nuisance in the regulation of relations among nations and in the orderly functioning of world society. The discussion of the problem in terms of legal norms tends to transpose a degree of formalism into it that obscures the human drama and urgency of the issues involved.[8]

What I am trying to convey with the preceding brief survey of approaches and modes of analysis is basically a dissatisfaction with the available ways of conceptualizing the problem. The fundamental issue contingent on the problem of minority integration concerns the preconditions of political community, and this has been explored with a good deal of formalism. I do not propose to try to correct all this through the elaboration of an alternative theory. On the contrary, I suggest that the attempt be made to bring a corrective to theory by proceeding inductively from the failures of practice. In this connection, I propose to put forward some reflections based on a consideration of the experience of Cyprus. This is a classic case of two articulate ethnic communities, one demographic majority and a substantial minority (in a ratio of approximately 4 to 1) having to coexist in a state, with the easy solution of separation precluded from among their choices by the facts of geography, ethnic demography and economic viability, yet failing to achieve political community and consequently shouldering the appalling costs of conflict, foreign invasion and violence on a large scale.

The facts of the case have become generally known to the informed observer by recent tragic developments and need not be repeated here. Furthermore, they are covered in a voluminous and easily accessible literature.[9] What I should like to do is identify the major problem areas that, in my judgement, caused the failure of minority integration and on the basis of this evidence venture some suggestions on what might be needed to make political community in ethnically plural societies possible. I should like to stress, nevertheless, that my tentative suggestions derive primarily from critical reflection upon past strategies and political options and therefore are not meant as a generalized policy blueprint either for the shaping of Cyprus's future or for the resolution of conflicts in parallel cases such as Lebanon or Northern Ireland. My diagnosis, in short, is much more a criticism of the past than a specific vision for the future.

A first major impediment to political integration might be considered constitutional formalism and rigidity. The institutionalization of communal representation, the distribution of offices on the basis of communal criteria and the stipulation of ethnic quotas in public services by writ of the constitution make ethnic divisiveness a part of the formal political culture and undermine political integration by stressing ethnic identity over democratic citizenship. Furthermore, the overdetailed specification of institutional arrangements and minority privileges writes rigidity and intransigence into the constitution and undermines the possibility of liberal solutions. The respect of the rights and the equal treatment of the minority should be made the major test of the majority leadership's statesmanship, not an institutional brake on the democratic functioning of the state. The choice of corporatism over democracy precludes piecemeal political solutions and preserves an all-encompassing dynamic in the settlement of political problems whereby the whole can collapse over a minor practical issue which might not otherwise put in question any fundamental constitutional principles.

Such had precisely been the experience of Cyprus. When the island became an independent state in 1960, it was endowed with a constitution built upon rigid bicommunalism in order to meet the requirements of the minority and to assure their participation in the republic. In this manner, it incorporated and institutionalized in the new state structure the traditional ethnic communities and identities which had been preserved and politicized by the British colonial administration. The most characteristic ideological expression of this configuration was the recognition by the constitution of membership in one of the ethnic communities, not of the status of individual citizenship, as the primary and decisive basis of the political identity of the citizens of the new state. In this manner, the classic liberal basis of political democracy, the primacy of the individual and his or her rights as a person independent of special characteristics, was delegated to a secondary place while predominant weight was ascribed to ethnic, religious and racial attributes in the organization of political life. Racial discrimination became, in a way, the price of the minority's agreement to participate in the bicommunal partnership of the republic.

All this meant that the preconditions of liberal political life and democratic change away from the inherited structures of colonialism were excluded constitutionally from available political choices at the inception of the republic. Instead of embarking on a quest for a political and cultural identity of its own, the republic remained a practically inconvenient and symbolically uninspiring bicommunal compromise. By officially preserving traditional ethnic identities, the republic could not capture the emotional allegiances of its subjects and failed to nurture a shared loyalty for the common homeland.

The respective nationalist legacies of the majority and minority communities which remained intact in the new political structure constituted a powerful ideological factor which pushed the republic in a direction opposite to that of an "integrative revolution".[10] The clash of two symbolically antagonistic, mutually exclusive and highly authoritarian nationalisms provided the ideological content of ethnic conflict. On the eve of her independence in the context of the anticolonial struggle of the 1950s, Cyprus had experienced the crystallization of ethnic confrontation that stretched from the ideological to most other levels of public life. Furthermore, political role inversion between the two ethnic communities bred mutual paranoia: the Turks who had been the master race in the three centuries of Ottoman rule in Cyprus found themselves in the position of a minority under the republic, while the Greeks changed from oppressed subjects to the dominant community in a state whose existence stood in the way of their national aspiration for union with Greece. Each side consequently found itself locked into the fear that willingness to compromise and cooperate might lead to even greater symbolic losses. Thus the bicommunal experiment of the Republic of Cyprus had to face from its inception serious subverting forces in the dynamics of local politics.

The effects of the dialectic of intolerance which divided the two communities were deeply felt in the political culture of independent Cyprus. All timid voices raised against communal isolation and antagonism and evoking the survival of the republic were simply stamped out. On the Greek Cypriot side, the dominant nationalist orthodoxy thriving on the absence of liberal values was ruthless in discrediting as treason all dissenting voices. On the Turkish Cypriot side, the extremists, firmly entrenched in the leadership of the community, did not limit themselves to moral and psychological coercion but went all the way in using their terrorist gangs to achieve the extermination of their critics who advocated interethnic cooperation. Alternative forms of social organization such as professional associations, trade unions and the units of local government that could bring members of both communities together and had an important record of interethnic cooperation under the colonial administration were blocked from developing any further and undermined under the republic. The fact that these agencies of intercommunal cooperation were consistently under the ideological influence of the Left precipitated the strong reaction of the nationalists of both sides against them.

Besides the constitutional and ideological impediments to the creation of political community in the republic of Cyprus, a structural source of division and minority antagonism toward the majority has been the socioeconomic inequalities between the two communities. Although the Turkish Cypriots had been politically and socially the dominant element in the three centuries of Ottoman rule (1571–1878) and experienced privileged treatment under the British (1878–1960), the form of capitalist development followed by Cypriot society in the twentieth century left them at an economic disadvantage. The Greeks as a more enterprising element, free from the cultural obstacles that hindered the economic development of the Turks, profited from an earlier start on mercantile activities and then reaped the benefits of economic modernization. Ethnic separation in the republic after 1963 and the self-imposed isolation of the Turkish Cypriots deprived the minority community of the fruits of the economic boom and prosperity brought by development planning after independence. These structural inequalities blended with other forms of antagonism to further obstruct the feeling of political community from developing. In the absence of timely gestures of generosity in the minority's favour, and since material condition and political status are inextricably interconnected, the fears and insecurities of the Turkish Cypriots about a precarious future in the republic despite their excessive constitutional privileges were, at least subjectively, not without foundation.

The previous observations point to what could be considered the most critical factor in the attainment of political community. On the evidence of the Cyprus case, the motivations of political leadership appear as the decisive element in the determination of political outcomes. Comparative evidence suggests that the motivation of political leadership constitutes the critical variable in the achievement of conflict regulation in segmented societies.[11] On this factor hinges the workability of constitutional formulas, the exploitation or abeyance of ideological tensions, the rectification of structural inequalities through planning and affirmative action and the alleviation of fears and insecurities in the collective psychology. The motivation of political leadership makes all the difference in the achievement of compromise. This was precisely what Cyprus lacked. The Greeks felt they had sacrificed too much. The Turks feared they had too much to lose. None trusted the motives of the other. The vicious circle of ideological rhetoric never failed to provoke mutual mistrust. Maximalist goals on both sides precluded all serious efforts to make the republic work. Naturally, it broke down with a little help from outside. But I want to stress that the assignment of the major responsibility to "outside interference" which has provided the Cypriots with a convenient scapegoat for their own failures, is no more than comforting self-deception. British colonialism, American imperialism, Turkish expansionism, Greek fascism—all played their role to a catastrophic degree at the expense of an innocent and good-hearted people. But on the evidence of the historical record, especially since 1960, I tend to suspect that all these overpowering forces might have failed to work out their poisonous schemes, had they not found the appropriate conduits in the contradictions of local society. The major channel through which foreign conspiracies were made operational was the lack of motivation on the part of local leadership groups to make the republic work, however difficult this might have been. In this, at least, the majority and the minority leadership, each motivated by their respective maximalist goals, were for once united. The force of this fact turned Cyprus into a classic example of a Thucydidean political tragedy: self-destructive blindness and violent human passions were let loose to wreck a whole civilization and sink hundreds of thousands of men, women and children of both races into appalling suffering.

The conclusions that emerge from the foregoing considerations, as far as the prerequisites of political community in plural societies are concerned, suggest basically a counterpoint to the experience of Cyprus. First and foremost, political community might be achieved if democratic citizenship is given precedence over communal membership as the basis of political identity. The vexing issue of the effective protection of the minority would be achieved through the full democratization of society and not by resorting to corporatism which is the certain avenue to the preservation of the infrastructure of conflict. Second, affirmative action programmes to redress communally based social inequalities might provide the needed evidence of good intentions on the part of the majority leadership to allay the fears of the minority and to disprove the arguments of its extremists. Furthermore, this might be the only way to cope with the fundamental component of the minority's social experience, objective and subjective exclusion. Third, a serious effort to cultivate loyalty to the common state by stressing shared rather than divisive symbols might act as the catalyst for the emergence of a viable psychological and cultural context within which majority and minority can coexist. This is probably the greatest challenge of all. The argument for the transcendence of group values, mentalities and stereotypes raises the question of how much people can sacrifice in terms of their emotional attachments without risking large-scale anomic consequences. This problem has not been adequately appreciated by those who think of nationalism as a purely artificial and largely contingent contrivance.[12] It is at this point that one of the greatest tests facing the effort to construct political community in plural societies arises. If a national society is made viable, both the tyranny of the majority must be avoided and the risk of driving minorities into rebellion should be pre-empted by generous recognition of their desire for differential treatment. Concurrently, however, the majority's sensitivities must be respected by not yielding "too much and at the wrong time"—something that might encourage separatist forces to shatter the fragile national community while it is still in the making.[13]

It might be suggested against the line of argument developed above that what a minority fears most is full democratization itself. Constitutional formalism and corporate recognition might be exactly what minorities are striving for. Democratic decisions may turn against affirmative action policies, and the chances of individual mobility in a democratic society may undermine minority's cohesion by encouraging its members to integrate in the majority's political culture, thus abandoning their heritage and tradition. It is quite conceivable that the minority's claims would focus on the safeguard of precisely these constitutive elements of its identity against the amalgamating pressures of an open society. This, of course, is morally and politically a highly debatable claim in that it poses the issue of individual autonomy and self-determination versus corporate pressures for conformity. I should like to stress that this is the

fundamental issue at stake which gets ideologically clouded—not entirely inno-
cently—by appeals for ethnic rights.

A few analytical distinctions might be helpful in placing the problem in
perspective. First, I think it must be recognized that so long as we are
honestly concerned with basic humane options, the individual's right to
belong, but also to modify or change allegiances, should be given priority
over   all   corporate   aspirations.   Otherwise,   the   case   becomes
a straightforward issue of coercion: the preservation of cultural heritages
in terms of personal identity should be made an individual option, not
a constitutional compulsion. Naturally, if a group of individual citizens
wants to preserve and transmit a particular tradition, it should be free
and also assisted through state subsidies to its cultural institutions to do
so. This, however, as a form of free individual expression, should be
limited to what Hegel has defined as civil society and should not be
allowed to introduce particularist values into the public domain. State aid
to minority institutions should be premised on the ideal of equality and
not on the recognition of corporate legitimacy. Should the state, however,
attempt to stifle, either positively or negatively, such initiatives in civil
society, the minority would be the victim of persecution and tyranny and
would have legitimate claims to revolt and secession. If the multiple
majorities which control the state want to avoid such eventualities, they
have no other option but to respect the minority's sensitivities and make
their goodwill felt through affirmative action. It is at this point that the
greatest political failures usually occur in plural societies.

Fundamentally, the issue of the creation of a viable community is
a question of political justice. Safeguard of basic civil liberties, respect for
equal political rights and the enjoyment of the protection of citizenship by
all can answer the question of community. Their absence amounts to tyranny, and community under tyranny is impossible, as ancients and moderns
recognized too well. It is precisely over the willingness to strive for political
justice that the motivations of leadership can best be appraised in connection with the attainment of community. I conclude with this issue because,
beyond the structural and cultural parameters of the problem, it opens the
possibility of political criticism.

Notes

1 John Dunn, *Western Political Theory in the Face of the Future*, Cambridge:
  Cambridge University Press, 1979, pp. 55–79.
2 Eric Hobsbawm, "Some reflections on nationalism," In *Imagination and Precision in the Social Sciences*, ed. T.S. Nossiter, London: L.S.E. Publishers, 1972,
  pp. 385–406.
3 Horace B. Davis, *Nationalism and Socialism*, New York: Monthly Review Press,
  1967. See also the selections from Otto Bauer and Karl Renner, in *Austromarx-
  ism*, ed. by T. Bottomore and P. Goode, Oxford: Clarendon Press, 1978, pp.
  102–125.

4 Reinhard Bendix, *Nation Building and Citizenship*, Berkeley: University of California Press, 1977. Also, see S.P. Huntington, *Political Order in Changing Societies*, New Haven: Yale University Press, 1968.

5 Rupert Emerson, *From Empire to Nation*, Cambridge, MA: Harvard University Press, 1960.

6 Cynthia H. Enloe, *Ethnic Conflict and Political Development*, Boston: Little, Brown, 1973. Also, see C.M. Young, *The Politics of Cultural Pluralism*, Madison: University of Wisconsin Press, 1976.

7 A.M. Rose, "Minorities", *International Encyclopedia of the Social Sciences* 10 (1968), pp. 365–371.

8 I should like to note a recent work which treats this aspect of the problem in a remarkably humanist perspective: Georges C. Ténékidès, *L'action des Nations Unies contre la discrimination raciale*, in Académie de Droit International. *Recueil des Cours* 168, 1980: 271–487.

9 For a survey of the bibliography see Paschalis M. Kitromilides and M. L. Evriviades, 1982. *World Bibliographical Series* 28: *Cyprus*, Oxford: Clio Press, pp. 53–98.

10 Clifford Geertz, "The integrative revolution", *The Interpretation of Cultures*, New York: Basic Books, 1973, pp. 105–157.

11 E.A. Nordlinger, *Conflict Regulation in Divided Societies*, Cambridge, MA: Harvard University Center for International Affairs, 1972.

12 E. Gellner, *Thought and Change*, London: Weidenfeld and Nicolson, 1964, pp. 147–178.

13 Cf. Emerson, *op. cit.*, pp. 332–333.

13 Relevance or irrelevance of nationalism?

A perspective from the Eastern Mediterranean

Motivation

In this chapter, I will attempt to sketch tentative answers to two questions. One is the question in the title of the meeting in which an earlier draft of this chapter was originally presented: are we in sight of the end of the nation-state? The second question is announced by the title of this chapter: how can we judge the relevance or irrelevance of nationalism for understanding the contemporary world? There is a third, more historically oriented, question that is in a way subsumed in the other two, and this raises the issue whether at present, in the world of the early twenty-first century, we have entered a process leading away from the state-system established by Westphalia. This is certainly a difficult question that can only elicit controversial answers. It will not be raised in what follows but some tentative responses to it may emerge, in an indirect way, from what will be said about the other two.

These questions may appear embarrassingly broad and ambitious, and their very formulation may sound — at least to the present author — presumptuous. What is not announced in the title, however, is the method by means of which I propose to approach them, and on this methodological basis, the whole project could perhaps be accorded the saving grace of historical realism and operational feasibility.

I have thought that it might not be impertinent to the substantive issues I wish to address to attempt my answers to the two questions through a synopsis of the work I have devoted over almost four decades of research and reflection to the question of nationalism and its role in political and cultural change. Inevitably, there is an autobiographical dimension to this approach, which becomes a second source of embarrassment, and this prompts me to begin with a few words of apology by quoting some lines from John Stuart Mill's *Autobiography*:

> In an age of transition in opinions, there may be somewhat both of interest and of benefit in noting the successive phases of any mind which was always pressing forward, equally ready to learn and to unlearn either from its own thoughts or from those of others. But a

motive which weighs more with me [...] is a desire to make acknowledgement of the debts which my intellectual and moral development
owes to other persons.[1]

Accordingly, in the spirit of the passage just quoted, I do not want to raise
any claims of whatever nature for what I am going to outline below, except
for its possible interest as an illustration in the sociology of knowledge.

An intellectual trajectory

The original motivation to turn to the study of nationalism, which developed into a lifelong engagement, derived from a study of electoral politics
in Cyprus in the early 1970s.[2] That work involved basic empirical research
inspired by the models of electoral analysis elaborated by the Michigan
school of survey research and by the classic approach of V. O. Key. It was
directed by a great political scientist, Fred Greenstein, who taught me at
Wesleyan University. From this research emerged the normative dominance
of nationalist discourse in local politics, a dominance that overpowered and
neutralized the basic sense of democratic politics: it set the limits of consen-
sus and legitimacy beyond which dissent could not be tolerated. For my
youthful mind, this was a realization, both captivating and traumatic,
because it placed question marks upon many of the accepted truths with
which my generation — and other generations before and after — had
grown up and had been socialized in the political culture of Cyprus.

It was by means of this basic empirical approach to political research
that I came to appreciate the *relevance* of nationalism as a force in
modern politics and the need to understand it as a ubiquitous and
unrelenting factor shaping the context of political choices and political
decisions. It was at this point that an important intellectual debt was
incurred: a debt to Shlomo Avineri, who had taught me political theory
at Wesleyan. Shlomo Avineri encouraged me to reflect upon the political
significance and the political operation of the basic anthropological
notions by reference to which I had attempted to interpret forms of
electoral behaviour. This conceptual approach was based on the Mediterranean anthropology of "honour and shame" elaborated by John
Campbell, Jean Peristiany and other followers of Evans-Pritchard.[3]
"Honour and shame" was an influential approach in the 1960s, and
some interesting work had been informed by it, but it was obvious that
its explanatory power in political analysis was limited as it could be
mostly operationalized as an interpretative tool in rural contexts and
peasant communities. My debt to Shlomo Avineri was not a superficial
one: it involved looking at the question of nationalism in political rather
than anthropological terms and opened to me the exciting perspective of
political theory upon actual political practice.

Even more substantively, this early intellectual debt meant putting the history of political ideas at the centre of any interpretative approach to nationalism, which in turn meant taking the intellectual aspects of the phenomenon seriously rather than trivializing them as has been done in a considerable part of pertinent writing by sociologists, anthropologists and political scientists who for the most part work with a reductionist sense of the role and status of ideas in collective life.

Three contexts

The work on nationalism in the Eastern Mediterranean to be outlined in what follows can be considered on three levels, defined by successively broadened contextualizations:

(I) Cyprus. The study of nationalism in Cyprus, if at all seriously attempted, soon reveals that pertinent manifestations since the nineteenth century were not intellectually autonomous phenomena; they depended to a considerable degree on the growth and expansion of Greek nationalism and the movement of national definition emanating from the Greek nation-state. This is a very interesting phenomenon of nation and state building through a process of exportation of ideas and normative discourse. From the "national centre," formed by independent Greece, to the eastern periphery of Orthodox, Greek-speaking society still under Ottoman rule this process involved an expanding phenomenon of the socialization of distant, isolated and unconnected populations, related theoretically by language, into a new normative culture that exposed them to modernity. I say "theoretically" related by language in order to recall the multiple forms of modern Greek dispersed over a vast distance in the Eastern Mediterranean, which as linguistic substrata could sustain the development of several neo-Greek languages on the model of the several neo-Latin languages of Europe. This development proved abortive largely as a result of the propagation of a standard form of Modern Greek emanating from the Greek state and thus possessing the great normative authority that allowed it to be adopted as a formal medium primarily of written expression by communities geographically ranging far afield and speaking widely divergent forms of the Greek language.

The phenomenon of the interplay of language and state and the story of the abortive development of multiple neo-Greek languages constitutes, I believe, one of the most interesting aspects of the history of the growth of Greek nationalism in the Eastern Mediterranean. It also possesses broader interest concerning the role of the state in language cultivation — which we tend to assume — but also in language destruction — which we tend to forget. A separate Greek Cypriot language appeared as an immanent possibility in the society of Medieval

Cyprus, as documented by important surviving sources, and this could provide a hypothetical basis for a distinct Cypriot "nation." This possibility was aborted by the Ottoman conquest of the island, which integrated it into the broader Orthodox Greek-speaking society under Ottoman rule, the Rum millet. This development taught the Cypriots that they belonged to a wider ethnic and eventually national community. Meanwhile, the cultural expansion of Greek nationalism reduced Cypriot Greek from a potential language to the status of a dialect.

A caveat is necessary at this point to avoid misunderstandings. The expansion and reception of Greek nationalism in contexts beyond that of its original inception was not an imposed process. On the contrary, it was a welcome and heartily adopted form of cultural mutation in Cyprus, in Asia Minor, in the Balkans and elsewhere, a form of cultural change that brought to isolated, backward and oppressed populations the promise of modernization and freedom. It also provided a cognitive framework for making sense of their identity and their history and for visualizing their future. It supplied what Clifford Geertz has aptly described as a "cultural system" for making sense of reality and of historical experience.[4] This explains the power and tenacity of nationalism in Cyprus and elsewhere in the regions inhabited by unredeemed Greeks.[5] For these populations, nationalism supplied a framework of social meaning, and it has been a grave error both of British colonial officials and historians but also subsequently of anthropologists and political scientists to dismiss it as an artificial externally imposed or concocted phenomenon.

Two factors make the Cyprus case interesting. First, the total success of the implantation of Greek nationalism, with the consequence of cancelling out alternative possibilities in the development of local collective identity, eventually leading up to collision with the group that was inevitably excluded from this course of development, the Muslim community in Cyprus. As a consequence, instead of becoming Cypriots, Muslims became politically Turks, as the Orthodox Cypriots became politically Greeks. British colonial policies in the period 1878–1960 encouraged this development through the employment of divide-and-rule tactics, so typical of British imperial administrative methods, or in any case, by the failure or programmatic unwillingness to encourage any form of co-operation or concerted political action by the two Cypriot ethnic communities.[6]

The second factor that makes the Cyprus case interesting is its tenacity and long-term survival, keeping a nineteenth-century irredentist political mentality alive into the twenty-first century. Hence, the problem of incongruity between the Cypriot liberation movement in the 1950s and 1960s and other anticolonial movements. The consequence of this was the failure of the liberation struggle to unite Cypriot society. On the contrary, it cemented the multiple ethnic and political divisions marking the society of the island, creating the basis for the development of a "dialectic of intolerance" as the ideological context of political life in independent Cyprus.[7]

(II) Greek nationalism. The realization that the main dynamic of Greek Cypriot nationalism was imported from Greece directs our interest to the study of Greek nationalism, its history and successive phases of growth. Another major intellectual debt was incurred in this connection: a debt to Elie Kedourie, who could be considered, without risking serious exaggeration, the founding father of the critical study of nationalism in contemporary scholarship on account of his analysis of the political translation of the Kantian idea of self-determination into the distinctly Western doctrine of nationalism.[8] Within the context of his research on the intellectual history of nationalism, Kedourie discovered the significance of the political thought of Adamantios Korais, the great liberal political thinker of the early nineteenth century.[9] He encouraged me, at our first meeting in London in June 1974, to look at the Enlightenment origins of Greek nationalism and this became a lifelong project of which I have not become tired or bored, mainly because the Greek Enlightenment has left us such an exciting literary heritage.

There is one important aspect of Greek nationalism that I believe to be the major explanatory variable of its success in Greek society: it has over time been the central axis of the transition to modernity in Greek society and culture. It has been in this sense the major force shaping modern politics, meaning democratic politics, the politics of mass society. This can explain its appeal, both within but also outside the Greek state, in the course of the nineteenth century. It was the promise of modernization, liberty and justice that made nationalism such a powerful, indeed irresistible force in Greek politics.

(III) The Balkan context. Greek nationalism did not develop in a vacuum. As a historical phenomenon, it cannot be understood in isolation from its broader Balkan context. Reflecting upon and researching its expression and manifestation in the wider Greek world of the nineteenth century, one inevitably comes to consider it to be a Balkan phenomenon, one of the multiple forms of the advent of modernity in Southeastern Europe and certainly the main one. This was a story of conflict and confrontation on many levels:

- Conflict with the Ottoman masters of the region as expressed in the national revolutions and wars of liberation in the area;
- Conflict among the liberated Christians over territorial spoils and ambitions;
- Conflict between secular nationalism and the Orthodox Church.

Conflict on this third level, between secular nationalism and the Church, is a most interesting aspect of the problem because it directs attention to the fundamental incompatibility between religion and nationalism and to the eventual triumph of nationalism and co-opting of religion into its ideological and psychological quiver.[10] Research on this topic has been perhaps the most exciting component of my preoccupation with nationalism over the years; it has offered the possibility to reconsider critically many conventional truths, to place question marks before many ideological certainties and finally to draw distinctions that clarify the historicity of social and political experience. A central preoccupation of this critical perspective has been to question the identification of Orthodoxy with nationalism, an identification produced by the co-opting of religion, in this case Orthodoxy, into the ideological baggage of Balkan nation-states in the nineteenth century.[11] Orthodoxy, however, like all religions, is universalist in its outlook and values. It stands in stark contrast to the moral partiality of nationalism; national Orthodoxies constitute a political, not a religious construct, which in fact belies the ecumenical values of Christianity.[12]

Meanings of relevance

What is absolutely clear I think from the historical case studies outlined above is that nationalism is a major force in modern history, certainly the major force in modern politics. It cannot be wished away by just "deconstructing" it. In this sense, it is a *relevant* problem that invites serious thinking and responsible research, which means research that focuses on the sources that register the collective experience of societies, not upon the subjective impressions of individual observers, journalists, anthropologists and so on. Nationalism as a social and political force, a force of change in societies — not necessarily for the better — needs to be thought about critically, but not demonized. Demonization does not contribute either to the understanding or the proper direction of nationalism. With the recognition of the relevance of nationalism comes the response to our other question. We are not facing the end of the nation-state, which has demonstrated a remarkable resilience and resourcefulness in adapting to a whole range of modern challenges. Nation-states are going strong and they retain their power, primarily because their legitimacy in the collective conscience of the societies over which they rule remains dominant and meaningful. For as long as nations as human communities retain their meaning and legitimacy, supranational structures, movements and organizations have to find ways to accommodate them. This is a clear lesson of the experience of the European community since its foundation and since the creation of the European Union in our own time.

One significant dimension of this *problématique,* which needs to be uppermost in our mind if we wish to pass serious and fair judgement based on understanding rather than on arbitrary subjectivism, has to do with the recognition of the fact that societies and more partial human communities crave nationalism because it nurtures expectations that they treasure, including the expectation of justice. This has been the experience of Cyprus that many observers have failed to appreciate. Let us remember as a further illustration the aspirations of colonial peoples, aspirations that have very often, almost as a rule, been bitterly disappointed by the political outcomes of their struggles.

These are nevertheless real, fundamental aspirations that guide and shape the destinies of societies.

This brings up another issue: the antinomy, very often dramatic indeed, between intellectual criticism and democratic commitment. Do we respect the will and expectations of the majority and the reasons for them, or are we satisfied to indulge in our intellectual complacence regardless of the needs and aspirations of the community around us? This is a question intellectuals, especially those who consider themselves "progressives" (always keen to dismiss nationalism and its significance) need to ask themselves.

This said, we should exercise discretion lest our democratic commitments lead us to a kind of normative rehabilitation of nationalism as a form of public discourse that superficially appears to provide alternatives and correctives to individualism. This, it seems to me, has been a temptation with which some communitarian critics of liberalism appear prepared to flirt in the course of their critique of the moral failures of individualism. This is a misguided expectation. Nationalism may move societies but it remains a morally outrageous doctrine. It elevates partiality against universalism, celebrates expediency against the claims of the categorical imperative, and obscures, very often dishonestly, the values of toleration and human dignity. On account of its moral makeup, nationalism can easily slide toward extremism, fanaticism and aggression. As a consequence, it is a doctrine that very often turns against itself and can lead communities to self-destruction, as is very sadly illustrated, among innumerable other examples, by the experience of Cyprus in the twentieth century. In this sense, it is and perhaps ought to be considered an *irrelevant* moral doctrine, which needs—because it remains such a powerful social and political force—to be guided and instructed rather than flattered and rekindled. This is an urgent task, incumbent upon responsible political and intellectual leadership in democratic societies.

Notes

1 John Stuart Mill, *Autobiography*, Indianapolis: The Library of Liberal Arts, 1957, p. 3.
2 Paschalis M. Kitromilides, *Patterns of politics in Cyprus*, Middletown, CT: Wesleyan University, 1972; Peter Loizos, *The Greek Gift: Politics in a Cypriot Village*, Oxford: Blackwell, 1975, p. 286.
3 *John K. Campbell, Honour, family and patronage: a study of institutions and moral values in a Greek mountain community*, Oxford: Clarendon, 1968; John K. Campbell "The Greek hero", *Honour and grace in Anthropology*, J. G. Peristiany & J. Pitt-Rivers, eds, Cambridge: Cambridge University Press, 1992, pp. 129–149; John G. Peristiany, *Honour and shame: the values of Mediterenean society*, London: Widenfeld and Nicolson, 1965.
4 Clifford Geertz, *The interpretation of cultures*, New York: Basic Books, 1973, pp. 193–233.
5 Paschalis M. Kitromilides, *Enlightenment, nationalism, orthodoxy: studies in the culture and political thought of Southeastern Europe*, Aldershot: Variorum, 1994, study no. XII.

6 G. S. Georgalides, *A political and administrative history of Cyprus (1918–1926): with a survey of the foundations of British rule,* Nicosia: Cyprus Research Center, 1979; G. S. Georgallides, *Cyprus and the governorship of Sir Ronald Storrs: the causes of the 1931 crisis,* Nicosia: Cyprus Research Center, 1985; Robert Holland, *Britain and the revolt in Cyprus 1954–1959,* Oxford: Claredon, 1998.
7 Paschalis M. Kitromilides, *Enlightenment, nationalism, orthodoxy: studies in the culture and political thought of Southeastern Europe,* study no. XII.
8 Elie Kedourie, *Nationalism,* London: Hutchinson, 1960.
9 Elie Kedourie, *Nationalism in Asia and Africa,* New York: Meridian, 1970, pp. 37–43, 153–188.
10 Paschalis M. Kitromilides, *Enlightenment, nationalism, Orthodoxy: studies in the culture and political thought of Southeastern Europe,* study no. XI.
11 Paschalis M. Kitromilides, "The legacy of the French revolution: Orthodoxy and nationalism", *The Cambridge history of Christianity: Eastern Christianity,* M. Angold, ed., Cambridge: Cambridge University Press, 2006, pp. 229–249.
12 Paschalis M. Kitromilides, *An Orthodox commonwealth: symbolic legacies and cultural encounters in Southeastern Europe,* Aldershot: Variorum, 2007.

14 Milestones in the historiography of the Cyprus question

The recent public debate in Greece and Cyprus provoked by the UN plan proposed in November 2002 for the settlement of the Cyprus Question has rekindled interest in a problem of long standing, a problem that has been occasionally described as the "last phase of the Eastern Question". In thinking about the Cyprus Question it would be well to remember that the long history of the problem, since at least the British occupation of the island of Cyprus in 1878, has provided the background to a remarkable scholarly literature, which has appraised, in considerable depth, the successive phases and the multiple aspects, domestic as well as international, of a convoluted conflict. It should be remembered, therefore, that the Cyprus Question besides being a political and international problem is also an important scholarly problem, which should be approached according to the norms of scholarship in order to be fully understood and fairly debated.

What follows is an attempt to recall some of the major scholarly contributions to the historiography of the Cyprus Question in order to illustrate the breadth of the pertinent bibliography. The methodological approach is based on a periodization, dictated by the major phases in the evolution of the Cyprus Question since the 1930s. The phases that form the basis of the periodization of the scholarly literature were shaped by the interplay of domestic factors with international politics, which created a dynamic that invariably complicated the problem.

By way of introduction I should note two fundamental works, which really constitute the milestones that map out the territory of serious scholarship on the Cyprus Question: the fourth volume of the *History of Cyprus* by Sir George Hill (*The Ottoman Province, the British Colony*, ed. Harry Luke, Cambridge, 1952) and the two-volume work by François Crouzet, *Le conflit de Chypre 1946–1959* (Brussels, 1973). Although now dated, Hill's work is indispensable for the wealth of historical detail it makes available and for its criticism of the sources, both features contributing to a serious understanding of politics in colonial Cyprus. François Crouzet, an eminent French historian, worked on Cyprus in a project of the Carnegie Endowment for International Peace and attempted to show the structural factors that contributed to what turned out to be an ethnic conflict made intractable by the involvement of international forces that amplified local conflicts into much vaster confrontations. These two works constitute the obligatory starting bibliographical point of all serious work on the Cyprus Question and the ability to do this is a yardstick for measuring the reliability of all subsequent work.

The Cyprus question in the 1930s

The uprising of 21 October 1931 in Nicosia and other cities but also in parts of the Cypriot countryside could be considered the modern origin of the Cyprus Question. The rising, the reaction of the colonial power to it and its consequences for local politics set in motion a series of crises that account for the subsequent complications and contradictions that still plague the Cyprus problem. The 1931 events in Cyprus attracted the attention of a historian of the pre-eminence of Arnold Toynbee, who in two reports in successive volumes of the *Survey of International Affairs* (for 1931 and 1932) he compiled at the time recorded very perceptive and acute observations on the socio-political dynamics of the problem. In particular Toynbee pointed to the growth of Greek nationalism among the rural population of Cyprus as a factor that added significant dynamism to the *enosis* movement on the island, a dynamism ignored by the imperious attitude of the colonial power with disastrous consequences later on. This early phase of the Cyprus Question has formed the object of a truly magisterial historiographical contribution by G. S. Georghallides, who could be considered, without risk of exaggeration, the most authoritative historian of the period of British rule in Cyprus: G. S. Georghallides, *Cyprus under the Governorship of Sir Roland Storrs*, Nicosia, 1985 [Cyprus Research Centre, Texts and Studies of the History of Cyprus XIII]. This major work completes the survey of the early period of British rule in Cyprus by the same historian: *A Political and Administrative History of Cyprus, 1918–1926, with a Survey of the Foundations of British Rule*, Nicosia, 1979 [Texts and Studies, VI]. The handling of the rising in 1931 by Greek diplomacy and in particular by Prime Minister Eleftherios Venizelos, who had the courage to stand up to the pressures of nationalist emotionalism, is the object of the most significant contribution to the subject in Greek by Yiannis Pikros, *Ο Βενιζέλος και το Κυπριακό* [Venizelos and the Cyprus Question], Athens, 1980.

The Cyprus question under the impact of World War II: the 1940s

The Second World War brought about fundamental changes to the definition of the problem, on two levels. First on the international level following Britain's fight for freedom against the Axis and the Cypriots's response and support for the British effort it was difficult to ignore their own wishes for self-determination. On the domestic level the emergence of the organized Left as a decisive factor in local politics, as made plain by the landslides of the Left in municipal elections in 1943, 1946 and 1949, added an important new player to Cypriot politics. The new political landscape that emerged in Cyprus in the 1940s is considered in detail on the basis of extensive documentation by Rolandos Katsiaounis, *Η Διασκεπτική 1946–1948* [The Consultative Assembly 1946–1948], Nicosia 2000 [Texts and Studies XXVIII].

The decade of internationalization and the liberation struggle: the 1950s

Greece's appeals to the United Nations for the recognition of the right of self-determination to the people of Cyprus (1954, 1955, 1956 and 1957) and the armed liberation struggle initiated in Cyprus (1955–1959) turned the Cyprus Question from a bilateral Greco-British problem into an international issue, with Turkey and the United States and other players drawn in. The international climate of the Cold War inevitably drew the Soviet Union, but also the nonaligned countries into the picture as it emerged from the debates on Cyprus in the Security Council and the General Assembly of the United Nations. The Cyprus Question was led to a — temporary as it turned out — settlement with the Zürich and London Agreements of February 1959. These developments generated a considerable literature from among which stand out two imposing works by Stephen G. Xydis, *Cyprus: Conflict and Conciliation 1954–1958*, Columbus Ohio, 1967 and *Cyprus: Reluctant Republic*, The Hague and Paris, 1973.

The international aspect of the Cyprus Question in the 1950s forms also the object of two other more recent studies: Robert Holland, *Britain and the Revolt in Cyprus 1954–1959*, Oxford, 1998 and Ioannis D. Stephanides, *Isle of Discord. Nationalism, Imperialism and the Making of the Cyprus Problem*, London, 1999. Both of these studies are distinguished by the quality of writing, the extensive research and the critical perspectives that inform them on British and Greek diplomacy respectively. Robert Holland contributes substantively not only to the appraisal of British policy on Cyprus which he judges short-sighted and vindictive, but more importantly he provides a reappraisal of the armed liberation struggle in Cyprus pointing to its comparative significance and placing it in a broader context of political interrelations and options in the age of decolonization. He thus offers a more substantive understanding of the dynamics of the problem that leads beyond the image of a terrorist campaign as the struggle was depicted by British diplomacy and reflected for instance in the detailed study by Nancy Crawshaw, *The Cyprus Revolt*, London, 1978. I. D. Stephanides's monograph on the other hand represents a remarkable exception in the plethora of writings by Greek and Cypriot authors who avoid to pass judgement on Greek and especially on Cypriot policies and decisions in the successive crises and tend to put the blame squarely on the "imperialist factor", depicting the Greeks as mere victims of the machinations of foreign powers.

The 1960s: statehood and ethnic conflict

The 1960s represent a critical phase in the evolution of the Cyprus Question, marked by the island's advent to independent statehood. Independence presented the Cypriots with a test of their ability to responsibly govern themselves. To Greece Cypriot statehood presented a test of her will and ability to tolerate an independent Cyprus as an equal partner in international relations. The psychology underlying this test is sketched out with great virtuosity by Alexander Xydis, "Το ψυχολογικό πλέγμα" [The psychological complex] in the collective volume A. Xydis et al., *Ο Μακάριος και οι σύμμαχοί του* [Makarios and his Allies], Athens 1972. Xydis's perceptive essay in political psychology has retained over a thirty-year period its topicality as a source of explanation of the periodic tensions and crises in the relations between Greece and Cyprus.

The most important study on the early history of the Republic of Cyprus is Diana Weston-Markides, *Cyprus 1957–1963. From Colonial Conflict to Constitutional Crisis. The Key Role of the Municipal Issue*, Minneapolis, 2001. This is a dispassionate analysis of the issue of separate municipalities introduced in the principal cities of Cyprus by the London agreements — an issue that turned out to be the major cause of the breakdown of the 1960 constitutional settlement in 1963. The author elucidates the inception and early discussion of the idea of separate municipalities and the subsequent problems in attempting to apply it in the new republic.

The 1970s: tragedy and survival

The 1970s was for Cyprus a period of tragedy brought about by the coup of 15 July 1974, engineered by the Greek military regime, and the Turkish invasion that followed. The dramatic events generated an extensive literature, predictably of unequal quality. From the plethora of pertinent contributions one might single out two collective volumes, based on conferences that met in Nicosia in June and September 1976 respectively. These two collections are of significance as early attempts at a self-critical examination of the problem by the Cypriots themselves: M. Attalides, ed., *Cyprus Reviewed*, Nicosia, 1977 and Peter Worseley and P. M. Kitromilides, eds., *Small States in the Modern World: The Conditions of Survival*, Nicosia, 1979. Mention should also be made of an important contribution by the distinguished American journalist Laurence Stern, *The Wrong Horse. The Politics of Intervention and the Failure of American Diplomacy*, New York, 1977, which offers a chronicle of covert American action aiming at destabilizing the Republic of Cyprus and points to the irrationalism and short-sightedness of US attitudes toward President Makarios.

Besides scholarly literature the successive crises of the Cyprus Question have generated important accounts by some of the principal participants. Inevitably some of these works are better than others, but a few among them are of fundamental significance for an understanding of the problem: E. Averoff-Tosizza, *Lost Opportunities: the Cyprus Question 1952–1963*, New York: New Rochelle, N.Y. 1986 and Glafkos Cleridis, *Cyprus: My Deposition*, 4 vols., Nicosia 1989–1992. Of sources available only in Greek the serious student of the Cyprus Question cannot overlook the writings of three important critical observers and participants: C. Christidis, *Κυπριακό και*

Ελληνοτουρκικά. Πορεία μιας εθνικής χρεωκοπίας [The Cyprus Question and Greek-Turkish Relations. Trajectory of a National Bankruptcy], Athens, 1967 and *Κυπριακό 1968–1980* [The Cyprus Question 1968–1980], Athens, 1984; Ploutis Servas, *Κυπριακό. Ευθύνες* [The Cyprus Question. Responsibilities], 4 vols, Athens, 1980–1993. Christidis, a distinguished lawyer and intellectual, was a legendary pamphleteer from the 1950s to the 1970s, producing under the pseudonym Damonides acute appraisals of the Cyprus Question, full of perceptive judgements and prescient warnings on the policy options adopted by successive Greek governments and Cypriot leaders. Servas was a veteran Cypriot communist leader, who was expelled from the party in the late 1940s and in this work he apportions blame and responsibility to all those who had played an active role in handling the Cyprus problem over the critical decades from the 1940s to the 1970s. Finally of special value is the testimony of M. Dekleris, *Κυπριακό. Η τελευταία ευκαιρία 1972–1974* [The Cyprus Question. The Last Chance 1972–1974], Athens 1981, 2nd edition 2003. The author, a senior Greek judge, participated as a constitutional expert in the intercommunal talks in Cyprus on the eve of the invasion and in his book he outlines the narrowing of differences between the two communities which would have made an agreement possible had it not been for the coup and the invasion.

* * *

This has been a rather condensed survey of an extensive literature, pointing out what, in the present author's judgement, is required reading by the scholar, journalist or observer who wants to develop a serious understanding of a complex, often contradictory and tragic problem. Part of the problem has been due to cognitive inadequacies and for this reason there is no other remedy than a serious self-education by all those who aspire to judge and to act in the Cyprus Question. What has been offered above is no more than a chart for apprentice navigators in a sea with many reefs and shallows.

Part Three

Bibliographical and critical notes

Study 1: "Cyprus in History".

This chapter on the trajectories of Cyprus in history is a revised version of an introductory survey originally published in *Cyprus: The Book of Maps*, ed. by Artemis Scutari, Athens: Adventure SA, 2016, pp. v–x. The impressive volume is a catalogue of early printed maps of Cyprus (15th–16th centuries) from the collection of the Sylvia Ioannou Foundation. This is an invaluable source of insights into the fortunes and perception of late Medieval and early modern Cyprus. It is pointless to try to add bibliographical documentation to this survey, which records the present author's understanding of the historical destinies of the island after almost half a century of research on the subject. A few allusions in the text, nevertheless, could be made clearer by citing the sources to which reference is implicitly made in the narrative.

The chronology of ancient Cyprus outlined in this chapter has now been re-established and clarified on the basis of a reappraisal of richer archaeological evidence. See Nota Kourou, George Bourogiannis, *Ρυθμοί τῆς κυπριακῆς κεραμικῆς*, Nicosia: University of Cyprus, 2018, pp. 2–5.

The flirtations of Cypriots with the ideas of the Reformation and the collection of prohibited books in Nicosia are discussed in Paschalis M. Kitromilides, "Βιβλία καὶ ἀνάγνωση στὴ Λευκωσία τῆς Ἀναγέννησης. Ἡ μαρτυρία τῆς βιβλιοθήκης τοῦ Μάρκου Ζαχαρία", *Κύπρος –Βενετία. Κοινές ἱστορικές τύχες*, ed. by Chrysa Maltezou, Venice: Hellenic Institute of Byzantine and Post-Byzantine Studies, 2002, pp. 263–275. The subject is revisited at much greater length and detail by Evelyn Chayes, "Carriers, Companions, Accomplices. The Zaccaria Network", *Cyprus and the Renaissance (1450–1650)*, ed. by Benjamin Arbel, Evelyn Chayes, Harald Hendrix, Turnout, Belgium: Brepols, 2012, pp. 231–272. This whole collection is absolutely essential for the knowledge of the "Cypriot Renaissance". Father Agostino Famagostano's report on the martyrdom of Marcantonio Bragadin on 17 August 1571 is published in *Κυπριακές πηγές για την ἀλωση της Ἀμμοχώστου*, ed. by Paschalis M. Kitromilides [Sources of Cypriot Learning and History, no. 2] Athens: Institute for Neohellenic Research/NHRF, 2011, pp. 91–113. The broadsides (avvisi) of the War of Cyprus have been collected by Aik. Koumarianou, *Ενημερωτικά Δυτικά Φύλλα (1570-1572). Ο Πόλεμος της Κύπρου*, Nicosia: Cultural Foundation of the Bank of Cyprus, 2004.

The idea of Venetian Cyprus as a "colonial economy" was first suggested by the great French historian of Medieval Cyprus, Jean Richard, in "Une économie coloniale? Chypre et ses resources agricolles au Moyen Age", *Byzantinische Forschungen* 5 (1977), pp. 331–352 and has provoked considerable debate among specialists.

On society and economy in Venetian Cyprus a major new contribution is the collection of Benjamin Arbel's papers, *Studies on Venetian Cyprus*, Nicosia: Cyprus Research Centre, 2017, which brings into focus many neglected aspects of the social history of the island under the republic of Saint Mark.

Study 2: "Early Modern Cypriot Learning (1571–1878)".

This study is an updated English language adaptation of part of the introduction to my work, *Κυπριακή λογιοσύνη 1571–1878. Προσωπογραφική θεώρηση*, Nicosia: Cyprus Research Centre, 2002, pp. 42–62. An earlier version of the same section of the work appeared in French translation, "Esquisse d' une périodisation de la vie intellectuelle chypriote 1571–1878", *Cahier du Centre d'Études Chypriotes* 36 (2006), pp. 125–141. A much longer and substantial treatment of the same subject appears under the title, "Η παράδοση τῶν Ἑλληνικῶν γραμμάτων καὶ ἡ Κυπριακὴ λογιοσύνη», *Ἱστορία τῆς Κύπρου*", ed. by Theodore Papadopoullos, Vol. VI, Nicosia: Archbishop Makarios III Foundation, 2011, pp. 489–517. The pertinent phenomena discussed in the present study were mostly intellectual expressions of the diaspora. A very important contribution to the subject is Zacharias N. Tsirpanlis, *Ὁ Κυπριακὸς ἑλληνισμὸς τῆς διασπορᾶς καὶ οἱ σχέσεις Κύπρου – Βατικανοῦ (1571–1878)*, Thessaloniki: Stamoulis, 2006.

A further important contribution to the subject is George Kechagioglou, "Κάτω από τον αστερισμό της κοινής νεοελληνικής: Συγγραφείς, γραμματεία και λογοτεχνική παραγωγή στην Κύπρο, την Οθωμανική αυτοκρατορία και την ευρωπαϊκή διασπορά (1571–1821)", in George Kechagioglou, Lefteris Papaleontiou, *Ιστορία της νεότερης Κυπριακής λογοτεχνίας*, Nicosia: Cyprus Research Centre, 2010, pp. 127–182.

In connection with the issues of intellectual history raised in this study two truly monumental editions of works by Cypriot scholars active in the period under review should be mentioned:

- *Ioakeim Kyprios' Struggle. A Narrative Poem on the "Cretan War" of 1645–1669.* Editio princeps, ed. by Tassos A. Kaplanis, Nicosia: Cyprus Research Centre, 2012.

- Markantonis Dagres (Darkes), *Συντυχία (α)πάνω στα προσκυνήματα του Ιεροσολυμάτου*, ed. by George Kechagioglou, Nicosia: Archbishop Makarios III Foundation, 2017.

These two works set the philological standards for a total re-examination of intellectual life and creative traditions in early modern Cyprus.

The emblematic work of Renaissance literature in Cypriot culture, the sixteenth-century anthology of Petrarchan poetry, is now available in a new edition, Ἡ Κυπριακὴ συλλογὴ Πετραρχικῶν καὶ ἄλλων Ἀναγεννησιακῶν ποιημάτων, ed. by Paschalis M. Kitromlides, introduction Elsie Tornaritou-Mathiopoulou [Sources of Cypriot Learning and History no. 5], Athens: Institute of Historical Research/NHRF, 2018.

Study 3: "The patriotism of the expatriates".

Originally published in *Il Pensiero Politico* 48/3 (2015), pp. 506–514.

The works by Tsirpanlis and Kechagioglou cited in the Bibliographical Note to Study II are completely relevant to Study III as well. They both provide extensive additional bibliography pertinent to the subjects discussed in the present study.

Study 4: "Repression and protest in traditional society: Cyprus 1764".

Originally published in Κυπριακαὶ Σπουδαί, Vol. 46 (1982), pp. 91–101.

The events of the revolt of 1764–1765 in Cyprus elicited considerable interest from European diplomacy at the time. The French Consul's report, dated 18 November 1764 from the French *Archives Nationales* is published here for the first time in the Appendix to the present study.

The Levant Company's Consul also produced reports to the British Embassy in Constantinople, which were transmitted to London, using cryptography. On the basis of these documents all dated 1766 it appears that the revolt was not quelled until the Spring-Summer 1766. See The National Archives, United Kingdom, State Papers 97/43, 15 March 1766, 15 July 1766, 16 October 1766, 15 December 1766.

Extensive prosopographical details concerning the *dramatis personae* (Caprara, Crutta, Vondiziano *et al.*) mentioned in the Venetian Consul's report have been made available thanks to the publication of the parish register of the Fransiscan church of Santa Maria delle Grazie in Larnaca by Mia Gaia Trentin, ed., *Animam Deo reddit. The Parish Register of the Dead Santa Maria of Larnaca (1729–1824)*, [Sources of Cypriot Learning and History, no. 4], Athens: Institute of Historical Research/NHRF, 2016. Many of the persons appearing in this episode are also encountered in the Greek documents from the Archive of the Venetian Consulate at Larnaca published in Paschalis M. Kitromilides, Κοινωνικές σχέσεις καὶ νοοτροπίες στὴν Κύπρο του δεκάτου ογδόου αιώνα, Nicosia 1992.

Study 5: "The anonymity of a prominent woman in eighteenth-century Cyprus".

Originally published in *Historical Poetics in Nineteenth and Twentieth Century Greece: Essays in Honor of Lily Macrakis*, ed. by Stamatia Dova,

Washington, DC: Center for Hellenic Studies, Harvard University, 2014, pp. 293–300. Translated by Panayotis League.

Substantial new information on the enterprising Dragoman Christophakis Constantinou has come to light from the Ottoman documents published by Theocharis Stavridis, ed., *Ottoman Documents from the Archives of the Venetian Consulate of Cyprus, 1671–1765*, Nicosia: Cyprus Research Centre, 2016, pp. 17–24 and passim.

The deeper question of gender inequality and female anonymity which is a diachronic issue not just in Cypriot history, but in the history of the human condition in general, remains the substantive subject raised by this study. I cannot resist the temptation to recall here an ancient Athenian inscription discovered at the metro-construction works in Athens, now on show at the Constitution Square station exhibition space:

ΩΣΑΡΙΟΝ
ΕΡΜΙΠΠΟΥ
ΖΩΕΙΛΟΥ
ΚΗΦΙΣΙΕΩΣ
ΓΥΝΗΙ

The Hellenistic or Roman stele to the woman of Hermippos son of Zoeilos from Kifisia informs us precisely about the identity of the husband but tells us absolutely nothing about the dead wife, who is remembered only as the female accompaniment of the male sponsor of the monument.

The ancient inscription raises, two thousand years earlier, exactly the same moral issues as the family portrait of the Christophakis clan at St George of Arpera.

Study 6: "A Moldavian connection to the introduction of the Enlightenment in Cyprus: the contribution of Archbishop Kyprianos (1810–1821)".

Originally published in *Istoria: Utopie, amintire şi proiect de viitor. Studii de istorie oferite Profesorului Andrei Pippidi*, ed. by Radu G. Paun, Ovidiu Cristea, Iasi: Editura Universitătii Alexandru Ioan Cuza, 2013, 167–176.

The subject of the "ecclesiastical Enlightenment" in the Orthodox Church, with references to Cyprus, is revisited in my book, *Religion and Politics in the Orthodox World. The Ecumenical Patriarchate and the Challenges of Modernity*, London and New York: Routledge, 2018, pp. 12–24, 51–52.

Study 7: "Cyprus in 1821: a report to the Levant Company and the layers of historical memory".

Published in *Revue des études Sud-Est européennes* 51 (2013), 321–328.

In addition to the works cited in the notes to this chapter, Cyprus's place in the Greek Revolution is also considered in a collection of documents by Emmanuel Protopsaltis, ed., Ἡ Κύπρος εἰς τὸν ἀγῶνα τοῦ *1821*, Athens, 1971.

A recent collection of French documents by Anna Pouradier Duteil-Loizidou, ed., *Chypre au temps de la Revolution Grecque d'après la correspondence consulaire et diplomatique française – Année 1821*, Nicosia: Cyprus Research Centre, 2018, also adds a host of details on the events of that fateful year. See especially pp. 142–148 for the report dated 27 July 1821 by Consul Méchain on the martyrdom of Archbishop Kyprianos and the other prelates and dignitaries.

Study 8: "Collective consciousness and poetry: three moments in the literary tradition of modern Cyprus".

This short chapter, originally published in *Neo-Hellenika*, Vol. IV (1981), pp. 159–170, was written like many other pieces in this collection under the climate caused by the catastrophe of 1974. My judgment is now modified concerning the appraisal of some of the poets treated in the essay, but the text is left in its original form, on the basis of the general principle followed in compiling this collection. It was probably the earliest discussion of politics and literature in Cyprus to be attempted in English and it is reproduced here mainly for its historiographical interest. The treatment of Cypriot literature has been greatly enhanced in George Kechagioglou, Lefteris Papaleontiou, Ιστορία της νεότερης Κυπριακής λογοτεχνίας, Nicosia: Cyprus Research Centre, 2010, esp. pp. 213ff.

An annotated selection of writing on Cypriot literature in English appears in Paschalis M. Kitromilides, Marios L. Evriviades, *World Bibliographical Series*, Vol. 28: *Cyprus*. Revised edition, Oxford and Santa Barbara: Clio Press, 1995, pp. 190–194, entries nos. 775–793.

This short critical chapter concludes by pointing to the emergence of generation of poets whose inspiration was painfully shaped by the bitter experience of the catastrophe of 1974. The achievements of this generation of Cypriot poetry have been remarkable in the almost half a century since the tragedy. This claim is now impressively borne out by the publication of the imposing volume of the collected poetry of Kyriakos Charalambides, Ποιήματα *1961–2017*, Athens: Ikaros, 2019.

Study 9: "From Coexistence to Confrontation: The dynamics of ethnic conflict in Cyprus".

Published in *Cyprus Reviewed*, ed. by Michael Attalides, Nicosia: Zavallis Press, 1977, pp. 35–70. This study is a considerably expanded version of a conference paper entitled, "Cyprus: The nature of ethnic conflict", originally presented at a meeting in Washington, DC in February 1975 and included in the proceedings: *US Foreign Policy toward Greece and Cyprus. The Clash of Principle and Pragmatism*, ed. by Theodore Couloumbis and Sallie M. Hicks, Washington, DC: The Center for Mediterranean Studies, 1975, pp. 83–97. In a much expanded version and with a revised title the article was included in *Cyprus Reviewed*, ed. by Michael Attalides, Nicosia: Zavallis Press, 1977, pp. 35–70 from where it is reproduced here.

In its successive incarnations the study represents an evolving attempt to develop a conceptualization of ethnic conflict in Cyprus in order to establish a historical sociology of the Cyprus Question, away from often simplistic power politics interpretations, ignoring the internal dynamics that eventually shape to a significant degree the nature of social and political conflicts. The article, along with the pertinent writings of Michael Attalides, is critically discussed by Mete Hatay, Yannis Papadakis, "A Critical Comparison of Greek and Turkish Cypriot Official Historiographies (1940s to the present)", *Cyprus and the Politics of Memory. History, Community and Conflict*, ed. by Rebecca Bryant, Yannis Papadakis, London and New York: I. B. Tauris, 2012, esp. pp. 38–40, noting the novel approach to writing on the history of ethnic conflict due to the consideration of the issues involved through the perspective of theories of nationalism.

The study had a considerable impact and was extensively cited in the literature on the Cyprus Question. Since the original publication, nevertheless, there has been an enormous amount of writing on the subject and it would not be realistic to expect to produce in this Note even a moderately satisfactory update. I will record, therefore, what I was reminded of as I was reading the text in its original form and I will also note some works which I consider essential for the broader understanding of the problem in its multiple contexts.

As it will be noted, the theoretical conceptualization of the phenomena of ethnic relations, ethnic politics and conflict in Cyprus presented in this paper was shaped to a considerable extent by the writings of Walker Connor on the subject. His writings have since been collected in an insightful volume, *Ethnonationalism. The Quest of Understanding*, Princeton: Princeton University Press, 1994. I acknowledge my debt to this great pioneer of the study of nationalism and ethnic politics in a recent article, "The modernity of nations. A tribute to Walker Connor", *Nations and Nationalism* 24 (2018), pp. 506–512. The study of ethnic conflict has further produced important works, notably by Donald L. Horowitz, *Ethnic Groups in Conflict*, Berkeley, CA: University of California Press, 1985, 2000, an important source in which Cyprus makes a negligible appearance. I might also mention Stefan Wolff, *Ethnic Conflict. A Global Perspective*, Oxford: Oxford University Press, 2006, with more substantial references to Cyprus.

The main argument the chapter is trying to outline through the historical sociology of the Cyprus Question suggests that ethnic conflict emerges as the result of sectional nationalism in plural societies. In the case of Cyprus ethnic conflict was the result of the growth of two rival nationalist movements, which politicized traditional religious differences and turned them into incompatible modern value systems. I have tried to reconstruct this process in a twin article to this one, "The Dialectic of Intolerance. Ideological Dimensions of ethnic conflicts", *Journal of the Hellenic Diaspora* VI, 4 (Winter 1979), pp. 5–30. A longer version, including some normative suggestions, appeared in *Small*

States in the Modern World. The Conditions of Survival. Revised edition, ed. by Peter Worseley, Paschalis M. Kitromilides, Nicosia: Cyprus Sociological Association, 1979, pp. 143–184.

One major methodological principle I believe should be followed in the study of nationalism if the pertinent phenomena are to be understood, is to see the process of cultural and symbolic transformation involved in its implantation in societies as part of their transition to modernity, through the lens of intellectual history. An intellectual history approach is necessary for a substantive understanding of nationalism. In the present study and its twin, "The Dialectic of Intolerance", I have tried to follow this path. Intellectual history can help us understand the growth of national consciousness and the elaboration of collective visions that make social and political change understandable in the broader society, beyond intellectual elites. Elites of course are the initial carriers of the forms of intellectual change that eventually bring about the national transformation of societies. In the case of Cyprus one such group had been Cypriot volunteers in the Greek armed forces — that fought in the wars of the Greek kingdom in 1897 and in 1912—1913. Detailed pertinent evidence is presented in Petros Papapolyviou, *Φαεινόν σημείον ατυχούς πολέμου. Η συμμετοχή της Κύπρου στον ελληνοτουρκικό πόλεμο του 1897*, Nicosia: Cyprus Research Centre, 2001 and *Η Κύπρος και οι Βαλκανικοί Πόλεμοι. Συμβολή στην ιστορία του κυπριακού εθελοντισμού*, Nicosia: Cyprus Research Centre, 1997. It is by looking at this kind of detail that the scholar of nationalism might come to understand the transformation of individual persons through the gripping experience of partaking in national sentiment and then through the actions of individuals one can observe the transition of societies to the ideological novelty of nationalism. A valuable documentary record on the growth of Greek nationalism in Cyprus in the early phases of British rule is supplied by Theodore Papadopoullos, ed., *Ἡ Διοργάνωσις τοῦ ἐθνικοῦ κινήματος 1901–1931*, Nicosia 2009 (Cypriological Library no. 18).

Nationalism as a fully fledged movement in Cyprus emerged in the 1930s as discussed in a well-researched monograph by Alexis Rappas, *Cyprus in the 1930s. British Colonial Rule and the Roots of the Cyprus Conflict*, London: I. B. Tauris, 2014. The further escalation of the problem through the intensification of nationalism in the 1950s is considered by Ioannis D. Stefanidis, *Isle of Discord. Nationalism, imperialism and the making of the Cyprus Problem*, London: Hurst, 1999, while David French re-enacts the final tragic and heroic act of the drama of nationalism in colonial Cyprus in *Fighting EOKA. The British Counter-Insurgency Campaign on Cyprus, 1955–1959*, Oxford: Oxford University Press, 2015.

Still despite the growth of Greek nationalism in Cyprus and Turkish Cypriot reactions to it, multiple forms of traditional coexistence survived at the grass roots as suggested by extensive evidence from folklore and popular religion, well into the twentieth century. For understanding literally the dynamics of ethnic conflict it is essential to understand the evolution of the

Turkish Cypriot community. On this, two works are essential: Altay Nevzat, *Nationalism amongst the Turks of Cyprus. The First Wave*, Oulu, Finland: University of Oulu, 2005 and Sotos Ktoris, *Οι Τουρκοκύπριοι. Από το περιθώριο στο συνεταιρισμό (1923–1960)*, Athens: Papazisis, 2013. To this should be added an earlier work by a senior Turkish Cypriot scholar, Ahmet C. Gazioglu, *The Turks in Cyprus: A province of the Ottoman Empire (1571–1878)*, London: K. Rustem and Brother, 1990, which is free to a considerable extent of the propagandist tone that marked for much too long most Turkish and Turkish Cypriot writing on Cyprus and provides an important account of the origins the Turkish Cypriot community and its development during the period of Ottoman rule in Cyprus. Also important for understanding the Turkish Cypriot community is James Norman Dalrymple Anderson, "The family law of Turkish Cypriots", *Die Welt des Islams*, N. S., 5 (1958), pp. 161–187.

The growth of nationalism and the reactions it provokes among groups which feel threatened by it eventually escalate in ethnic conflict. Since the original publication of this study in 1977 there has been an outpouring of writing on ethnic conflict in Cyprus. From this literature two truly important works stand out: François Crouzet, *Le conflit de Chypre 1944–1959*, Brussels: Bruylant, 1973, 2 volumes and Harry Anastasiou, *The Broken Olive Branch: Nationalism, Ethnic Conflict, and the Quest for Peace in Cyprus*, Syracuse: Syracuse University Press, 2008, 2 volumes.

Of the legion of writings on the 1974 tragedy two works of political criticism stand out and should not be forgotten by the serious study of the Cyprus problem:

- Laurence Stern, *The Wrong Horse: The Politics of Intervention and the Failure of American Diplomacy*, New York: Times Books, 1977
- Christopher Hitchens, *Hostage to History. Cyprus from the Ottomans to Kissinger*, New York: The Nounday Press, 1989.

The extensive literature on the 1974 crisis is surveyed and critically commented in Paschalis M. Kitromilides, Marios L. Evriviades, *World Bibliographical Series*, Vol. 28: *Cyprus*. Revised edition, Oxford and Santa Barbara: Clio Press, 1995, pp. 110–132, entries 458–834.

Nationalism and the politicization of ethnicity have been major factors obstructing resolution of the Cyprus problem. From the extensive literature the following sources consider the pertinent issues from multiple angles: Michael A. Attalides, *Cyprus: Nationalism and International Politics*, Edinburgh: St. Martin's Press, 1979; Norma Salem, ed., *Cyprus: A Regional Conflict and its Resolution*, New York: St. Martin's Press, 1992; Adamantia Pollis, "The Social Construction of Ethnicity and Nationality: The Case of Cyprus", *Nationalism and Ethnic Politics*, 2, 1 (1996), pp. 67–90; Caesar Mavratsas, "Approaches to Nationalism: Basic Theoretical Considerations in the Study of the Greek-Cypriot Case and a Historical Overview", *Journal of the Hellenic Diaspora*, 22, 1 (1996), pp. 77–102; Vangelis Calotychos, ed., *Cyprus and Its People: Nation, Identity, and Experience in an Unimaginable Community*, Boulder: Westview

Press, 1998; Alexis Heraclides, *Το Κυπριακό Πρόβλημα, 1947–2004: Από την Ένωση στη διχοτόμηση;* [The Cyprus Problem, 1947–2004: From union to partition?], Athens: I. Sideris, 2006; Takis Hadjidemetriou, *The 24 April 2004 Referendum and the Solution of the Cyprus Problem*, Nicosia: IKME, 2008; Alexis Heraclides, "The Cyprus Gordian Knot: An Intractable Ethnic Conflict", *Nationalism and Ethnic Politics*, 17, 2 (2011), pp. 117–139; James Ker-Lindsay, ed., *Resolving Cyprus: New Approaches to Conflict Resolution*, London: I.B. Tauris, 2015.

Study 10: "Ethnic Conflict in a Strategic Area".

This paper, coauthored with Professor Theodore A. Couloumbi, was originally published in the *Greek Review of Social Research*, no. 24 (May-August 1975), pp. 271–291. In a slightly shorter version it was also included in *Ethnicity in an International Context. The Politics of Disassociation*, ed. by Abdul Said, Luiz R. Simmons, New Brunswick, NJ: Transaction Books, 1976, pp. 167–202. Professor Couloumbis has revisited the Cyprus Question in his more broadly focused book, *The United States, Greece and Turkey: The troubled triangle*, New York: Praeger, 1983. On the entanglement of the Cyprus conflict with American domestic politics, which brought into focus another facet of ethnic politics see Paul Watanabe, *Ethnic Groups, Congress and American Policy: the Politics of the Turkish Arms Embargo*, Westport, Connecticut: Greenwood Press, 1984.

The present study overlaps with the previous one (Chapter 9) in this collection, but given its main focus on the geopolitical dimension of the Cyprus Question and the international aspects of the problem, the bibliographical update in this Note will be limited to the mention of works on mediation efforts which have attempted over the almost half a century since the tragedy of 1974 to bring about a settlement of the problem. Works on mediation attempts include the following:

- Farid Mirbagheri, *Cyprus and International Peacekeeping*, London: Hurst & Co, 1998 and
- Michális Stavrou Michael, *Resolving the Cyprus Conflict: Negotiating History. Revised and Updated*, New York: Palgrave Macmillan, 2011.

On the challenges of conflict resolution by means of the re-education of public opinion and the restructuring of collective attitudes in the two Cypriot communities the writings of a dedicated peace activist are characteristic:

- Maria Hadjipavlou, "The Cyprus Conflict. Root Causes and Implications for Peacebuilding", *Journal of Peace Research* 44 (2007), pp. 349–365.
- and Lenos Trigeorgis, "Cyprus. An Evolutionary Approach to Conflict Resolution", *Journal of Conflict Resolution* 37 (1993), pp. 340–360.

Two works by diplomats with an active involvement in the problem are also very useful and revealing:

- Oliver Richmond, *Mediating in Cyprus: The Cypriot Communities and the United Nations*, London: Frank Cass, 1998.

- David Hannay, *Cyprus: The Search for a Solution*, London: I. B. Tauris, 2005, while Ingemar Lindahl, *Notes from the Graveyard of Diplomats. Cyprus 2002–2004*, Nicosia: Heterotopia, 2019 brings a uniquely humane perspective on a very critical period in the history of attempts at a Cyprus solution, by publishing selected sections of his diary from that period.

Study 11: "An Unexplored Case of Political Change: A research note on the electoral history of Cyprus".

This short chapter, from the *Greek Review of Social Research*, no. 38 (January-April 1980), pp. 187–190, was originally a communication at the meeting of the European Consortium of Political Research in Florence in March 1980. It puts forward one of the most fertile ideas I had in the whole of my intellectual and research career. The idea was taken over by one of my best doctoral students in the Department of Political Science of the University of Athens, Vasilis Protopapas, who devoted to it his truly impressive work, *Εκλογική ιστορία της Κύπρου. Πολιτευτές, κόμματα και εκλογές στην Αγγλοκρατία (1878–1960)*, Athens: Themelio, 2012, which covers the subject exhaustively and with great professional skill. I feel sincerely proud for having supervised this work.

On the history of the Legislative Council, which provided Cypriots with their first experience of electoral politics a significant recent contribution is Christos K. Kyriakides, *Το Κυπριακό Νομοθετικό Συμβούλιο (1878–1931). Ίδρυση, λειτουργία και κοινοβουλευτικές αντιπαραθέσεις: Συνταγματικές ελευθερίες υπό περιορισμό και αμφισβήτηση*, Nicosia: House of Representatives, 2016.

On the "remaking" of Cypriot politics and the electoral history of the 1940s an additional significant contribution is Anastasia Yiangou, *Cyprus in World War II*, London: I. B. Tauris, 2010.

On two particular issues arising in the discussion, Robert Holland, *Britain and the Revolt in Cyprus, 1954–1959*, Oxford: Oxford University Press, 1998, should be added to the sources cited in note 14 of the article, while on constitutional analysis the several works by Polyvios G. Polyviou should be added to note 15. P. G. Polyviou has written extensively on the problems of constitutional order in Cyprus. See most notably his *Cyprus in Search of a Constitution*, Nicosia, 1976; *Cyprus. Conflict and Negotiation 1960–1980*, New York: Holmes and Meier, 1980; and more recently, *Cyprus on the Edge. A Study in Constitutional Survival*, Nicosia, 2013.

Study 12: "Political community in plural societies".

This chapter was originally published in the volume, *Minorities: Community and identity*, ed. by Charles Fried, Berlin, Heidelberg, New York and Tokyo, 1983, pp. 341–351. The volume grew out of one of the Dahlem Konferenzen, which met in December 1982, and it includes also the report, "Humane incorporation: The Shape of Acceptable Options for Relations between Majorities and Minorities", coauthored by the members of the study group which discussed this particular theme at the conference (H. Shue, Rapporteur and V. Erchner, P. M. Kitromilides, R. Marx, H. Rau, M. G. Smith, R. Sondhi, S. Thernstrom, S. Uran, M. Walzer, A. R. Zolberg).

On the subject of minorities I should like to recall the significance to my thinking of a seminal essay by Elie Kedourie, "Minorities", *The Chatham House Version and Other Middle Eastern Studies.* New edition, Hanover and London: University Press of New England, 1984, pp. 286–316.

Study 13: "Relevance or irrelevance of nationalism? A perspective from the Eastern Mediterranean".

The original article was published in *International Journal of Politics Culture and Society* 24 (2011), pp. 57–63.

Nationalism again! On the occasion of a meeting in June 2010 at Kibbutz Kfar Blum in northern Galilee, organized by Shlomo Arineri, a former teacher of mine at Wesleyan University and one of the great intellectual influences on my thinking, I had a chance to revisit in this short piece many of the problems and preoccupations that had marked my earlier writings on nationalism and the Cyprus Question. I am by now convinced that no definitive answer can come up to any of these questions and concerns but our understanding can be enhanced and our awareness deepened by means of raising the questions again and trying new approaches to them, occasionally counterfactual, as a method of control over conventional wisdom through the consideration of alternative possibilities.

Since my earlier attempts at understanding nationalism in Cyprus, a whole new generation has emerged on the academic scene with interesting and brave work to their credit. I cannot record everything here obviously but the following sources I think represent essential contributions to the subject:

- Ceasar Mavratsas, *Όψεις του ελληνικού εθνικισμού στην Κύπρο,* Athens: Katarti, 1998.

- Marios Thrasyvoulou, *Ο εθνικισμός των Ελληνοκυπρίων,* Thessaloniki: Epikentro, 2016.

Study 14: "Milestones in the historiography of the Cyprus Question".

Published in *The Historical Review/La Revue Historique* I (2004), pp. 287–292.

A twin historiographical essay to study XIV by the present author has been, "The Historiography of modern Cyprus and Robert Holland's place in it", *Cyprus from Colonialism to the Present: Visions and Realities. Essays in Honour of Robert Holland,* ed. by Anastasia Yiangou, Antigone Heraclidou, London and New York: Routledge, 2018, pp. 15–22.

On British rule in Cyprus which forms the immediate background of the Cyprus Question, two later works by Robert Holland, which place the subject in the broader framework of British imperial policy, are essential: *Blue-Water Empire. The British in the Mediterranean since 1800*, London: Penguin, 2012 and *idem* and Diana Markides, *The British and the Hellenes. Struggles for Mastery in the Eastern Mediterranean 1850–1960*, Oxford: Oxford University Press, 2006.

Index